PRIVILEGED VIEW

The Confessions of Madeleine Brown, Mistress of LBJ and Witness to History

Madeleine Brown

Foreword & Introduction by **Jim Marrs**

Published by:
Trine Day LLC
PO Box 577
Walterville, OR 97489
1-800-556-2012
www.TrineDay.com
trineday@icloud.com

Library of Congress Control Number: 2024948978

Brown, Margaret & Brown, Madeleine Duncan
Privileged View —1st ed.
p. cm.

Epub (ISBN-13) 978-1-63424-497-8
TradePaper (ISBN-13) 978-1-63424-496-1
1. Kennedy, John F. 1917-1963 Assassination. 2. Brown, Madeleine Duncan 1925-2002 3. Johnson, Lyndon D. 1908-1973. I. Brown, Margaret & Brown, Madeleine Duncan . II. Title

First Edition
10 9 8 7 6 5 4 3 2

Cover Photograph: Greg Lewis

Distribution to the Trade by:
Independent Publishers Group (IPG)
814 North Franklin Street
Chicago, Illinois 60610
312.337.0747
www.ipgbook.com

Publisher's Foreword

A-tisket a-tasket
A green and yellow basket
I wrote a letter to my friend
And on the way I dropped it,
I dropped it, I dropped it,
And on the way I dropped it.
– Nursery Rhyme, 18th century

When it happened it was dramatic, traumatic, and sad. As a kid, just waking up to the world, I knew it was serious, I was let out of school to sell papers on the street. Then later Martin Luther King, Jr., and Bobby Kennedy were publicly murdered. *It was all too much.* Our lives, our history has been terribly impacted by these events. Why did *it* happen and *who* did *it*?

These questions still reverberate today. They haven't been answered. Or have they? A multitude of books, films, articles and PowerPoint-presentations have delved into the subject of the assassination of John Fitzgerald Kennedy, the 35th president of the United States. None so decisive as the memoir of Madeleine Duncan Brown, a long-time Texas paramour of Lyndon Baines Johnson, the 36th president of the United States. *Privileged View* isn't simply a reprint of her book, *Texas in the Morning*, but also includes an earlier foray to realize her story in print with the help of the estimable Jim Marrs.

There were many attempts to bring Madeleine's explosive book to print. She and her daughter in law, Peggy Brown, sent the manuscript out to publishers – no one would take it on. Then finally Harriston Livingstone put it on his shoulders and with the help of other JFK researchers released, *Texas in the Morning* in April of 1997.

There have been detractors to Madeleine's story. I have read through many of the objections and found them lacking. The greatest criticisms have concerned Madeleine's account of "the party" the night before JFK's assassination. The doubters castigate her witnesses and timelines, accusing her of making it up. The disparagement that I found most amusing was about her statement on relationships between some players:

"It was my understanding that the event was scheduled as a tribute honoring his life long friend, J. Edgar Hoover, whom Murchison had met decades earlier through President William Howard Taft, and Hoover's companion and assistant, Clyde Tolson"

The critics mock this sentence. But the facts are Tolson was the confidential secretary for three Secretaries of War. Taft had been Secretary of War, before serving as President, and later as Chief Justice of the Supreme Court. Taft was in Washington, D.C. and friendly with his fellow Secretaries of War. Tolson and Hoover both received their law degrees from the same college in D.C. during this period. So the notion that Murchison meet Hoover through Taft and Tolson is quite compelling.

I first went to Dallas in 2013, the fiftieth anniversary of killing of JFK, accompanying Judyth Vary Baker, another lady whom some JFK researchers and poo-bahs denigrate. The resistance to narratives that implicate LBJ and other aspects of the criminal plot to kill our president has kept the American people in the dark, left perpetrators unpunished and damaged our country at home and abroad.

Judyth, after being rudely dismissed from one conference, and denied speaking at another, started her own. Gathering at a senior center in Arlington, Texas, her efforts are still going strong. TrineDay supported these assemblages and I have attended almost all.

I met Peggy Brown at one, she came with a friend and always just sat quietly – smiling. We became friends and when she told me about lunches and dinners that Madeleine had with Marina, Jean Hill, Billy Sol Estes and others in Dallas. I said, "Oh my gosh, that's play," and went home thinking about how wondrous and educational such a show could be.

Then I learned that Peggy was the holder of Madeleine's legacy, and Madeleine's wish that *Privileged View* would be published.

TrineDay is honored, humbled and *privileged.*

Onward to the Utmost of Futures,
Peace,
R.A. "Kris" Millegan
Publisher
TrineDay
November 1, 2024

In loving memory of my son,
Steven Mark Brown
December 27, 1950 –September 28, 1990
and his father
Lyndon Baines Johnson
August 27, 1908-January 22, 1973

Acknowledgements

I want to thank my family, Jimmy, Steven, Christopher, and Jeffrey for all their understanding during my long stint as a working mother during the time it took to write this manuscript. I am most grateful to Edgar Tatro, one of the finest JFK assassination researchers in the country, for his patience, and for his editing, correcting, revisions, and suggestions, and for faith fully standing by me. He deserves a standing ovation.

The same is true of Rita M. Dinsmore, Mr. Tatro's trusted associate, who spent endless hours devoting her full support and efforts to typing and proofreading the manuscript.

I want to thank Kevin Walsh, and my attorney, Miles H. Brown for their support during the traumatic days after Steven filed his lawsuit as well as during the critical two months he was declared a missing person. I must also thank them for helping us with Steven's tragic encounter with the U.S. Navy.

This book never would have been completed without Francis Rabon of Copy Pro Copies, who supplied countless copies of this manuscript as it was edited.

I also wish to thank Norma Langley of *Star* magazine, Hal Wingo, Kent Demaret of *People* magazine, Lillian Smith and Phil Donahue, Lori Weiss of Kelley and Company, and Gertrude Houston of *P.M. Magazine,* Walt Brown and Anthony Summers.

And last of all, I want to thank Bill and Kathleen Pulte for their long time support, help, and friendship.

– Madeleine Duncan Brown

Contents

Foreword

by Jim Marrs

The struggle for a title is, at once, the most elusive and frustrating pursuit, and the most seductive. For an author approaching the life story of a historically significant person, title- chasing is often a horror, sometimes a trade-off, seldom satisfactory. In the case of Madeleine Duncan Brown, however, the title so aptly covers the subject, that once having met Madeleine and experienced Texas through her eyes, I could think of her biography in no other way. She had a *Privileged View*.

From the pages of a journal kept with scrupulous attention to detail and updated when the passage of time added to perspective, Brown's Texas is a rich tapestry from which I am *privileged* to work. Her insight into Texas history, from the Lone Star's earliest days to the present, is a lesson in the politics of power and greed, leading to a devastating conclusion: that a small group of men, interested in perpetuation of personal wealth and deeply rooted conservative lifestyle, fashioned U.S. policy for decades and changed the history of the world forever.

Some names are familiar – J. Edgar Hoover, for example, who built himself an empire within his walled fortress, the F.B.I. Others have names that are not-so-familiar, but their stranglehold extended to the creation and election of candidates for high office, and the selection of appointees to regulatory agencies. They dictated the terms by which the "business" of America was conducted. They controlled the money and made the laws; they owned the country's oil, its industry, and its policymakers. They hailed, not from Washington, where laws are made, or New York, a center of banking and business, but from Texas.

Madeleine Brown knew these men, knew their collective mind; she had met them and learned their creed at her grandfather's knee. She was politically savvy; she was smart. And above all, she was accepted within the cloistered walls of this "Texas-men's world." Lyndon Johnson, with whom she would share a business and personal relationship for more than two decades, once said of her: "She is Annie Oakley with a gun, Bobby Jones with a golf club ... and sharp enough to shave fuzz off a Georgia peach."

Brown, an account executive at a prestigious Dallas advertising agency from 1948 on, bears witness to a period of history which is little understood. Her accounts are first-hand, her revelations explosive as she profiles the men and the lawless conduct that culminated in the assassination of America's most popular president.

As a writer and a journalist, I am struck by the utter simplicity of it all. At last, here is a reasoned way to synthesize and comprehend so many "wrong" things – the McCarthy hearings, the cold war, Vietnam and "acceptable losses," political assassination, the de facto overthrow of our government. All homegrown, all inextricably tied to the Texas oil fraternity known as the "8F Group," and to the elected and appointed officials the oilmen kept in their hip pockets.

And Brown is the living witness to it all.

* * *

Having established her bona fides beyond any question, I was still concerned for her welfare. But she told me it was time to "make it right," and since the death of her son, that she had "nothing left to lose."

After many hours of riveting "edge-of-the-seat" journal reading, and interviews with Brown, who is still attractive, vibrant, and sharp as that "Georgia peach," I have concluded that her *PRIVILEGED VIEW* is essential if we are ever to comprehend the shadow world that brought us, literally, the brink of the Twenty-first Century. She is one of the few left to tell the story, perhaps the only one willing to tell it. And she has made available to me, not only her writings, but her correspondence, hundreds of valuable photographs and documents, as well as a long list of willing interview subjects, many of whom have the most highly respected investigative and journalistic credentials. In addition to the scholars and the historians, Brown will facilitate interviews with those who have special knowledge, such as Billie Sol Estes, and Marina Oswald (Porter), with whom Brown shares a very special and most unusual friendship.

From a journalist's perspective, and as someone who always felt there was something "different, strange, foreign" about Texas, the pictures I carry in my mind from a recent trip are both bittersweet and haunting. I shall always remember the '50s-style larger than life figure of a black and white steer standing watch atop an appropriately '50s-style Oak Cliff burger joint. And across the street, on the opposite corner, a huge blackbird rotating on the roof of the Lamar Building, doing its service to the environs in clockwise perpetuity. Between the two landmarks, the "Alamo-style" Texas Theatre, where Lee Harvey Oswald was cornered less than an hour after the Kennedy assassination, a half hour after the death of Officer J.D. Tippit ... three blocks from Austin's Bar-B-Que, where Tippit worked part-time and where his married girlfriend worked. Less than a half-mile distant, Jack Ruby, the man who introduced Tippit to his girl, had an apartment. And within shouting distance of Ruby's, two of Lee Harvey Oswald's various residences.

Madeleine Brown grew up in the same Oak Cliff neighborhood, a stone's throw from the infamous Dealey Plaza across the river in Dallas. Here in the well-kept Catholic cemetery, I watched her kneel at her parents' grave. I averted my eyes until she finished her devotion, then followed her ten feet across a stone path to another grave, J.D. Tippit's.

It was a moment of high emotion. Yet, more than the "small world" rush of feelings and impressions, it was another thread in that rich tapestry. As we started to leave, Madeleine, who is prescient, took my arm and said, "Alanna, whenever someone dies, I take inventory."

After *Privileged View*, the country itself will be taking inventory – of its scoundrels and its heroes. In telling her most remarkable story, Madeleine Brown, a woman in the world has waited to hear from for more than 30 years, places herself squarely in the second category. It is an honor to chronicle her story.

INTRODUCTION

by Jim Marrs

On November 22, 1963, the day President John F. Kennedy was assassinated, many people in Texas whispered to each other, "LBJ had a hand in this."

I know this to be true. I was there. I heard those people. And, yes, even as a young college student, that thought crossed my mind too.

It was a gut-level reaction, not based on knowledge but based on the stories and rumors which had circulated about Lyndon B. Johnson through the years in Texas. Stories of shady deals, political corruption and even murder contracts.

In the late 1960s I met a young woman whose family was well connected and who had attended elaborate barbecues at the Johnson ranch. I was amazed to hear her description of three eavesdropped conversations. She said LBJ and his cronies would discuss putting out a murder contract as casually as other people discuss the weather.

This was a completely different side of politics and business than I had learned studying in school and reading the newspapers.

At the time Lyndon Johnson was president and the Vietnam War was in full swing. I began to pay close attention to the man, his politics and his past.

Stories abounded in Texas regarding Johnson's first major victory in politics – the "stolen"senate election of 1948. The charges that Johnson's political pals in South Texas had stuffed the Jim Wells County ballot box with 202 votes could never be proven because the ballots in Box 13 disappeared. Yet it was *obvious* to all what had happened.

Johnson's opponent, former Texas Governor Coke Stevenson appealed the election result in court. After hearings, federal Judge R.T. Whitfield Davidson ordered further investigation of the election, stating, "There has not been one word of evidence submitted to disprove (Stevenson's) claim that he has been robbed of a seat in the United States Senate."

But before a conclusion to the issue could be reached, Johnson approached Supreme Court Justice Hugo Black, a former member of the Alabama Ku Klux Klan and a Johnson supporter, who issued a sweeping order ending the election fraud investigation.

Black's order prompted Judge Davidson to comment, "The United States Supreme Court has altered my opinion, but it hasn't changed my mind." Veteran Texas newsman J. Evetts Haley noted, "The Black order, hurriedly issued in chambers ... brazenly abridged the Constitution and the Bill of Rights.... But perhaps most terrible of all, it sanctified corruption as public policy. There is nothing in American history like it."

If there were ever any serious questions regarding what really happened in 1948, they were laid to rest in 1977 when a guilt-ridden Luis Salas, the Jim Wells election judge, stated publicly that he had certified fictitious ballots for Johnson. "Johnson did not win that election. It was stolen for him," said Salas.

Attempts to reveal the truth of that election were stymied after a series of murders thinned investigator ranks.

It is ironic to consider that so much of America's recent nightmares, the JFK assassination, Vietnam, etc., are intertwined with a politician who would never have been there but for a stolen election in 1948.

By 1954, a wealth of information concerning Johnson's finances and payments to him from Brown and Root Construction Company of Houston had been gathered by the Austin District IRS Collector Frank L. Scofield. Suddenly Scofield found himself the object of charges that he had violated federal law by requiring employees to make political contributions. The charges were swiftly dismissed, but while Scofield was absent defending himself, the Johnson files were moved to South Austin Quonset hut which mysteriously caught fire, destroying the evidence. This episode has a familiar ring to those who have noted the missing and destroyed evidence in the Kennedy assassination.

During this same time-period, Johnson had offices in Fort Worth's Texas Hotel, the same hotel where Jack and Jackie Kennedy stayed the night before the assassination. According to local police who provided security there, one man who had unlimited access to Johnson was veteran Texas gambler W.C. Kirkwood.

Johnson, along with his mentor, House Speaker Sam Rayburn, and Texas oil giants, H.L. Hunt and Clint Murchison, would spend hours playing high-stakes poker at Kirkwood's notorious Four Deuces club.

This may be the most significant connection as the Kirkwood's claimed friendship with Jack Ruby, the man who killed accused assassin Lee Harvey Oswald, and Dallas gambler Lewis J. McWillie, a close friend and mentor of Ruby. According to the FBI reports, McWillie was linked to Mafia boss Santo Trafficante, one of the men involved in the CIA-Mafia assassination plots against Fidel Castro, as well as New Orleans crime chief Carlos Marcello.

Also, it was Kirkwood's son, Pat Kirkwood, who hosted Secret Service agents at his "Cellar" club the night before Kennedy was killed. Kirkwood has said that the agents were drinking heavily and stayed until the early morning hours of November 22, 1963, perhaps explaining their slow reactions in Dealey Plaza.

Another Johnson connection to the Mob came to light in the confessions of Houston Gambler Jack Halfen, a reported bag man for Carlos Marcello, New Orleans Mafia leader. Under charges for income tax evasion in the mid-1950s, Halfen admitted that his Houston gambling operations netted almost $15 million a year, with 40 percent going to Marcello, 35 percent to Halfen and 25 percent to Texas police officials and politicians. One of these politicians was Lyndon Johnson, who received more than $500,000 over a 10-year period for his efforts to kill or water down anti-rackets legislation, according to Halfen.

It is a fact that with Johnson becoming president after Kennedy's death, the all-out war against crime within the Justice Department initiated by Attorney General Robert Kennedy came to an abrupt halt.

In addition to organized crime, by the fall of 1963 Johnson was being linked to several criminal scandals involving some of his closest associates – Senate Majority Leader secretary Bobby Baker was accused of influence peddling, banking and real estate scams; Fort Worth Banker Fred Korth (named Secretary of the Navy by John Connally after Connally won the Texas governorship in 1962) was implicated in the TFX (F-111) fighter-bomber scandal and Billie Sol Estes, the Texas fertilizer tank tycoon, convicted of fraud and income tax evasion.

It is extremely doubtful that Johnson could have politically survived truthful investigations into any one of these scandals. Interestingly enough, these investigations were cut off after Johnson's ascension to the Presidency.

The Estes scandal deserves particular attention since it involved the murder of Federal Department of Agriculture official Henry Marshall, who had begun to link Estes' illegal government cotton allotment payments to his friend Lyndon Johnson.

In 1985, Estes, freed from prison and granted immunity from prosecution, claimed that he, Johnson aide Clifton Carter and a third unidentified man (thought to be Malcom Wallace) met with the vice president in his Washington home in early 1961. According to Estes, after hearing fears that Marshall might have evidence linking Estes to the vice president, Johnson said, *"Get rid of him."*

On June 3, 1961, Marshall was found shot to death on his farm near Franklin, Texas. He had been shot five times in the abdomen. Lying nearby was a bolt-action .22-caliber rifle. The death was ruled a suicide, launching a storm of controversy in Texas. A belated autopsy revealed Marshall had suffered carbon monoxide poisoning as well as a blow to the head, but the "suicide" ruling was upheld by a conflictive Texas grand jury.

This story, if true, illustrates Johnson's willingness to join in a conspiracy of murder and this incident fits squarely with other allegations and rumors which dogged Johnson's career.

There is also evidence indication Johnson's involvement with people directly connected to the JFK assassination, both before and after the fact.

The last-known close friend to accused assassin Lee Harvey Oswald was Dallas geologist George de Mohrenschildt, himself connected to powerful Texas oilmen and the CIA.

In de Mohrenschildt's personal address book can be found the phone numbers of Johnson, Johnson's then military aide, Col. Howard Burris, and George H.W. Bush (de Mohrenschildt even put down Bush's nickname "Poppy," known only to close friends).

This, coupled with Johnson's activities in the immediate aftermath of the assassination, provoke strong suspicions in the minds of researchers regarding LBJ's involvement.

These activities include:

- Johnson's claim that Robert Kennedy told him it was necessary to delay the flight of Air Force One from Dallas to Washington so that LBJ could be sworn into office by a Dallas federal judge, a claim later disputed by the younger Kennedy.
- The swift rebuilding of the Presidential Lincoln Continental convertible on Johnson's orders which effectively destroyed it as vital evidence as to the number and direction of shots.
- The dry cleaning of John Connally's clothing, after being picked up on orders of Johnson aide Carter, which also destroyed vital forensic evidence.

- Personal Phone calls from Jonson to people in the Dallas area urging a quick wrap up of the assassination investigation. (Dr. Charles Crenshaw drew considerable criticism after his claim that he received a personal call from LBJ while trying to save Oswald's life – yet I know of others who also claim to have received LBJ calls in the days following the assassination.)

In Texas today, LBJ remains the chief suspect in the minds of many. But this belief is based on rumor and the published literature. And while it presents a disturbing portrait of the man who succeeded Kennedy, it is far from ironclad proof of his complicity.

Now, with this book, we have Madeleine Brown's riveting first-hand account of Texas power politics, of the days leading up to the Kennedy Assassination, the days that followed, the role of H.L. Hunt, Clint Murchison, other Texas oilmen, and sadly, the all-important role of LBJ.

Upon hearing her account, I contacted newsmen who had covered Johnson on the political trails in the 1950s and 1960s. I asked them if they knew of Madeleine Brown. And indeed they did. It seems it was an open secret among newsmen at the time that LBJ and Madeleine Brown had been lovers since 1948.

I now have had the opportunity to review correspondence between Johnson's Dallas attorney and confidante Jerome Ragsdale and Madeleine, sufficient to convince me – a skeptical researcher – that the "open-secret" was a *bona fide truth.* I also had the honor of meeting Madeleine's son – the next surprise – a carbon copy of his famous father down to the gangling form, large ears and hands and aggressive humor. A resemblance far beyond possible happenstance. Tragically, Steven died in 1990 of lymphatic cancer, a disease that plagued the Johnson family line.

In summary, I wish to declare that I have found Madeleine Brown to be a delightful, articulate and witty Southern gentle lady, whose recollections and insightful grasp of Dallas and of Texas in the Forties and Fifties are crystal clear. Her book, which should be of abiding interest to JFK assassination researchers, historians and the public, is a fascinating look into the inner workings of Texas business and politics – the corruption of money, self-interest, and power – at a pivotal point in U.S. history. It is also the story of a seething love affair spanning decades, linking a dedicated career woman, dazzled by the spectacle of wealth and seduced by authority, with one of the most powerful and ruthless men of the Twentieth Century.

1

Privileged View

There are people who eat the earth and eat all the people on it like in the Bible with the locusts. And there are other people who stand around and watch them eat it.

– Lillian Hellman, *The Little Foxes*, 1939"

Avarice, ambition, lust … are nothing but species of madness."

– Spinoza, *Ethics*, 1677

On Thursday night, November 21, 1963, Madeleine Duncan Brown, a media buyer and advertising account executive for a Dallas public relations firm, attended a gala party given by Clint Murchison, and unofficial chairman of the board of the now infamous 8F group – a powerful fraternity of independent oilmen who'd earned their stripes wildcatting in the post Teapot Dome oilfields of East Texas.

The way the Texas born and bred redhead understood it, the event, held at oilman Murchison's Dallas home, was a tribute to Murchison's longtime friend, F.B.I. Director J. Edgar Hoover, and Hoover's companion Clyde Tolson. The oilman had introduced the director to Tolson many years before and had built them a vacation cottage on his retreat in La Jolla, California. There, every year, the F.B.I. men would indulge their passion for gambling at the nearby Del Mar Racetrack, which Murchison also owned.

The oilmen had always taken care of their friend Edgar, but on the night of November 21, 1963, the guest list was designed to be impressive: California Senator Richard M. Nixon, banker and oilman R.L. Thornton, H.L. Hunt, considered one of the richest men in the world, Judge Roy Hofheinz, former mayor of Houston and philanthropist, John McCloy, who would later be appointed to the Warren Commission, George and Herman Brown, owners of Brown and Root, which manufactured oil drilling machinery, and a host of others from the so-named 8F Group, which routinely met in suite 8F at the Lamar Hotel.

The party was just breaking up when the Vice-President Lyndon Johnson made a surprise appearance. For reasons Brown didn't understand, tension immediately filled the room. The 8F men retired behind closed doors, and a short time later, Johnson, anxious and red-faced, reappeared.

It would remain a secret to the world for many years, but in Dallas, it was common knowledge that ad executive Brown had been LBJ's lover since 1948. Still, the two were discrete in public. So, when Johnson approached her that evening, she said nothing, not even that she was happy to see him. The Vice-President squeezed her hand and spoke in a grating whisper. Not a fond hello, but words she would never forget: *"After tomorrow, those goddamn Kennedys will never embarrass me again. That's no threat – that's a promise."*

* * *

Within 24 hours, the public would be watching Johnson take the oath of office as the 36th President of the United States. John F. Kennedy, perhaps the most popular President in the history of the country, was dead. His beautiful young wife, Jacqueline, stood shocked into silence, her stylish pink suit stained with her husband's blood. Judge Sarah Hughes, known as "the hanging judge," and a friend of LBJ, administered the oath in the cabin of the presidential jet, Air Force One. Brown, watching the proceedings on television with her two young sons, thought she saw Congressman Albert Thomas wink at the new president. Lady Bird, Johnson's wife and the new First Lady, smiled smugly. Her husband, who had wanted to be President of the United States more than anything in the world, had finally reached his goal.

Through the years, Madeleine Brown had cultivated many important friendships, this was, after all, Texas, where oil was money, money talked, and the world listened. It spoke loudest in Washington D.C., where 80 percent of the administrators overseeing oil production were $1 a year men who kept government controls on oil prices and production off the back of the industry. Many of these men, whose allegiance was owed to interests in South and Southwest, were members of the Dallas 100, a group of well-to-do, well-connected citizens who were considered off-limits to the authorities. Madeleine Brown, who was herself a member, says today, "If you had the money and the connections, you were immune."

From the age of 22, Brown had a *Privileged View* of Texas politics and the workings of the rough-and-tumble men who ran it – men who considered themselves Texans first and Americans second. She regularly rubbed shoulders with some of the most powerful of the group, courting their friendship and their advertising dollars.

Of all the Texas wheeler-dealers in Lyndon Johnson's political life, George and Herman Brown were the dominant figures. When Johnson ran for the Senate in 1941 and again in 1948, Brown and Root, having greatly expanded their operations through government contracts, really laid the cash on their candidate's line, as did Clint Murchison. With ready access to the best Washington sources and with advance information on proposed public works, the oil entrepreneurs were in excellent position to skim off the gravy at "cost-plus" prices. George and Herman Brown's private plane was always at Johnson's disposal, and the brothers had unbroken participation in government ventures. They built, during Johnson's political career, roads, dams, bridges, ships, tanks, railroads, tunnels, ocean and navigation locks, offshore drilling rigs, air bases, pipelines, and automatic energy plants. And according to columnist Drew Pearson, that's how they financed Johnson's many campaigns.

Diversifying like most American mega-businesses, Brown and Root came to own hotels, oil and gas production, real estate and office buildings. KTBC Radio, which was owned by the Johnsons, had its offices in the Brown Building in Austin until the station moved to a street level corner of the Driskill Hotel, another Brown and Root property. Clint Murchison, H.L. Hunt, and other oil people, also prospered, purchasing railroads, food plants, racetracks, and huge oil and storage tanks.

* * *

Madeleine found agency work exciting. She linked being where the action was. And the action was often in dives like Vick' Coffee Bar in downtown Dallas. There she would purchase up to ten Roi-Tan cigars for her boss. Her "coffee cronies" included policemen on the Dallas street beat, an attorney whose father had been a bookkeeper for Chicago gangsters, as well as the oilmen who made up the 8F Group.

For example, Sid Richardson was the stereotypical Texas good-ol'-boy, equally at ease negotiating oil leases while drinking buttermilk with Baptist ranchers or bartering land while downing more potent beverages. Though a shrewd businessman, he liked to convey the impression that he was just plain folks. "Luck," he once remarked to Madeleine, "helped me every day of my life. And I'd rather be lucky than smart cause a lot of smart people ain't eatin' regular."

Richardson owned a fleet of Cadillacs and loved living in hotels, unlike H.L. Hunt, who ignored his riches and continued to dress like a bum and to drive faded jalopies.

H.L. stood almost six feet tall, weighed approximately 170 pounds, and always wore clothes that looked as if they had been purchased from the local thrift shop. Before Brown began attending social functions and learned Hunt was the richest man in the world, she used to buy him a cup of coffee every morning – not only because she thought he was homeless and couldn't afford a ten cent cup of coffee, but because he could charm the birds out of the trees. Brown says he was almost excluded from patronizing Vick's because of his appearance.

H.L., a school dropout, learned to play poker from cotton planters on the Mississippi River. He gambled in Chicago in the days when he was a young hobo drifting across the country.

Later, he parlayed a $4,000 pot into a successful oil business in El Dorado, Arkansas. After he hit it big in the oil business, he started traveling to gambling joints in Chicago more frequently. Because of the high stakes, as well as his skill at poker, he was treated respectfully by a young Al Capone, and was often seen at Capone's gambling emporium, the Four Deuces.

Although Hunt and Capone came from different backgrounds, according to Madeleine Brown, they followed the same ground rules in life and business – their own peculiar code of honor. "H.L. and Capone were more alike than either man would care to admit," she says. "But they had a lot in common, including a relationship with a man named Jack Rubinstein, who would later change his name to Jack Ruby. Back in the forties, Jack was merely a source of beautiful girls for H.L., who could never resist a pretty face.

"They were all tremendous gamblers," according to Madeleine, "the whole 8F group." Brown remembers walking through the lobby of the Lamar Hotel one day. Hunt and Murchison were playing gin-rummy, while the hotel's owner, Jesse Jones, and Judge Roy Hofheinz sat on a nearby couch, smoking cigars. H.L. was dressed in his usual attire, an ill-matching baggy suit and white socks, puffing on his ever-present cigar. He broke out a deck of cards and the two men played for a dollar a point. H.L. took Clint for a quick $800 in the first game. As they began a second round, Brown took a seat beside the Judge. Other members of the 8F Suite of the Lamar Hotel, were sitting around the lobby, their ears tuned to pick up information about the latest gusher.

"I need my checkbook," Clint said when it was apparent he had lost the second game as well.

"Clint, where's your running buddy, Sid Richardson?" Madeleine asked. "I thought you all went everywhere together."

Clint never looked up from the card game. "He's out in La Jolla at the racetrack watching Hoover and Tolson play house."

Through the decades, Brown, now [1995] a healthy 70-year-old, kept the secrets of the 8F as well as those of her lover, Lyndon Baines Johnson, for whom she bore a son, his only male heir. Now, in *PRIVILEGED VIEW*, she finally prepared to open the window on their world, and to solve the greatest mystery of the 20th Century – who killed Jack Kennedy, and why? Madeleine Brown knows that one of the men behind the assassination plot was none other than Lyndon Johnson. He told her so himself.

"I want history to be corrected," Brown says as her reason for writing *PRIVILEGED VIEW*. "I want the world to know that Lyndon had two families. I want the world to know what really happened in Dallas, that Lyndon and some of our friends planned and carried out the president's assassination. When I confronted him about it, he had a ballistic fit. He slammed the bathroom door so hard he almost took it off its hinges. Then he said, It was the fat cats ... you know them, Madeleine."

> *"I lived through it all, including having a pipe bomb explode in my car and my brake lines cut – warnings not to tell the story, I'm sure. But I think Lee Harvey Oswald's name should be cleared. Lee was a patsy, just as he said. He was not guilty. Lyndon told me that, as well."*

In an introduction to this book written by Jim Marrs, author of the book *Crossfire*, the basis for Oliver Stone's *JFK*, the acclaimed reporter verifies that Madeleine Brown is an essential eyewitness to history. Writes Marrs, "In Texas, LBJ remains suspect in the minds of many. But this belief was based largely on rumor and speculation. And while it presented a disturbing portrait of the man who succeeded Kennedy, hitherto it was far from iron-clad proof of complicity.

"Now with this book," he continues, "we have Madeleine Brown's riveting first-hand account of Texas power politics, of the days leading up to Kennedy's assassination, the days that followed, the role of H.L. Hunt, Clint Murchison, another Texas oilman, and sadly, the all-important role of LBJ.

"Upon hearing her account, I contacted newsmen who had covered Johnson on the political trails in the 1950s and 1960s. I asked them if they knew of Madeleine Brown. And indeed, they did. It seems it was an open secret among newsmen at the time that LBJ and Madeleine Brown had been lovers since 1948.

"I now have had the opportunity to review correspondence between Johnson's Dallas attorney and confidante Jerome Ragsdale and Madeleine, sufficient to convince me – a skeptical researcher – that the "open-secret" was a bona fide truth. I also had the honor of meeting Madeleine's son – the next surprise – a carbon copy of his famous father down to the gangling form, large ears and hands and aggressive humor. A resemblance far beyond possible happenstance. Tragically, Steven died in 1990 of lymphatic cancer, a disease that plagued the Johnson family."

Like Jim Marrs, Madeleine emphasizes the Texas connection. She admires Oliver Stone – who interviewed her for his controversial film, *JFK* – but she says that despite his success in "opening people's eyes," there were parts "that should have been edited out. Anything dealing with New Orleans, for instance." When asked why, she says, "Because the plot was here."

Murchison and Hunt had many business dealings in Louisiana, according to Brown, and Jim Garrison, district attorney of New Orleans, whose point of view was reflected in *JFK*, may well have been encouraged to pursue false leads or to protect the oilmen. "I did see David Ferrie, a C.I.A. informant from New Orleans, in the Carousel Club," she says. "But if you made a diagram of all these peoples' lives, they would intersect over and over again."

However, Brown knows that the plot to kill John Kennedy was uniquely Texas in nature … and relatively uncomplicated. "It was simple and homegrown. But the cover-ups were many and tailored to suit different agendas. Yes, there were people whose names came up who had C.I.A. associations, of F.B.I., or Mafia, or Cuban. And for each name, however unrelated to the assassination, an elaborate cover was constructed. This satisfied the government's purposes, and the purposes of those who were actually guilty, even if it left the public hungry for the truth – an amazing 90 percent of them today don't believe in the lone-assassination, single-bullet theory. What the public has come to understand is that on November 22, 1963, the government of the United States was overthrown. What they don't know is that it wasn't just an assassination – it was a coup, designed and carried out by Texas."

East Texas. A tough country. A place where every man believed himself a king, where populist politics thrived, where the law of nature reigned supreme. A place of raging self-interest, barely civilized in the troubled days of November 1963, when the world cast a horrified eye in its direction. Dallas was, after all, its jewel. And those who made it shine were brutal men who scratched the earth and profited mightily by the gushing oil they brought forth.

The politics of pride. Steeped In tradition, stung by the economics of the Depression, embittered by the government slights dating back to

Reconstruction, the men of East Texas feared the government control of their industry.

Then, suddenly, there was too much oil. Flooding the market, more expensive to pump than it was worth to sell, the object of government scrutiny, possibly of government control.

It would take the Depression, a World War, the seeds of a cold war that were sown before the fighting ended, and America's emergence as a world power to set the stage for "the other" – the unspeakable evil that culminated on the streets of Dallas. The potential was always there, a troubled pot simmering for a hundred years, a frontier justice acceptance of "the way things were done" that didn't comport with the rest of the country.

Madeleine Brown was born to the Texas hill Country, privy to its culture, history, and the vicissitudes that led liberal Democrat and establishment Republican to join hands in a lawless vulgar dance with the Devil. She grew up steeped in its politics. Summers spent on her grandfather's veranda, sitting on the whitewashed oak planks rolling cigarettes for Sam Rayburn (Speaker of The House of Representatives from 1940-1957) on a Roi-Tan roller and watching, during Prohibition Days, the ever-present jug of "white lightning" pass between the two men.

"I knew it was time for Mr. Sam to leave when he would tell my grandfather: 'See the red barn over there? Any jackass can kick it down, but a carpenter has to build it. I'm going back to Washington and kick some barns down!' Mr. Sam may have been the only honest politician to come out of Texas," Madeleine says today. She would come to know the others, to be accepted among them, and to fear both their hunger for power and their capacity for violence.

As Madeleine writes in her diary, "In those days, the fields of East Texas were graced with cattle, watermelons, peanuts, sugar cane, tobacco and pumping oil wells, with gas flares that burned like giant candles lighting up the sky. I delighted in visiting my grandparents, where, as the youngest grandchild for fourteen years, I received preferential treatment. I learned how to throw horseshoes and shoot pistols, rifles and shotguns. (Years later I would even outshoot Lyndon Johnson, who was an excellent marksman.) Every Christmas my Uncle Chester would dress up and play Santa Claus for me. Our home was festive with music, bountiful with good food, and filled with high-spirited family.

"My aunts, Billye and Pauline, with college boyfriends, would come by the house in rumble seat automobiles, with their radios blaring out tunes and I would yearn to go with them. The fun-loving, wild side of me was apparent, I'm afraid, from the beginning.

"*My* mother, Mary Priscilla, was beautiful, petite, and frail as a China doll. She had big brown eyes and jet-black hair. Her redheaded mother, Laura Tipps, was a descendant of the family that established the Ben Franklin Stove Company outside of Memphis, Tennessee. My grandfather, Joe E. Lee, a tall, slender, black-haired man with the pronounced characteristics of his Indian blood, was closely related to the heroic Confederate General Robert E. Lee.

"George, my father, who worked for Dallas Power and Light, and supplemented our income with rental properties, was a handsome man with coal black hair and steel blue eyes. He was a gentle, sincere man, who strove to make our small and ultra-conservative Oak Cliff community a better place in which to live.

"When my mother learned that she and George were about to add another child to their brood, I'm told she announced she already had her three children. That left me mostly to George, and as I grew up, I was definitely my father's daughter. A marksman, an avid golfer, I liked to fish and hunt and fly a plane. I was a happy child, very independent and very determined to have a career."

Madeleine displayed none of the characteristics of the stereotypical southern belle, preferring instead the company of men, and the subjects of business and politics. She began her "career" at the Republic National Bank. And by the time she had mastered every manner of banking machine, she was hired away from Republic by the advertising entrepreneur, Ray K. Glenn.

"Working at Glenn Advertising required midnight-oil, salesmanship of the highest order, deep keel, guts, and a desire to work in a continuous state of anxiety. But I had no illusions. I was 22 years old, tall and slim, with shoulder length red hair and better than average looks. I was a Texas-man's kind of woman. I also had a bad marriage to an alcoholic husband, and a young son, Jimmy.

"Although I was media director, I functioned as an account executive. One of the benefits of working at Glenn was that all the accounts were in different industries. In the morning we discussed the problems and opportunities of a client who made chili. In the afternoon it might be a bank, an airline, or a manufacturer of potato chips. Every time we saw a client, we had to be sufficiently briefed on his business to give relevant advice. Changing gears that quickly was a constant challenge. But my first real challenge – one that would change my life forever – was not a challenge at all, but an invitation. It came from Jesse Kellam at radio station KTBC. Jesse was a close friend of Lyndon Johnson's and managed the congressman's radio station in Austin. Glenn Advertising frequently purchased blocks of airtime for our clients and, Jesse and I had become good friends. He said, 'I know it's late notice, but I would love for you to be my guest this evening at a party KTBC is throwing at the Adolphus Hotel to celebrate Lyndon's senatorial victory over Coke Stevenson.' I told him I would be honored. 'Eight o'clock sharp,' he said. 'The Crystal Ballroom ... and don't forget your dancing shoes.'"

While only a footnote to history, the 1948 Senate election in Texas would always be subject of controversy and cynical speculation. It was a political hinge, providing Lyndon Johnson with the Senate career that ultimately led to Presidency. By a margin of 87 votes out of 900,000 cast, Lyndon was proclaimed the winner. Governor Coke Stevenson immediately charged his opponent with illegal ballot-stuffing and the Texas Secretary of State was enjoined from placing Lyndon's name on the general election ballot.

Just a few days before the KTBC party, two U.S. Senate investigators arrived in Texas. Fourteen subpoenas were issued to officers in Jim Hogg, Starr, Duval, Zapata and Jim Wells Counties; yet only seven subpoenas were served. All the ballots and records in Duval County had already been destroyed and some were missing in other counties. In the end there was no real investigation. Crucial witnesses were nowhere to be found, and ballots from "Box 13," a large Mexican precinct, were burnt by South Texas election boss George B. Parr, who was later found murdered by a single gunshot.

An F.B.I. investigation conducted after the election would reveal that 202 of Lyndon's South Texas supporters had voted in alphabetical order in the "Box 13" precinct.

"On the night of the KTBC party, it was hardly a secret that Lyndon had stolen the election.

"At the Adolphus, I made my way through a crowd of the wealthiest and most influential citizens of our state, and everywhere I witnessed the supreme confidence that characterized this privileged assembly, the backslapping and the occasional remark to the effect that 'Old Coke (Stevenson) would have to find another target ... the Box 13 scandal had been laid to rest.' I saw Jess Kellam across the room – a grand ballroom that had the wild and smoky air of a casino. Ladies and gentlemen, formally attired, tables scattered around the dance floor under a large brass-and-crystal chandelier. Cigarette girls with long legs, wives with long faces, gourmet food, tuxedoed waiters, champagne, all enveloped by five thousand square feet of flawless French Renaissance decor in the Crystal Ballroom.

"All the tables along the Flemish Tapestries were twosomes, except for the grab-bag table – Jesse's table, so-named for its odd mix of people and personalities. There, I joined Jesse Kellam, Sid Richardson, who was my Uncle Johnny Bowen's business associate, John Connally, a congressional aide to Lyndon Johnson, H.L. Hunt, and Clint Murchison, who was a stalwart supporter of the man of the hour, Lyndon Johnson.

"We watched Lyndon, a big, Texas-tanned hunk of a man wearing a white dinner jacket with a red carnation in the lapel, black pants, vest, bow tie, and boots, reach the top of the stairs. He was still a stranger to me, and yet, there was something familiar about him. The year was 1936, George was holding me on his shoulders so I could see President and Mrs. Roosevelt, who were guests of the Texas Centennial celebration at Dallas' Fair Park. Lyndon was a handsome young man with lots of black wavy hair, carrying a National Youth Association poster. George told me his name, and that he was the Texas director for the NYA [National Youth Administration], an agency that President Roosevelt had created to help young people stay in school and out of the ranks for the unemployed. 'A magnificent program,' George had remarked. 'And a fine young man, that Lyndon Johnson.'

"Yet, I was not prepared for the Lyndon I saw that night in 1948. His appearance startled me. He looked every inch a congressman who was about to become senator. He greeted everyone at our table with a smile and a handshake. Then he nonchalantly walked around the table and rested a hand on my shoulder. 'Aren't you going to introduce me to this lovely young lady. Where are your manners, Jesse?'

"'Mr. Johnson, this is Madeleine Brown, one of my favorite people in the advertising business.'

"Lyndon leaned forward and spoke in a soft drawl, 'So you're the beautiful redhead at Glenn Advertising that Jesse has been hiding from me. It's about time that I have the honor to finally meet you.'

Before the evening was over, Madeleine had accepted an invitation to Johnson's official Box 13 victory party at the Driskill Hotel, and without knowing it, had become an important part of his life. At this second celebration, she saw the oilmen again – Sid Richardson and Clint Murchison – and sitting with them, Clyde Tolson and a man with a bull-dog face.

"Isn't that J. Edgar Hoover sitting over there with Clyde Tolson?" she whispered. Lyndon arched an eyebrow and said, "Little girls shouldn't have such big eyes and ears."

Johnson and Madeleine became lovers the night of the Driskill Hotel party, an affair that would span more than two tumultuous decades.

There would be many beautiful moments in the months and years to come. During one of their first evenings together, Lyndon told Madeleine about buying the old Martin homestead, close to his birthplace. He had always wanted to be a rancher and was like a little boy with a new toy. "Hell, it is so run-down," he told her, "Chickens can run their necks up through the floor of the old house, but I grew up here on the Pedernales River, with family and cousins. I can identify with everything in the rolling hills, with beautiful wildflowers and wildlife. I bought this old place at a real bargain, only twenty thousand. You know, Madeleine, my old man rode countryside the day I was born and told everyone a United States Senator had been born."

Few people fully understood Johnson, according to Madeleine. "His family, his friends, his political associates, the members of his Senate staff and especially me – each of us had his or her piece of the Lyndon Johnson puzzle. John Connally once said of him: 'There is no adjective to describe him. He was cruel and kind, generous and greedy, sensitive and insensitive, crafty and naive, ruthless and thoughtful, simple in many ways, yet extremely complex, caring and totally uncaring; he knew how to use people in politics in a way nobody else could that I know of. As a matter of fact, it would take every adjective in the dictionary to describe him.'"

And that includes ruthless. Johnson once told Madeleine that he held a second trust deed for fifty thousand dollars on another senator's home. When a routine investigation of financial affairs almost exposed the loan, Johnson called in his marker. He went to see the senator and demanded payment, in full, on the loan before the incriminating document proved bribery. Johnson was off the hook, but the senator lost his home.

"Lyndon, who was a great admirer of Huey P. Long (populist governor of Louisiana), used to say, 'If a job had to be done, and if there were obstacles in the way, just get rid of them, and let it go.' His view was shared by most of the men I knew, men who belonged to the powerful oil fraternity known as the 8F group." Madeleine would often be frightened of the terrible power Johnson and his friends wielded. But oil "talked" in Texas – louder than anything else, even justice.

* * *

It was in 1950 that Madeleine noted a change in Lyndon. "I'm so damn tired and run down," he told her. "I work all night reading transcripts and writing questions to ask at the next day's hearing on (General Douglas) MacArthur. I haven't slept in three days, but I think it's paying off. The public emotion for that arrogant son-of-a-bitch seems to have subsided. And I'm still running the goddam hearings of the defense preparedness subcommittee. I felt like the most popular whore at Miss Mona's Chicken Ranch."

But Madeleine knew there was more on his mind.

"I'm so goddamn upset over my family problems with my sister, Josefa," Lyndon confided. "I'm gonna tell you, Madeleine, but remember ... you hear nothing, say nothing and don't ever repeat a goddamn thing."

Lyndon revealed that his younger sister, Josefa, had been having an affair during 1949 and 1950 with Malcom E. "Mac" Wallace, a former University of Texas student body president who was working as an economist for the Agriculture Department. Wallace was generally known as one of "Lyndon's boys." Josefa, at the time, was getting a divorce and had just been released from a Washington D.C. alcohol rehabilitation center.

During 1951, according to Lyndon, Josefa had stopped dating Wallace and began a relationship with John Douglas Kinser, a thirty-three-year-old Austin gold pro, Kinser owned Butler Park, a scenic spot across the Colorado River from the center of Austin, where he operated the Pitch and Putt Golf Course. Kinser began dating Josefa hoping to get a federal small-business loan, a typical Texas back scratching deal, a variation on the classic "It isn't what you know, it's who you know."

One mid-afternoon, Lyndon said, Mac Wallace drove up to the Pitch and Putt course, walked up to Kinser and shot him dead in front of a hundred witnesses. Wallace fled but was caught and indicted for murder with "malice aforethought." He was released on $30,000 (later reduced to $10,000) bond arranged by Lyndon.

"Goddamn, Madeleine, can you believe this fuckhead Wallace?" Lyndon was pacing the floor now and waving his hands for expression. "No one loves to drink and fuck more than me, but shit, I wouldn't kill anyone over a piece of ass. The world's full of ass!"

Lyndon sat back down and loosened his necktie. "Hell, I've got friends in Austin who owe me favors. I'm going to call in my markers for Wallace's trial. I can't have this bullshit embarrassing my family."

Fix a murder trial! Madeleine says she was astounded by the power Lyndon wielded in Texas. And power, for him, was an aphrodisiac. The telling of the Wallace-Kinser story resulted in the wildest and most provocative night of lovemaking she would ever experience. And even though Lyndon had always been a vigorous, strong lover, she was shocked by his roughness. He stripped her gown from her body and flung her on the bed. Then, he reached up with both hands and ripped his shirt open. His tie was still draped around his neck. He slid the knot down and drew the tie over his head. Madeleine was terrified when he lowered the tie and traced it across her breasts. He pinned her down and used his tie and her stockings to tether her to the bedposts.

In 1951, Lyndon saw to it that Mac Wallace was brought into the 98th District Court of Travis County before Judge Charles A. Betts. John Cofer (Lyndon's lawyer during the "Box 13" voter fraud case in 1948), was Wallace's defense attorney, and District Attorney Robert J. Long, another ally of Lyndon's, prosecuted Wallace without offering a motive. The defendant did not take the stand and no evidence was presented to suggest either cause or extenuating circumstances. Cofer simply filed a one-page motion for an instructed verdict, pleading that there was no evidence upon which the State could "legally base a judgement of guilty." Long said nothing whatever in rebuttal, merely asking the jury to "punish Wallace in whatever degree you can."

Thus, after one of the briefest and most perfunctory trials on record, even for Texas, the jury found Wallace "guilty of murder with malice aforethought." Wallace's punishment, however, was an astonishing *five-year suspended sentence* in a jurisdiction where the death penalty was mandatory. It is interesting to note that Josefa Johnson's name was never mentioned in connection with the trial.

Years later, after the tragic events at Dealey Plaza, Madeleine was horrified to learn that photos taken in Dallas on November 22, 1963, clearly showed a Wallace Plumbing truck parked at the scene of President Kennedy's assassination.

The death of America's youngest president was the end play in a high stakes game of ultra-conservative domestic politics and cold war intrigue. The early Fifties were troubled years. On June 25th, 1950, North Korea' army crossed the 38th parallel, invading South Korea. On June 30th, American troops were committed and the first of many "police-actions" with tragic consequences had been launched.

On the home front, President Harry Truman was increasingly crippled by the so-called "red-scare" and the "red-baiter" Senator Joe McCarthy. America had come to understand another president's declaration: "The only thing to fear is fear itself."

According to Madeleine, there were many who played upon that fear, even as they profited from the oil and war machines required to conduct an aggressive foreign policy, H.L. Hunt was particularly rabid.

"H.L. became a public figure for the first time when *Fortune* and *Life* ran articles on America's super rich, identifying him as the wealthiest man in the country. The magazine estimated H.L.'s income to be one million dollars a week and his total assets to be from $400-700 million. According to our own Texas friends, the figures were a little on the light side. To determine the exact extent of H.L.'s fortune would have required a regiment of accountants, but his holdings included some of the largest oil reserves in the world, including the Far East, vast tracts of land in Texas, Louisiana, Arkansas, Florida, Mississippi, Montana, Wyoming and North Dakota. And recently, H.L. had put up the money to create a publishing division to print and distribute anti-Communist pamphlets and a monthly magazine called *Facts Forum News*. He also produced radio and television programs in a similar vein, called *Life Line*. These were aired on more than three hundred and fifty radio stations and eighty television stations across the country."

Ten years later, when the Dallas police searched Jack Ruby, after he murdered Lee Harvey Oswald on live TV, they found two *Facts Forum* radio scripts in his jacket pocket.

When Ruby was asked where he got them, he replied, "In a sample package of HLH food (HLH Foods was H.L. Hunt's health food company)." The police also discovered that Ruby had visited the offices of Lamar Hunt (H.L.'s son), a short time before the Kennedy assassination. "I first met Jack Ruby in the early fifties," Madeleine says. "I had been shopping at Neiman-Marcus during my afternoon break and I bumped into Jerome Ragsdale and another man, who Ragsdale introduced as Jack Ruby. Over the course of the next few years, I often saw the two of them together on Commerce Street or in the King or University Clubs. Occasionally, I spotted them huddled with H.L. Hunt."

* * *

It was the same time period that Madeleine also met Billie Sol Estes, who was considered the "new" King of the Texas Wheeler-Dealers, and who would someday be a tripwire to history. Billie Sol had been introduced to Lyndon and the inner circle by Clifton Carter, an attorney from Smithville.

"There are many memorable Billie Sol anecdotes," Madeleine says. "My favorite is the time promised Lyndon a $500,000 campaign contribution and was slow in delivering it.

Lyndon called before dawn one morning, 'Where the hell is that cash?' he bellowed from our site at Driskill.

"Lyndon, do you know what time it is?" Billie Sol replied.

"Hell, I didn't call you to find out what time it is. I called you to find out where the hell the cash is. I want you to get out to the fucking airport and get the goddamn cash on its way now."

Billie Sol went on to become one of Madeleine's best Texas friends, once telling her, "Madeleine, you know as well as I do that Lyndon would do anything for you that he could – if you paid him enough."

On July 1, 1955, as the Senate's youngest majority leader, Lyndon Johnson had a massive heart attack ("about as bad as a man can have and still live," as he described it). It put him on the sidelines for six months, but as Jesse Kellam quipped, "He recovered like one of his political campaigns."

According to Madeleine, Lyndon gave up the chili dishes he favored and his three- pack-a-day cigarette habit, trimmed down from 220 to 180 pounds and cut his normal working day in half. Meanwhile, out at the LBJ ranch, where it was quiet and still, he considered the impact of his health on his political career, and stayed in close contact with the oilmen and with J. Edgar Hoover who was busy running a "one-man government" within the government.

"I told Lyndon that I didn't think he should retire from politics," Madeleine says. "He was depressed because the heart attack had put a damper on the rumor that he was a leading contender for his party's presidential nomination."

Speculation had arisen mainly because Lyndon had seemed to be trying to divest himself of the image that he was a segregationist. Acting independently of his fellow Southerners, he refused to sign the "Southern Manifesto," denouncing the Supreme Court decision on desegregation of public schools. In 1957, he would pilot through the Senate the first Civil Rights Bill since Reconstruction.

Madeleine recalls that Lyndon was fond of recounting one particular anecdote:

> In Houston, the Southern Pacific Railroad had applied for a permit to build a railway station in the downtown area, but the city council vetoed the permit because "blacks and whites would have to stand on the platform together." A trainload of Marines had arrived in Dallas just after World War II. On board, all the military men, both black and white, were laughing and joking with each other until they

> crossed the border into Texas. The conductor, with the assistance of the M.P.s, told the men that they were now in Texas and the blacks and whites could not intermingle. When the M.P.s tried to separate the men by races, they became belligerent and tied up both the conductor and the M.P.s – basically commandeering the train.
>
> When the Union Pacific train pulled into the railroad station in Dallas, all the white marines left the train with the black Marines on their shoulders. "We fought side by side in muddy foxholes around the world," one of the white Marines said, "and saved each other's lives as if we were blood brothers. We're not about to turn our backs on them now just because we are in America! It doesn't make any sense to me how a black man can go to war to risk his life for all Americans – of every color – and then return home to sit in the back of a bus or have to drink from a separate water fountain."
>
> "Since we are Americans," Lyndon would add at the end of the anecdote, "we must stand side by side, from the foxholes to the mountains." Johnson, like his friend Judge Hofheinz, who saw to it that several of Houston's public facilities and lunch counters were racially integrated, may have been many things. But neither man was a racist.

In October of 1959, Sam Rayburn scheduled a press conference in Dallas during which he announced that the "Johnson for President Committee" would open in Austin under the auspices of Governor Price Daniel and himself. Publicly, Lyndon ignored the move, but privately, Jesse Kellam began coordinating plans with Jack Valenti for Madeleine to work on the campaign placing radio and TV schedules.

"Lyndon's decision to seek the presidential nomination in 1960 was handled as cagily as most political decisions in his life. He withheld his own announcement until July fifth – coincidentally my birthday – shortly before the opening of the 1960 convention.

Many observers contend that Johnson never seriously believed he could take the nomination away from Senator John F. Kennedy, starting as late as he did in his attempt to win delegates. Kennedy went into the convention in Los Angeles with impressive primary victories, plus the solid results of hard work and sharp dealing with state conventions by his staff and most notably his younger brother, Robert, whom Lyndon despised.

There were three main issues in the campaign: Cuba, Quemoy and Matsu (There is reason to believe that the C.I.A. trained, equipped and financed Chinese nationalist commando raids on the mainland which were launched from these offshore islands), and the questions of whether

President Eisenhower should have apologized to Khruschev after the U-2 spy flight of Francis Gary Powers.

Lyndon believed there was a fourth issue – Kennedy's Catholicism – that would keep the Harvard-educated senator from getting the nomination. Secretly, Johnson hoped that the media would then turn to him. But in the end, they did not. Kennedy was nominated, and both his selection of Johnson as a running mate and Johnson's acceptance came as a surprise. It was common knowledge that there was no love lost between the two men, but Kennedy, as a Roman Catholic Easterner, was shaky in the Southern Bible Belt and in the West.

"Lyndon understood that his whole political future depended on his ability to deliver the South to the Democrats," Madeleine explains. "And immediately after the convention in Los Angeles, Jesse Kellam was optimistic. He put great stock in the marketing expertise of the brilliant Jack Valenti, and he instructed me to begin purchasing blocks of broadcast advertising time for the Kennedy-Johnson campaign throughout the entire southwest region.

"By then, my dear boss, Mr. Glenn had died, and I had joined the staff of George Bevel and Associates, bringing with me the new Kennedy-Johnson account.

* * *

"In September, Kennedy and Johnson stole the show at the Alamo. Demonstrators carried signs that read: *They Want The Bible and The Constitution and We Don't Want The Kremlin or The Vatican*. Lyndon countered by introducing Kennedy with his 'Little ole war hero' speech: 'And then that little ole Massachusetts boy took his little ole torpedo boat and rammed it into the side of a Japanese cruiser, and there wasn't nobody around askin' what religion he was. And when he was savin' those American boys that were in his crew, they didn't ask what church he belonged to…'

"Kennedy's speech, perfectly suited for the Alamo, said, among other things, that 'side by side Bowie and Crockett died, McCafferty and Bailey and Corey, but no one knows whether they were Catholics or not. For there was no religious test at the Alamo.'"

But regardless of what was said or how it appeared to be received, Madeleine insists that there was a very strong anti-Catholic current in Texas. Throughout the 1960 campaign, H.L. Hunt brought radio time and personally went on-air, denouncing Kennedy as a Papist. The Pope, he intoned, would be moving into the White House.

Texas had not warmed up to Kennedy. The state might go one way, might go another. No one knew. But the Republican Party was growing by leaps and bounds in Texas.

On the other hand, the ultra-conservative H.L. Hunt, who had been anti-Johnson since the war (when Lyndon voted against the Disney bill which would have raised the ceiling price of oil), was having a change of heart. Johnson had never voted "wrong" on oil again, and he had proved himself to be a strong leader in Congress. Hunt felt that Lyndon could control what he viewed as the ever-present threat of communist subversion in the government.

On November 4, 1960, just four days before the election, Johnson carried the Democrats' campaign into Dallas. Madeleine witnessed the crowd of hecklers and demonstrators that gathered outside the Adolphus Hotel. Lyndon turned down an offer by a hotel official for a change in plans for security reasons and said that he was "coming in the main entrance, wherever that is."

Johnson and Lady Bird fought their way through a jeering mob waving signs that read: *LBJ Sold Out To Yankee Socialists, Smile Judas, Down With Lady Bird,* and *Remember Duval County and Box 13*. It took the Johnsons almost thirty minutes to inch their way to the Grand Ballroom where they were greeted by 2,000 cheering luncheon guests. But the warm reception aside, Johnson's supporters were deeply troubled by the disturbance.

Later that day, Madeleine and U.S. Attorney, Barefoot Sanders, accompanied the Johnsons to KRLD-TV, where Lyndon was to tape his statewide television speech to be aired the following night. Lyndon told the television crew, "We were hissed at and spit upon. It was hard to believe that this was happening in Dallas, Texas." Then, he scared the crew into total silence when he roared like a lion, "If you're against me, get the hell out of this studio. Did you hear me? Fuck the disloyal!"

There would be a Democratic victory in 1960, by the slimmest margin in a hundred years. Of the sixty-nine million votes cast, the Democrats won by approximately 113,000 votes. The Kennedy-Johnson ticket barely carried the Lone Star state, and observers credited the incident at the Adolphus for that victory.

On January 20, 1961, Lyndon Johnson joined John Kennedy, Chief Justice Earl Warren, Harry Truman, outgoing President Eisenhower, Jackie Kennedy and Lady Bird for the inauguration. Using a Bible given to him by his mother, Rebekah, Lyndon was sworn in as the Vice President of the United States by Sam Rayburn

But even before the inauguration, the jokes started circulating, about vice presidential trips to state funerals. Lyndon had become the favorite son of the Texas oil boys, but he found he had lost most of his former power in the Senate.

"Lyndon was often in a dark mood," Madeleine recalls. "He would return frequently to the tranquility of his beloved Hill Country, and I always thought it was because he could be with me. On one weekend, Jesse arranged for me to meet him at the Menger Hotel in San Antonio.

"By now, our son Steven was ten-years-old. When I first told Lyndon I was pregnant, he flew into a rage. His voice terrified me, and I wasn't sure what he would do. Finally, he growled, 'Did you tell anyone who the father is? Because if this bullshit somehow leaks out.... Hell, I'm just now getting over that fucking Box 13 shit! I waited a long time to have all the oil people in my corner, and I'm not about to sit here and let the press hang me out to dry because I couldn't keep my pants on! I promise you, Madeleine Brown, if you know what's good for you, you'll cooperate, or your ass will be in a hell of a lot of trouble.'"

Johnson's ravings that day ended with a declaration of love. He never suggested Madeleine have an abortion, and through his lawyer, Jerome Ragsdale, he continued full financial support of her and the boys. Dale Turner, a slender black beauty with a contagious smile, was hired as a live-in nanny, and Madeleine frequently took Dale and the boys with her when she went to meet Lyndon.

"That day at the Menger, the lobby was filled with Secret Service agents. They were even in the hallway upstairs, acting as oblivious to our appearance as the stone-faced guards at Buckingham Palace.

"I saw Lyndon's door open. He walked halfway down the hall, and literally swept me up in an affectionate bear hug. Then, his eyes caught something behind me. I turned around and saw Dale and the boys removing their overnight bags from the hall. Dale gently, but firmly, pushed the children back into the room and smiled politely at Lyndon before closing the door."

"Goddamn it," he muttered. "I never wanted her to know who you were meeting. The less people know, the better off we are. I'll have Ragsdale replace her on Monday."

"I pleaded with Lyndon not to have Dale discharged, but as we were getting ready to part, he coldly said, 'Tell Dale goodbye.'"

"A few days later, Dale called me at my office and asked for the remainder of the afternoon off. She had gotten an emergency phone call. I told her to take the boys to mother's house.

"Dale never returned. She disappeared without a trace. The boys cried for weeks, and I searched for her everywhere. I knew she was dead, or she would have called, but no one had ever confirmed it. Many years later, after Lyndon was gone, Billie Sol Estes told me the truth about Dale. "Don't you know what happened, Madeleine?" he said, a look of surprise crossing his face. "Mac got rid of her for Lyndon." I was incredulous, but I had to know how many other deaths there had been over the years. Billie Sol's words chilled me to the bone. "About eighteen, I guess."

Having a man like John Kennedy in the White House presented problems to the ultra- conservatives. The oil men feared changes in the oil depletion allowance and an end to the cold war. And F.B.I. Director Hoover faced a Kennedy move toward "mandatory retirement." Hoover, with extensive files on everyone, seemed unable to "motivate" John Kennedy or his brother Robert, the Attorney-General, and like the oilmen, Hoover soon turned his attention to the "crown-prince," Lyndon Johnson. Hoover's style was particularly effective with Lyndon, who had much to lose and much to hide.

"One weekend in 1961, Lyndon met me at the door of his suite at the Driskill, and after a passionate embrace we sat together on the sofa. 'Madeleine,' he said, 'I've got a fucking big problem, and you're the only one who can solve it.'"

"When I asked him what the problem was, he said, 'Hoover. Kennedy plans on making him leave the F.B.I. on New Year's Day, 1965. "Hoover knows about you and Steven and he's calling in his marker. If I don't get Kennedy to waive his mandatory retirement, Hoover's threatening to go public with our relationship. And I'd rather have Hoover inside the tent pissing out than outside pissing in. So, I've talked it over with Jesse and Jerome, and we think you should get married to take some of the heat off me.'"

I thought he was kidding, but he continued.

"Jesse says you've been shooting skeet and playing golf with a friend of mine by the name of West. He would be a likely candidate. It would strictly be a marriage for appearances' sake. He'll live in his house, and you'll live in your house."

"You make it sound like the man has already agreed to this arrangement. How much did you pay him?"

"Every man has his price," Lyndon said, smiling. "But when this bullshit is over, I'm going to make Hoover kiss my ass in Macy's window on the hottest day of the year and swear it smells like roses."

A few weeks later, Madeleine and Charles G. West (who many years later committed suicide), were married "on paper" by a justice of the peace.

The clash of political egos, including Hoover's, and the events engendered strong feelings for and against the Kennedy Presidency – Bay of Pigs, Cuban Missile Crisis, wheat deal with Russia – played into the hands of those who wanted a "new deal" in Washington. It seemed that everyone had a wish list *and a hit list*, and both Kennedy's, John and Robert, figured prominently on both.

John Kennedy, though tough on Cuba, had been perceived as an ultimate "peacemaker." It was known that he was preparing to withdraw advisers from Vietnam, and that he was seeking a thaw in the cold war – bad news to the government's various intelligence agencies. Refusing to be blackmailed by Hoover, who had used words such as "adulterer" and "fornicator" to describe him, Kennedy had begun the process of "excising" the director from an F.B.I. that had grown dangerously intrusive under his stewardship.

Hoover, the master extortionist, was himself a victim of extortion. Even as he continued to deny the existence of the Mafia – to the consternation of Bobby Kennedy, who as attorney general had mounted a major campaign against organized crime – Hoover was hobnobbing with known crime figures, gambling with them and accepting their favors.

Much as the Kennedys wished to rid themselves of Hoover, they also sought an opportunity to drop Johnson from the '64 presidential ticket. The opportunity to embarrass the vice-president arose when Billie Sol Estes' financial entanglement involving the United States Agriculture Department caused the biggest scandal in Texas history. The Kennedys ordered a thorough "investigation" and the Justice Department sent seventy-six agents into the state.

"Billie Sol had become one of the wealthiest men in Texas," Madelaine explains. "With some slick maneuvering, he then convinced prosperous farmers on the Cotton Allotment Program, and tank manufacturing companies into a complicated sale-and-lease-back arrangement so he could raise more capital for snowballing enterprises. His own capital was exhausted, so he started using the farmers' credit to enable the tank companies to get mortgages from finance companies for a 10% fee.

"When Henry Marshall, the U.S.D.A. official, started investigating Billie Sol, mayhem and murders started popping up overnight."

* * *

On June 3, 1961, Henry Marshall was found dead on a remote section of his farm near Franklin, Texas, shortly before his investigation became public. His death was ruled a suicide, despite the fact that he had been shot in the abdomen five times with a single shot bolt action rifle. Subsequently, Billie Sol Estes got the word that his allotments had been canceled, then reinstated through political maneuvering. But a year later, he was in jail in lieu of a half-a-million-dollar bond; grand jury charges were prepared, and suit and countersuits were filed.

When a "sculpted" Agriculture report with the results of the Marshall investigation was leaked, it fanned new fires of suspicion: "Did Marshall really commit suicide?"

Then, on the night of April 4, 1962, at the western end of Texas, a rancher came upon the body of George Krutilek in the sand hills near the town of Clint, slumped in his car with a hose from his exhaust pipe stuck in the window. He had been dead for several days and the El Paso County pathologist, Dr. Frederick Bornstein, held that he certainly did not die from carbon monoxide poisoning.

Krutilek was a forty-nine-year-old certified public accountant who had undergone grilling by F.B.I. agents on April 2, the day after Billie Sol's arrest. The investigation concerned the Billie Sol affair. Krutilek had worked for Estes and had been the recipient of his favors, but he was never seen or heard of again after the F.B.I. grilling until his badly decomposed body was found.

On May18, 1962, at Bryan, Texas, District Judge John Barron reopened a grand jury probe into "the mystery death" of Henry Marshall. The conclusion of murder was inescapable. But after almost two weeks, the Texas grand jury, impaneled with twelve "good men and true ... were unable to agree" on whether Marshall's death was a murder or suicide.

On February 28, 1964, just before he was to begin serving a prison term, Harold Orr, who had been key to Billie Sol's financial frauds, went out to his garage, ostensibly to change the exhaust pipe on his car. There, a few hours later, he was found dead. And another "Billie Sol" related murder occurred when Howard Pratt, a Chicago office manager of Commercial Solvents (an Estes company), was also found dead from carbon monoxide poison.

In a federal court on August 10, 1964, Billie Sol was convicted of conspiracy and mail fraud. He would remain loyal to Lydon Johnson even though Attorney General Robert Kennedy visited him in prison to persuade him to testify against the vice-president. It is interesting to note that while there, Kennedy also questioned Billie Sol about Hoover's association with oilman Clint Murchison.

Many years after the Marshall murder, Billie Sol told Madeleine that the coroner's jury had been rigged, much as the Mac Wallace trial for murder had been ten years before. When Brown looked at him, somewhat stunned, he added, "Wake up, Madeleine. This is Texas."

* * *

In 1984, twenty-three years after Henry Marshall's death, U.S. Marshal Clint Peoples encouraged Billie Sol to come clean. Testifying with immunity from prosecution, Billie Sol told a grand jury that he had attended at least three meeting with Lyndon Johnson – two in Washington and one at the Driskill hotel – during which they discussed the need to "stop Marshall from disclosing Estes' fraudulent business dealings and his ties with Johnson." Billie Sol named Malcolm "Mac" Wallace as Marshall's killer and declared that Johnson was "the nearest thing to a dictator that I have ever known."

* * *

Clint Peoples was killed in a freak automobile accident on June 23, 1992. It happened as Madeleine was escorting movie maker Oliver Stone's production manager to an interview with Peoples for the movie *JFK*.

For those who have followed the investigation into the assassination of John F. Kennedy, it will be difficult to comprehend the sinister implication inherent in the words, "Wake up ... this is Texas." But Madeleine Brown, as one of the privileged "Dallas 100," was able to monitor events as they unfolded in Dallas, even though she could not foreordain the history that would be made in Dealey Plaza.

"I know I felt unnerved by strange incidents plaguing Dallas, an atmosphere of "hate" boiling in a city controlled by a powerful oligarchy – Clint Murchison, H.L. Hunt, banker R.L. Thornton, Mayor Earle Cabell, and perhaps a hundred other influential people who were off limits to the Dallas Police. I had always known that organized crime operated in the city, including. All the nasty components were "ready-made" to assassinate President Kennedy or anyone else who got in the way.

"The oilmen had been gratified with Lyndon's performance in the Senate, particularly with his stand on importation of foreign oil. Clint and Sid used to joke that if Lyndon could get the support of Knowland of California, Nixon, and Hoover, he could control the United States.

"Meanwhile, President Kennedy and his administration were in big trouble with the independent oilmen, and with many more Texas Democrats who were upset over persistent rumors suggesting that Lyndon would be dropped from the 1964 ticket because of Billie Sol Estes and Bobby Baker (influence peddling) scandals."

In 1962, the Kennedy administration indicated its intention to reform the oil industry. On July 12th, a Treasury Department official acknowledged, "It is no secret that we are collecting financial data on percentage depletion in the oil and gas industry, and that we are considering this issue in connection with tax reform." By May of 1963, Attorney General Robert Kennedy was talking openly of "an apparent tendency toward concentration in this industry" and the need for an antitrust probe. A cabinet-level Petroleum Study Committee suggested radical changes which would be put into effect by January 1,1964.

"The oilmen knew they had Lyndon in their pocket," Madeleine says. "When he lost the presidential nomination but secured the vice-presidential spot, I heard H.L. proclaim, 'We may have lost a battle, but we will win the war.'"

Hunt's criticism of Kennedy was constant and reflected what the 8F group felt about him. Hunt was almost paranoid: "John Kennedy is a political phenomenon – a product of his old man, Joe, but he won't take any advice. This is America and we need to stop him before it's too late. Just look at the mistakes he's made."

Hunt could run through the Kennedy "treasons" in one breath: "Laos, Viet Nam, the Bay of Pigs. Look what he did to Charles Cabell and Allen Dulles. Civil rights, the Berlin Wall, Cuban missiles, wheat deal, Alliance for Progress, NATO, the coming missile gap, Indonesia ... and *lord*, the oil depletion. He's wanting to cut our pocketbooks by a fourth! How long are we going to let this goin' on? Are we goin' to have to shoot those bastards to get them out of office?"

According to Madeleine, everyone wanted Kennedy not to come to Texas. But the ugly atmosphere generated the wealthy ultra-right wingers, the independent oilmen, all three warring Texas Democrats (Senator Ralph Yarborough, Governor "Big John" Connally and Vice President Johnson), who possessed a colorful heritage of back-biting, backstabbing and bickering, would not deter the President. He had fences to med, an election in '64 and he was adamant about coming to Texas.

"It was common knowledge that Jack Ruby knew the 'goin' on's in 'Big D.' Jack was a gracious host and a barrel of fun to be around. He would greet us at his Carousel Club with the usual: 'You classy guys, come on in – it's colder than a well digger's ass in Alaska.' And Jack would hand you an ol' Southern peach brandy hot toddy, the kind that if it doesn't make you warm up – will make you feel good.

"One particular night, a week before the Kennedy trip, Andrew, the porter, was busy cleaning up the club, making it ready for the Wally Weston and Chari Angel (Bobby Lou) Show. It was always a contest between Jack and Abe Weinstein, the owner of the Colony Club, as to who could provide the best entertainment. Abe had recently employed a beautiful young girl named Beverly Oliver and she was generating lots of applause. It was during this time that we saw a man later identified as Lee Harvey Oswald in deep conversation with Jack.

"All of us so-called 'insiders' knew Jack's history with organized crime in Dallas, dating back to the early '40s. His main activity, of course, was a gun-running operation to Cuba. We used to tell him that he was playing with bad boys. His reply was always the same, 'You goin' to catch me?' And since Dallas operated so 'wide open,' Jack's activities probably would have been overlooked, had he not become a key figure in history.

"On this particular night, we had been at the Carousel an hour or so when Jack came over to our table waving a map of President Kennedy's motorcade route through Dallas. In fact, Jack had very specific information about the president's entire Texas trip. He said, 'Everyone's telling him not to come to Dallas. Don't you know someone's gonna blow his head off…'"

On Thursday night, November 21, 1963, the night before the assassination, Val Imm, the society editor for the now-defunct *Dallas Times Herald*, unwittingly documented one of the most significant gatherings in American history – the 8F party at Clint Murchison's. On Friday morning, Madeleine got a telephone call from Johnson.

"I woke up early on November 22. I had a meeting scheduled for 11:30 a.m. with some influential Democrats to finalize the Austin fundraiser. As I was packing my automobile, Lyndon called from the lobby of the Texas Hotel. the fury in his voice had not dissipated. I had barely eked out the words, 'About last night…' when he repeated what he'd said the night before, only in much more ominous terms: 'That son-of-a-bitch crazy Yarborough and that goddamn fucking Irish mafia bastard, Kennedy, will never embarrass me again!' He added, 'I've got about a minute to get to the parking lot to hear that bastard!' and he slammed down the phone.

"A few minutes later, I heard from Jesse Kellam, who gave me a rundown of the President's schedule. "Jesse," I interrupted, "the Democrats are in turmoil." We talked about what was going on in the city. There was the full-page ad in the paper that offered a sarcastic, 'Welcome Mr. President.' And then there were the circulars, saying, 'Kennedy – wanted for Treason.' I didn't let on to Jesse, but I had seen the circular before. H.L. had shown it to me. I had been getting out of my car, and spotted H.L. with something in his hands. 'C'mere honey, I've got something for you,' he called. I took one look, and I said, 'H.L., you're going to get in trouble.' And he just laughed. 'Not me,' he said. 'I'm the richest man in the world and no one gives me any trouble.'

"Jesse told me that a large crowd had gathered to hear the President's last speech in Fort Worth, and that Kennedy thought he had made some headway with feuding Democrats, Lyndon Johnson, Ralph Yarborough and John Connally, because they had finally agreed to sit together in the Dallas motorcade.

"Thirty-five minutes later, Lyndon arrived at Dallas' Love Field. He was sporting a broad smile as he joined Mayor Earle Cabell. Dearie Cabell presented Jackie Kennedy with an armful of American Beauty roses. After a short greeting and handshakes with the crowd, the party boarded the cars for the motorcade.

"Sheriff Bill Decker and Dallas Police Chief Jesse Curry took their places in the lead car. Others in the motorcade were the Vice President and Lady Bird Johnson, Mayor Earle Cabell and his wife, Lady Bird's White House Press Secretary, Liz Carpenter, Houston's P.R. man, Jack Valenti, East Texas lawyer, Senator Ralph Yarborough, who only moments before had settled the Democratic feud. The press, which usually was positioned near the President, was located near the end of the procession.

"As the motorcade turned onto Main Street, the ugly gray clouds briefly opened to a beautiful bright sun and vivid blue skies. Cheering multitudes of people, waving American and Texas flags, lined the streets. All the open hostility had vanished."

According to Madeleine, her longtime friend, Doris Clyce, standing on the corner of Main and Houston Streets, heard the first two shots that sounded like firecrackers. Other shots reverberated across Dealey Plaza. Kennedy fell slightly forward, then violently backwards, as Jackie cried out. "They've killed my husband" while climbing across the back of the limo to salvage pieces of the President's skull.

Madeleine says today, "there were at least three shooters. Mac Wallace was one of them. He was behind the picket fence on the grassy knoll. One was on the railroad trestle. Another was on the Dal-Tex building." An assassin's bullet struck John Connally, who cried out, "My God, *they* are going to kill us all..."

William Greer, the driver of the presidential limo, accelerated and sped to Parkland Hospital, passing Trammel Crowe's Apparel Mart on the way. There, 2,500 people had gathered to hear the president speak.

When the medical staff at Parkland realized the President's wounds were fatal, Father Huber, a Catholic priest from Holy Trinity administered the last rites. A heartbroken First Lady placed her wedding ring on the President's finger, and a sheet was pulled over his head by nurse Doris Nelson. A few minutes later, a public announcement was made. *President Kennedy was dead.* Governor Connally's condition was described as critical, but he was expected to survive.

"I had been at the old Red Courthouse listening to a group of angry Democrats," Madelaine recalls. "When I heard the news, I phoned my friend, County Judge Lew Sterrett (known as 'The Fixer' in the Dallas County Courthouse). Lew said both Lyndon and the President had been shot, 'Maybe everyone.'"

The first reports over the wire services said that Johnson, not Connally, was the second victim. Secret Service agent Rufus Youngblood had pounced on the Vice President, slamming him to the floor of the limo to protect him. The jolt had apparently injured Johnson, and he was still in pain when he arrived at Parkland Hospital. Seeing him bent forward and holding his chest, some reporters assumed he had been shot.

Johnson was told of Kennedy's death at 1:13 p.m., and thirteen minutes later, he was hustled into an unmarked police car to be driven to Love Field, where the presidential jet was waiting.

"At the time, I refused to consider the possibility that Lyndon had any involvement in the President's killing. I wept for the fallen President's family, but not just for them. I was sorry for Lyndon, who had just been catapulted into what – now – seemed the most dangerous job in the world. And I felt sorry for myself, because I knew I would rarely see him."

Thirty minutes after the President's assassination, a Dallas policeman, J.D. Tippit, was shot to death halfway between Lee Harvey Oswald's and Jack Ruby's apartments in Oak Cliff, a Dallas suburb. A few minutes later, Lee Harvey Oswald was apprehended at the neighborhood Texas Theatre. He was arrested by Officer Nick McDonald, and after a struggle was taken to the Dallas City Jail. During his interrogation, Oswald denied firing the shots that killed the President. He also denied killing Tippit. Oswald insisted that he was a patsy.

* * *

Two days later, it would stun the nation to see Jack Ruby, live on television, shoot the same Lee Harvey Oswald dead in the basement of the Dallas City Jail.

According to Madeleine, Jack knew all the Dallas policemen. He knew Tippit especially well, because Tippit was always at the Carousel Club.

"I think Jack decided to do it himself, because he figured he'd get away with it and he'd be a hero. But it was H.L. who called Jack and ordered the hit on Oswald. First, H.L. sent John Currington to check on security at the jail. When Currington reported back, he said, 'Mr. Hunt, there is no security.'

"In Dallas, everybody got away with everything, unless they had to take the fall for someone with more clout and more to lose. Poor Jack didn't know what he was getting into. He was a good friend to everyone, always helping people. But during his confinement in the county jail, when we wanted to visit him, Jerome Ragsdale advised us all to '*Stay away.*'

"We did meet Jack's flamboyant attorney, Melvin Belli, of San Francisco. We passed the hat at our coffee bar to help pay Belli's legal fees."

Jack Ruby stood trial for the shooting death of Lee Harvey Oswald. He was convicted of capital murder, and unlike Mac Wallace a decade earlier, was sentenced death. Ruby would cheat his executioner (perhaps), when he died at Parkland Hospital from cancer.

* * *

Five weeks after the Kennedy assassination, on New Year's Eve, Madeleine saw Johnson again. There had been much speculation about who had the most to gain from Kennedy's death and Johnson's name was often mentioned. After railing at her, he said, "Behind every success there is a crime. I hope you remember what I told you long ago … you see nothing, you hear nothing, you say nothing."

"I had my answer before I was actually told that Lyndon, Edgar (Hoover), H.L. and the oilmen had planned the assassination. They had taken care of business the way they always had, to protect their own interests. For the oilmen, it was the oil depletion allowance and the end of the cold war, for Edgar, his privileged job. And for Lyndon, it was the Presidency. If Lyndon had not become President that day, the Bobby Baker and Billie Sol Estes scandals would have out an end to his political career, The Kennedys would have had all they needed to remove him from the '64 ticket.

"According to a White House photographer there is only one photo of Lyndon totally losing his composure. It was after the assassination and

Bobby Kennedy had just walked up to Lyndon and said, 'You SOB, why did you have my brother killed?'"

Johnson, who wanted more than anything to be President, would enjoy sweet victories and endure bitter defeats. But one of his first duties was an obligation to protect the men who had helped put him in the White House, beginning with Hoover. Soon after the assassination, Johnson staged a ceremony in the White House Rose Garden to announce his waiver of Hoover's mandatory retirement. He said: "J. Edgar Hoover is a hero to millions of decent citizens and anathema to evil. No other American, now or in our past, has served the cause of justice so faithfully and so well … I have today signed an Executive Order exempting him (sic) from compulsory retirement for an indefinite period of time." For Hoover, who had played an active role in the events leading up to the Kennedy assassination, the pay-back had come.

Johnson further discharged his debt by selecting the right men to sit on the Warren Commission. Composed of eight members, several of whom were motivated by their own self-interest, the Commission included Representative Gerald R. Ford (The Fords were close friends of the Johnsons while in Washington), Representative Hale Boggs, Senator Richard B. Russell (bachelor and good drinking buddy of Lyndon's brother, Sam), Chief Justice Earl Warren (who had ties to organized crime), Senator John Sherman Cooper (Skull& Bones), John J. McCloy (a financial ally to the oil tycoons H.L. Hunt, Clint Murchison, and Sid Richardson, and a longtime chairman of the Chase Manhattan Bank), C.I.A. Director Allen W. Dulles, and Commission Counsel J. Lee Rankin.

According to Madeleine, "Long before their report was released, a group of "gun lovers" headed by C.G. West took the same kind of 6.5 mm Mannlicher-Carcano rifle Oswald was supposed to have used and set up a similar scene to the one at Kennedy's assassination. After test-firing the gun, each expert said it was *impossible* to fire this gun as reported. They stated there had to be three or more people firing rifles. Furthermore, Former Speaker of the House, Thomas P. (Tip) O'Neill, in a public forum, discredited the Warren Report completely."

The new President had the records sealed until the year 2029. When Madeleine asked why, he smiled and said, "Remember Box 13?"

* * *

The Oak Cliff community of Dallas isn't as close-knit as it was 30 years ago.

No longer a middle-class neighborhood with local ships and a vibrant community spirit, the suburb, with its decaying buildings (including the infamous Texas Theatre and Austin's Bar-B-Q, where patrolman J.D. Tippit worked part time) is but a shell of its former self. But Oak Cliff silently holds on to its secrets, including the reason so many of the principal players in the assassination drama – including Jack Ruby and Tippit – happened to live within its small radius. For not only did Madeleine Brown also live in Oak Cliff, but so did Marina and Lee Harvey Oswald. And stranger still, today, Madeleine Brown counts Marina Oswald among her very close friends.

They met some 15 years ago, when Larry Howard, Director and President of the JFK Assassination and Information Center in Dallas, declared that he thought "it was about time." Neither woman was quite sure what she'd find. "Marina is a little strait-laced and gentle, and she wasn't at all sure she wanted to associate with his mistress," says Madeleine, with a smile. "After 21 years of a relationship with Lyndon, I no longer considered myself a 'mistress,' but then that's another story. At first, with Marina, there was this little barrier. But after we chatted awhile, she laughed and said, 'You know, I like you *anyway*.' And I liked her, too."

On the surface, an observer might expect the women to resent, maybe even hate each other. Johnson, after all, had been instrumental in making Lee Harvey Oswald a "patsy." And since the events of November 22 had forever changed the course of Madeleine and Lyndon's relationship, Madeleine might not have wanted any reminders.

Yet the two women found surprising solace in each other, and much in common, despite their age difference. Marina had been a "love child", as Steven was, and while Madeleine was more confident and self-contained, neither was a stranger to shame. More than that, both women, along with Jackie Kennedy, had been "widowed" that day, left alone to rear their children, their famous men consigned in history. And most of all, they both knew that Lee Harvey Oswald was wrongly blamed for the most heinous political crime of the century.

"Marina's a mission to me," says Madeleine. "When I haven't seen her for a few weeks, I'll call and say, 'It's time for our lunch at the Top of the Cliff.' She loves that.

"My heart goes out to her. She's been persecuted for things that she was totally innocent of, and Lee, too. After his death, they took everything away from her, including her identification. She has no photos of Lee, or of Lee with the children. But I have seen them at the Dallas Police Department, and I'm trying to help her get them back.

"We wrote to Janet Reno asking for redress and asking that Lee's case be reopened. She's remarried now, and has a nice home, and a son with Ken [Porter]. But as she says, 'The world will always insist that I have two husbands.' I've asked her what would make a difference in her life, and she says, 'An act of Congress.'

"You know they locked her up in jail with her two baby girls after Lee was murdered. The day they released her, she had no home, no money, and spoke almost no English. Only one person stepped forward to help her – H.L. Hunt. He had her brought to his office, and he took care of her. Gave her money, made sure she was all right. He did it because he had a guilty conscience.

* * *

During Johnson's presidency, Madeleine's time with him was limited. He spent most of his days in Washington. "To get the legislation he wanted, Lyndon used what many of us in Texas recognized as the 'Johnson treatment.' It consisted of a combination of empty flattery, insistent coaxing, arm-twisting, threats and solicitous wooing, with an endless succession of telephone calls, booze-saturated lunches, vulgar and shocking barnyard jokes, physical contact, compassionate arm-around-the-shoulder camaraderie as well as the cold stare when he was crossed. The technique was very good at exposing the most sensitive nerve in a potential target. Lyndon often told me that the 'nerve' was the 'target's own self-interest.'"

Johnson had his own targets. In July 1964, he proudly signed into law the most sweeping civil rights bill since Reconstruction. Then in 1964, facing a tough election, he again fought the effects of the Bobby Baker and Billie Sol Estes scandals. Bobby Baker, a good and loyal friend who had served as secretary to the Senate Democratic majority when Lyndon was the majority leader, had ties to organized crime and had used official influence to amass a sizable fortune.

A Senate subcommittee investigation disclosed that Baker had arranged a deal between an insurance man and an LBJ Company, the Johnson family's communications empire in Austin. With Johnson as President, the Baker investigation never officially linked the Johnson name to Baker's alleged unethical practices, but the affair remained a source of embarrassment.

Another embarrassing incident involved Walter Jenkins, the chief assistant and coordinator of Johnson's White House staff. Shortly before the election, Jenkins was arrested on morals charge in the men's room of the downtown Y.M.C.A. in Washington. It turned out that he had previously been arrested at the same location. J. Edgar Hoover, as a closet homosexual, had failed to notify Johnson about the first incident.

On November 3, 1964, Election Day, Johnson voted at his ranch, then spent the day driving his Lincoln Continental around his lavish Texas spread.

That night, as the votes were counted, it quickly became apparent that tens of thousands of Republicans had deserted their party to vote for him. The nation had given him a record-breaking majority, sixty-one percent of the popular vote. The President elect called it a "mandate for unity."

"As usual when Lyndon had something to celebrate, he wanted me with him. I flew to Washington with several Dallas political dignitaries aboard Earle Cabell's personal DC-3.

Besides the main inaugural held at the Mayflower hotel, I attended the big fundraising gala at which Johnny Carson was the master of ceremonies.

"To the world Lyndon said: 'We aspire to nothing that belongs to others. We seek no dominion over our fellow man, but man's dominion over tyranny and misery.' I loved this man with all my heart, but the terrible irony was not lost on me.

"Whatever he had done to scratch his way to the top, Lyndon still believed that many of his dreams for a better America would become a reality. The landslide victory that put him into office had also given him a Democrat victory in the House and the Senate. And both houses were printed to follow his lead with little opposition. The fabulous 89th session soon began rubber- stamping his 'Great Society' program, passing legislation that had been denied for 30 years.

"During the rest of his term, Lyndon would realize many great successes before the crushing blow of Vietnam. His love for education expressed itself in federal funding for primary and secondary schools, as well as colleges. There would be new safeguards for black voting rights, reform of the immigration laws, grants for the 'model cities' development program, and a substantial start on efforts to rid the air and streams of pollution, an issue that was so close to our own son's heart.

"For Lyndon, the passing and shaping of legislation was the prime function of government, but he would be consumed by the ugly, seemingly endless war in Vietnam."

Lyndon's health was also suffering. He confided to Madeleine that the chest pains from his diseased heart were often unbearable. They spoke often about their son, who was now in college. There were many regrets, but no remedies.

Then, on her way to pick Steven up from a ballgame, Madeleine had a near fatal car accident. She spent three weeks in a coma, her arm, leg, and neck broken. Facing years of painful surgery and expense, she had bouts of bitterness and anger. It would be left to Steven to pull her out of her depression.

Battered by the ill fortunes of a misguided military mission, Lyndon announced that he would not seek re-election. Nineteen sixty-eight would be a dark year in American history, the specter of assassination returned with the murders of Martin Luther King outside a Memphis hotel room, and Bobby Kennedy in a Los Angeles hotel kitchen. Tensions came to a climax in Chicago with a violent anti-war demonstrators at the Democratic National Convention.

According to Madeleine, when John Connally came out with "Democrats for Nixon" and staged an extravagant fundraiser at his Forestville, Texas ranch, all the important wealthy kingmakers, be they Democrat or Republican, joined forces to support the Republican candidate. Lyndon, a dyed-in-the-wool Democrat, told her that he should have kept a closer eye on John Connally.

"I watched Lyndon yield his office and withdraw to his ranch in the Hill country – with no job, no political role to play – defeated, disgraced, ailing.

"In August 1969, I flew to Houston to be with him. He had brought NASA to Texas and Nixon had invited him to view the launch of Apollo. There was a knock at my hotel room door and I felt all the old excitement.

"I opened the door to find a crumpled, overweight, haggard-looking Lyndon, His bout with heart trouble showed clearly in the lines on his face. But the craggy face I know so well had mellowed. His graying hair was long, swept back and curling on the ends.

"He held me close, in one of his bear hugs. We sat together, hand in hand, on the sofa. I felt great sorrow for Lyndon. As he continued to talk about how good it was to be back at the ranch, I could see in his eyes that his mind and heart were far away in Washington. I asked him how he had been feeling.

"Just fair," he replied. "Chest pains hit me every fucking afternoon, a bunch of damn sharp jolts that scare the shit out of me."

"We sat together for hours, as friends not lovers; Lyndon was past that. But during that visit, which would be our last, I asked him to acknowledge Steven before it was too late.

"First, he got angry, and then terribly sad. I showed him an essay Steven had written about 'truth' and 'destiny.' Lyndon buried his face in his hands and cried. And for the first time, I realized it was too late. Steven's father was dying."

In March of 1970, Lyndon Johnson suffered angina and was hospitalized in San Antonio.

Two years later, he suffered another heart attack while visiting his daughter Lynda and her family.

"On January 22, 1973, I received a call from Jesse informing me that while resting in bed at his ranch, at 3:50 p.m., Lyndon had suffered a fatal heart attack. He had called the switchboard and Secret Service agents responded with a portable oxygen unit. They found him on the floor next to his bed and were unable to revive him. He had died alone.

"Lyndon's body lay in state for a day at the LBJ Library. He wanted lots of people at his funeral. He had once remarked, 'I want everyone to know who's in the box.'

"I was still mourning in May when Jesse Kellam called, requesting that I meet with Jerome Ragsdale and with him. The 'financial arrangements,' would continue, as they had for the past twenty-three years.

"In October of 1977 Jesse Kellam died. Then the following April, Jerome Ragsdale also died. Lyndon's will had disappeared, and the safe deposit box, with all its contents, had been drilled from the wall. I had authenticated proof of Steven's paternity in the form of letters, but that was all."

"For all those years, I had wrestled with the question of when to tell Steven about his father. Whenever the subject came up, I implied it was Jerome Ragsdale. But in 1985, Steven was diagnosed with non-Hodgkin's lymphatic cancer, the Johnson family disease, and I finally had to tell him the truth. Steven went through predictable stages: acceptance, regret, anger, denial. But, ultimately, he decided to fight for his father's name"

Steven died on September 28, 1990, before the issue could be resolved.

* * *

"After Steven's death, I had plenty of time for reflection. In this life, if you fancy yourself a good and decent human being, the guilt you feel over an illicit affair is something that you carry to your grave. I would never love anyone as a lover, except Lyndon, and I would bear many crosses because of our relationship.

"I know he loved me, or I wouldn't have been a part of his life for so long. And I think he was attracted to me on many levels. He could not abide dumb people, and I was aggressive, and what he wanted in a girl. As far as I was concerned, Lyndon was unlike any man I had ever known. Today, after realizing all the things that happened, I still have warm feelings for him. If you love someone, you can't turn your feelings off and on. You deny so much. Now, when one of our friends dies, I stop and take inventory for both of us. I know I truly had a *Privileged View.*"

2

Visions

The ballroom of Dallas' Adolphus Hotel had that wild and smoky air peculiar to a casino. Ladies and gentlemen sat, formally attired, at tables scattered around the dance floor under a large brass-and-crystal chandelier. Cigarette girls with long legs, wives with long faces, gourmet food, tuxedoed waiters, champagne and broken promises all were gathered in five thousand square feet of flawless French Renaissance decor in the Crystal Ballroom.

Three hours before, I had checked off the last item on my "THINGS TO DO TODAY" list, swung back in my swivel chair, and stretched my arms over my head, my tired stiff elbows cracking. It had been a long day, but now everything was buttoned up for the weekend away from the office. I had called Mr. (J.E.) Gene Sommerhauser, Vice President of Marketing for Lone Star Beer, to make another solicitation pitch, finished my notes for the Texas & Pacific Railway meeting on Monday, and drafted the first copies of new radio advertising campaigns for Gebhardt Chili.

The second floor office of Glenn Advertising was deserted. My boss, Mr. Ward Wilcox (who had a reputation in Texas advertising circles as the best man in marketing), had said "Goodbye, have fun" to me a half-hour before. The desk clock showed 5:35p.m. My work day had begun at seven in the morning, but now that I had cleared my notepad of the final nagging detail, I felt a sense of relief and accomplishment. I pushed back from the clean desk and crossed to the window.

Peering down two stories into the streets, my eyes rested on a young couple strolling hand-in-hand along the sidewalk. They stopped under a lamppost, and I watched as the man took off his neck scarf and tied it around the woman's face to protect her from the blustery late autumn cold. They were very much in love, I thought, and I wondered what it would be like to have a caring, loving man protect me from the chilly Texas wind. As I drew back from the window, I knew there never would be any chance of that happening to me. I was merely a spectator of love.

I was twenty-three in 1948 then, and had recently separated from my husband, James Glynn Brown, who had been my childhood sweetheart. He had served thirty-seven months in the U.S. Marine Corps during World War II on active duty under Admiral Nimitz, Commander of Naval Operations in the Pacific. Glynn's war experiences had shattered his nerves, and turned him into a hopeless, physically abusive drunkard, who was eventually institutionalized in a veteran's hospital for "chronic paranoid schizophrenia."

With my two-month-old son, Jimmy, I returned to the home of my parents, which, as a teenager, I had viewed as dreary and depressive, and from where I had fled four years earlier. I chose not to dwell on these painful moments in my life, priding myself on the stability and security of my newly achieved position as media buyer for Glenn Advertising.

I stole a last peek at the lovers on the street before I returned to my desk. Next to the telephone was a photograph of Glynn and myself on our wedding day, smiling radiantly during the happiest time of our love. I picked up the photograph and stared at it, remembering how the ravages of war had turned a sweet and caring young man into a fighting and killing machine ...

Once the war was over, he turned his aggressiveness on me. I remember coming home from work and hiding in a closet. On my knees, I begged God to let me wake up from this horrible nightmare. Instead, I heard a loud banging on the door. Glynn's voice was angry and cold.

"I know you're in there!I'm tired of waiting!You come out right now!" I crawled deeper into the back of the closet. He started pounding harder and cursing louder. Finally, he began throwing his body against the door. I was terrified and began screaming. The door burst open. He reached in, dragged me out and threw me on the bed. He ripped off my clothes until I was completely naked. I was so ashamed. I tried to cover up, but he spread my arms out and beat me. I fell against the wall, fighting to rise to my feet. It wasn't the blows that now weakened my legs; it was the humiliation.

Returning to the present, I tried to understand for the thousandth time why all this was happening-why Glynn had become such a Jekyll-and-Hyde character. Then the telephone rang. I caught one last glimpse of the happy couple in the photograph, wondering if elusive dreams would always be my curse, before I picked up the receiver with a feeling of annoyance.

"Glenn Advertising. This is Madeleine Brown."

"Madeleine-" I immediately recognized the familiar voice. "Jesse Kellam here. I figured you'd still be hanging around the sweat shop."

Jesse was a close friend of Lyndon Johnson's, and now man aged the congressman's radio station, KTBC, in the Texas capitol, Austin. Glenn Advertising frequently purchased blocks of airtime from KTBC for its many varied clients, and since my promotion to the position of "media buyer," Jesse and I had developed a close, mutually beneficial business relationship.

"Listen," Jesse continued, "I know it's late notice, but I would love for you to be my guest this evening at a party KTBC is throwing at the Adolphus Hotel to celebrate Johnson's senatorial victory over Coke Stevenson." This election came to be known as the infamous "Box 13" scandal, and Johnson's credibility was forever after questioned.

Visions of a lavish party at the grande dame of great hotels with women in fashionable, elegant gowns and oil-rich men in west em-style tuxedos made my blood rush, but I answered in a cool, measured tone of professionalism.

"Jesse, I would be honored. What time should I arrive?" "Eight o'clock sharp at the Crystal Ballroom."

I scribbled the name and time on the draft for the Texas &

Pacific Railway's new advertising campaign.

"Okay, Madeleine. See you tonight then ... and don't forget your dancing shoes!"

3

Dancing Shoes

The Adolphus Hotel was a unique creation of fortune, flamboyance, and fate. It was in 1912 that Missouri beer baron Adolphus Busch chose to honor Dallas, his adopted city, with a new hotel-twenty one stories of unabashed baroque.

I arrived at the carriage entry and a smartly uniformed door man welcomed me with gracious charm. At once I sensed the pervasive continental character of this world-class hotel. The Grand Lobby of the Adolphus was a beautiful lady who beckoned me into her parlor. Few other hotels in America offered such a unique harmony of comfort and high decor. Consider a 19th Century lacquered chinoiserie, a bronze Dore Gleridon table, a Napoleon II oval mirror. Scores of such fine aristocratic pieces adorned the lobby and its many random and intimate seating accommodations. Exquisite *objets d'art* were everywhere. Beautifully evident, too, was service in the grand manner, as the concierge personally escorted me to a separate mezzanine which housed the select Crystal Ballroom.

On the way to the magnificent foyer, with its white grand piano, I stole a glance at myself in the hallway mirror. Soft, shoulder-length, curly red hair fell around my baby face to ac cent my youthful innocence. I felt elegant in my first black-tiered or ganza eyelet with spaghetti straps, and wrapped about my shoulders was an equally elegant mink stole, which my father had given me. I hoped I was as attractive as the tall, creamy-skinned socialite Alice Glass from Marlin, Texas, who was always draped in emeralds, diamonds, and rubies. I wondered whether she would be in attendance with Charles Marsh, a rich newspaper tycoon who owned the street car franchise in Austin, the largest single block of stock in the Capitol National Bank, as well as vast tracts of real estate. He was also a partner in some of the most profitable oil wells in the West Texas Permian Basin, my uncle Johnny Bowen's country.

In his 1982 biography, *The Path to Power: The Years of Lyndon Johnson*, Robert Caro described an alleged secret romance between Lyndon and Alice Glass. Caro said the affair was known only to Alice's sister, Mary

Louise, and to Alice Hopkins, a cousin and best friend of Alice Glass. I attended many parties and social functions with Alice and her wealthy companion, Charles Marsh, over the course of years, and I know for a fact that their purported romance was groundless gossip-nothing more, nothing less. Besides, it strains one's imagination to picture Alice gambling the Sussez manor house that Marsh built for her and all his gifts of emeralds, diamonds and rubies for a sexual liaison with a Texas hill country congressman. That wasn't the Alice Glass whom I knew.

As the concierge politely opened the large ornate doors, I felt my stomach flutter with what seemed like a zillion butterflies. A quick head count told me that a large crowd of socially prominent Texans had crammed themselves into the ballroom. All the anguished prayers I had cried out from bent knees over the disaster of my marriage had finally been heard, and, in an unexpected way, God answered. The party was the dawning of a new world that ultimately would change the course of my entire life.

As I made my precarious way into this elegant but chaotic party, I was too far away for someone to call me, so Jesse Kellam could only stand at his table and wave a welcome. I beamed through the thick cloud of low-hanging smoke, my eyes straining to scan the room like a chary cat.

All the tables along the Flemish Tapestries were twosomes, but the others seated up to nine diners to promote togetherness. Near one of the entrances to the serving pantries from which the waiters emerged with their heaped-up trays, was the one later named by Jesse as "the grab-bag table," for its mixture of people and personalities.

Its full complement numbered a bachelor, Sid Richardson, who was my uncle Johnny Bowen's business associate: Charles Marsh; Alice Glass and Jesse Kellam, a Texas real estate oil millionaire and good friend to FBI director, J. Edgar Hoover. Other seated guests included John Connally, not merely a congressional aide to Lyndon Johnson, but a man who would eventually display political aptitude of his own as Texas governor, U.S. Treasury Secretary, and a presidential candidate; H.L .Hunt, an ultraconservative-oil man who was on his way to becoming one of the world's richest men; and Clint Murchison who had been supportive of and closely associated with Lyndon during the "stolen" senate election of 1948.

Clint recognized Lyndon's extraordinary talents as a politician. He often would say, "You can't keep a good horse under blankets forever-and Lyndon was a winner for sure!! !" Clint, known as a Texas oil man who had invested heavily in real estate ventures, owned

Henry Holt, a publishing house in New York which published J. Edgar Hoover's book, Masters of Deceit in 1958. Hoover and his associate director, Clyde Tolson, were guests of Murchison's each summer at his hotel in La Jolla, California. Murchison's son would years later establish and own the NFL's Dallas Cowboys for more than twenty five years.

As I took my seat between Jesse and Alice Glass, the men rose to greet me with typical gentlemanly southern hospitality.

Marsh started to say, "Welcome to-" but when Alice put her hand firmly on his arm, changed it to, "Hi, Madeleine! We knew you'd make it." As Jesse introduced me to everyone at the table, a waiter arrived with a large dish of caviar and a bucket of chilled champagne which he set beside Jesse.

"To old friends and new acquaintances . .." Jesse picked up the champagne glass, lifting it magnanimously in toast. T hen he turned his attention to Murchison, and they continued what had obviously been a vibrant discussion about football.

As waiters with food trays made their way through the aisles of crowded tables, Alice and I talked incessantly, as if we had known each other all our lives. Suddenly, something caught Alice's eyes. I followed her gaze to see what was diverting her attention.

It was a big,Texas-tanned hunk of a man accompanied by a petite,simply dressed,almost shy lady. He looked tough and sort of charming in a white dinner jacket with a red carnation in the lapel, black pants,vest,bow tie,and beautifully hand tooled leather cow boy boots. I did not notice more than that except that the man carried himself very well.

I saw him reach the top of the stairs where he was greeted by dozens of party-goers with outstretched hands. He was a stranger to me,yet there was something familiar about him ...Mentally,I went back in time. Yes ...the year was 1936, and my father was holding me on his broad shoulders so I could view President and Mrs. Franklin Delano Roosevelt,the honored guests of the Texas Centennial celebration at Dallas' Fair Park. T he First Couple had been invited by Texas millionaire Jesse Jones,the owner of the Houston Chronicle and the prestigious Lamar Hotel. Mr. Jones had recently donated $200,000 to the Texas Democratic Party.

As I scanned the parade line with all its bands and dignitaries, my eyes caught sight of a thin handsome young man with lots of black wavy hair,-carrying a National Youth Association poster. I tapped my father on the shoulder and asked him who the young man was. He promptly told me that the object of my attention was Lyndon Johnson, the Texas director for the NYA,which President Roosevelt had created to help young people stay in school and out of the ranks of the unemployed. The NYA gave young people out of school both jobs and the training for better jobs.

"A magnificent program," my father added,"and a fine young man,that Lyndon." My father was a staunch Democrat,a good friend of House Speaker Sam Rayburn,and in a position to know about government programs.

I could not take my eyes off Lyndon,even at the tender age of eleven. Then the carnival atmosphere of Texas' one-hundred-year old birthday,along with the pomp and circumstance of the presidential motorcade,distracted me.

"Madeleine;' Alice whispered into my ear,"where's your mind? That's Lyndon Johnson himself."

As he came striding to our table, his very presence dominated the ballroom. I, for one, was not prepared for Lyndon. His appearance startled me. He looked every inch a Congressman who was about to become Senator, an enormous man with enormous presence. He embodied Texas, in shape, form, and fashion. Lyndon was the classic Texan personified.

Arriving at our table, he greeted everyone with a smile and a handshake, bowing slightly to Alice and Mrs. Kellam. Then he nonchalantly walked around the table and rested a hand on my shoulder. "Aren't you going to introduce me to this lovely young lady, Jesse? Where are your manners?"

Obviously embarrassed, Jesse, who was known as Lyndon's "hatchet man," rose from the table with arms outstretched toward me. "Mr. Johnson, this is Madeleine Brown, one of my favorite people in the advertising business."

Lyndon leaned forward and spoke in a soft drawl, "So you're the beautiful redhead at Glenn Advertising that Jesse has been hiding from me. It's about time that I have the honor to finally meet you." Then he politely extended a handshake that felt as if it would crush my fingers with a fierce, dynamic energy. The handsome man squeezing my hand stood six feet, five inches tall-and his vigorous enthusiasm all but took my breath away.

"The honor is all mine, Mr. Johnson," I managed to reply. With a grin, he quickly replied, "Mr. Johnson is my father.

Please call me Lyndon. That is, if you will permit me to call you Madeleine?"

"Well, of course. Mr. John – er, Lyndon."

Like a gentleman, Lyndon then kissed my hand and held it. "Duty calls and I must leave you now and join Bird in making social appearances around the room. But I would be absolutely delighted if you could see fit to attend Austin's Box 13 victory campaign at the Driskill in three weeks."

I was about to reply when Jesse, winking at me, interrupted our brief conversation, "She' ll be there, Mr. Johnson. I'll see to it."

Suddenly the band broke into a rhythmic rendition of Cole Porter's hit, "Anything Goes," and party-goers moved onto the dance floor, chanting along with the music and clapping their hands. Lyndon pulled my chair back and took my hand. Evidently, he decided not to leave just yet!

"Let's dance," he said, pulling my arm. "No, Lyndon, I can't-"

I wanted to explain to him that because of my disciplined Victorian upbringing, I hadn't been able to dance much in my life. But he was so insistent that I relented.

Lyndon pulled me to the dance floor, put his arms around me, and pressed his body next to mine. With his hips he instantly taught me rhythmic movements and his strong arms spun me away from him and then pulled me back. He stared into my eyes the whole time. Eventually, he held me even closer and I thought I never wanted the night to end.

The band wrapped it up; the crowd applauded. Lyndon bowed graciously. And as he escorted me back to my table he whispered into my ear, "Anything goes! I'll see you in Austin." Then he politely excused himself to find Mrs. Johnson so they could mingle together with other guests.

I was so enraptured with this man that I was unaware the other guests at the table were staring at me. Finally, Jesse tapped me on the shoulder.

"See, I told you to bring your dancing shoes." He wickedly winked again.

I turned to talk to Alice once again, but all I received in return was a quizzical stare.

Later that evening, I lay on my bed with my arms around my self, drinking in my new found happiness. The warmth in Lyndon's voice, the tenderness in his eyes-it was still there as my heart soared. I took the intimate dance and the personal invitation to Austin as a sign that Lyndon wanted me, and the knowledge made me feel desirous, sensual ... even beautiful. For the first time in my life I felt special. I relived the whole perfectly wonderful night, then drifted off to sleep to dream of being in Lyndon's arms, kissing him, holding him and being with him at the Driskill Hotel.

4

Here's to New Beginnings

"Good morning!" I breezily greeted Bea Miller, Glenn Advertising's capable and attractive receptionist.

Bea smiled and cocked her head toward the comer of her desk as she spoke. "You must have made a big impression on KTBC Friday night, Madeleine."

Could it be? In front of me rested a bouquet of two dozen red roses. The florist's card said only, "Here's to New Beginnings." My familiar "zillion butterflies" went rampaging in my stomach once again. Attached to the card was a formal invitation:

Radio Station KTBC-Austin Requests the Pleasure of Your Company
at the Maximilian Room The Driskill Hotel
Dinner will be served – 8 P.M – Dancing to Midnight
October 29, 1948- RSVP

I was still blushing when I walked toward Ward Wilcox's of- flee.

"Come on in, Miss Madeleine." He motioned me into a leather chair directly across from his desk.

I handed him the invitation. "I've been invited to a party KTBC is throwing in Austin in three weeks. Then my heart quickened as I asked, "Do I have permission to attend?"

Mr. Wilcox, my boss, studied the piece of paper keenly, his shiny bald head reflecting the ceiling lights. It appeared for a seemingly long period of time that he was going to deny my request. Then he leaned back in his executive chair, chewing on his ever-present Roi Tan cigar. Finally, a teasing smile broke across his chubby face and I caught a tiny stir of humor.

"Go, Miss Madeleine! Go!" he chuckled and then added straight-faced, "Butjust a couple of ground rules to honor-"

"Yes, sir." My heart leaped and I leaned forward.

Mr. Wilcox continued to chomp on the cigar in the corner of his mouth. "No more than two drinks all evening. If someone forces more than two on you, pour them in the potted plants. Understand?"

"Yes, sir."

"Number two." He took the cigar from his mouth, looking at me candidly. "Don't, under any circumstances, fool around with any clients. Oh yes, Miss Madeleine, you're beginning to run in big social circles. I told you to read the *Wall Street Journal* and run with the rich people. Good advice, huh?"

I began counting the days, the hours, the minutes, and eventually the seconds before I would leave Dallas' Love Field Airport flying Trans-Texas Airlines to Austin to see Lyndon. Trans-Texas was known throughout the state as "Tree Top Airlines" in those days. Stories circulated that its passengers could actually count the ticks on the backs of prized red-and-white Santa Gertrudis cattle. Dick Kleberg raised this American breed on his own huge King Ranch, along with the ticks.

After boarding the non-pressurized DC-3, I hoped we would have a good tail wind that would shorten the flight about thirty minutes. Back in the Forties there was very little air traffic, so we did not have to worry about getting clearance to land.

The flight from Dallas to Austin was smooth. Only my stomach was turbulent, and soon the pilot announced we would be on the ground in seven minutes. As I stole a quick glance out of the window, I saw KTBC's mobile news unit awaiting my arrival as Jesse had prearranged. The anticipation was killing me.

Minutes later I ascended the Driskill Hotel's fabulous brass and marble staircase which led to the second floor mezzanine and the Maximilian Room. A night like this was something out of a fantasy, and I planned to take full advantage of it. Tuxedos and glimmering starched shirts, evening gowns by famous designers, the band playing, gleaming high-heeled pumps, the clink of glasses, the pop of champagne corks. The light from the chandeliers seemed to dance in soft luxury.

In the Maximilian Room there they were-some of the rich est and most influential men in Texas and America, along with their women: wives, mistresses, and rental dates. John McCloy, Chase Manhattan Bank chairman; Herman and George Brown, who through their nationally dominant construction company poured millions into Lyndon's political campaigns and won fat federal contracts for their generosity; Jesse Jones, newspaper and hotel tycoon, a Democratic kingmaker; Cliff Carter, a trusted LBJ friend; Walter Jenkins,Lyndon's young, ambitious and hard working congressional aide (Lyndon once bragged to me that he "worked Walter like a nigger slave"); John Douglas Kinser, a popular golf professional who was having an affair with Lyndon's younger married sister, Josefa; and the "Duke" of Duval county-George Parr. Also present were the "regulars" such as Jesse Kellam and Charles Marsh and the ever-elegant Alice Glass, literally dripping in diamonds.

Without checking in my compact mirror, I knew that my brown eyes had never been as bright, my ivory skin as glowing, nor my smile as happy. But I hoped my curly hair looked acceptable and that my mascara hadn't smudged. I hoped for so many things.

The band played dreamy Latin music that sent dancers dip ping and swaying around the dance floor. I watched one particular couple whose bodies moved with a singular fluidity and grace. As they spun around, their bodies seemed to become one.

"Madeleine Brown? May I have the honor?" Lyndon's voice startled me as he offered me his arm.

As we walked toward the dance floor, I couldn't remember if my feet had touched ground or not.

"You look absolutely beautiful," he smiled.

"Oh, come on, you don't mean that. You're embarrassing me," I said, bowing my head to avoid having him look in my eyes.

"You are young and beautiful and so full of fire." Lyndon kissed my hand and held it to my cheek.

"Are you sure?"

"I've got twenty-twenty vision." I was blushing at this point.

"You've got all kinds of beauty, especially the kind that ex cites a man. And besides, you got to me right away."

Lyndon's smile was a sexy teasing one, and he didn't have to say anymore to transform my pink blush to screaming scarlet.

After two dances I began to gain enough confidence to experiment with a few more steps. Lyndon was a wonderful teacher with a great deal of patience. I found that I loved not only dancing, but also the effect my swaying hips and undulating movements had on the man who swept me off my feet. He was in the best of spirits, enticing me to try new steps and relishing my success when I mastered them.

The music downshifted to an exotically sensual melody. With out coaxing, I placed both my arms around Lyndon's neck, wondering afterwards if Lady Bird was present. He looked into my eyes and pulled me so close that I felt we had melted together. When his foot moved, my foot followed; when his hips dipped, so did mine; and when he leaned me over almost in a backbend, his face was only inches from mine and his throbbing masculinity left no doubt about his intentions.

For a while I was completely oblivious to the party. I was lost in my own world as though I stood in a vacuum. The very air held it breath. Faintly, I once again returned to reality and perceived the hot music that was building to a crescendo. Lyndon looked at me, smiled, and squeezed me close against his chest as the band changed tempos to play, up beat and full force, his favorite song, "Alexander's Rag Time Band."

I glanced over his shoulder as we gyrated slowly around the dance floor. At one table, Sid Richardson and Clint Murchison, two oil field wildcatters who had made fortunes in Texas' richest land, hovered closely with two of the men who seemed so familiar to me. The four were completely lost in intense conversation.

Sitting intimately across from each other at a table for two was Judge Roy Hofheinz (he later owned the Ringling Brothers Circus, built AstroWorld and later merged his firm with the Mattel Toy Company) of Houston and a vivacious young lady who was obviously not his wife. She sipped champagne out of a thin crystal flute and gazed into the Judge's eyes with fascination. When a waiter came to clear their plates and asked them if they wanted dessert or coffee, the man had to repeat himself twice before the Judge responded. In Texas nighttime social circles, mistresses were certainly not uncommon commodities among the rich and influential.

Judge Hofheinz was a king in Texas wheeling and dealing. He told me that Lady Bird had asked his assistance which he was happy to provide. Acting on Lady Bird's behalf, it was he and the former Under Secretary of the Interior, Alvin Wirtz, who negotiated the purchase of the almost bankrupt 250 watt radio station, KTBC. Lyndon used Lady Bird and her $17,500 cash inheritance as cover for ownership of a potentially lucrative operation, pulling all kinds of strings for government approval. It was KTBC that laid the financial base which made the Johnsons millionaires, and as such, his attention to it was second only to his obsession with his political career.

T he crowd applauded as the band continued to play "Alexander's Rag Time Band." I asked about Lyndon's family. He replied they had been desperately poor farming and raising cattle, even though his father, Sam, served in the Texas State Legislature. Lyndon's mother, Rebekah, came from a prominent, educated Texas family and had worked in the local newspaper office. Lyndon gave his father full credit for sending him to Washington. Sam had campaigned for Dick Kleberg, owner of the one and a half million acre King Ranch, in exchange for procuring a job for Lyndon in Washington.

"You know, Madeleine, Dick's wife was the only woman in the world that hated my guts. I believe she could have stabbed me to death without blinking an eye."

Shyly I replied, "I can't believe you're telling me the truth." "Well, you just ask Mr. Sam;' as House Speaker Sam Rayburn was commonly known. "He'll tell you she didn't like me worth a shit." Lyndon continued, "I decided to stay in Washington at any price. Even Pappy O'Daniel's Senate victory in 1941 didn't hamper my spirits. You just watch me. T his Box 13 Scandal will be put to bed in Texas. Governor Coke Stevenson will find another job to do." While only a footnote in history, the 1948 Senate election would always be a subject of controversy and cynical speculation. It was a hinge of history, opening up for Lyndon the Senate career that ultimately led to the Presidency. To put it simply, the career of the President rested on the theft of that earlier election. By a margin of 87 votes out of 900,000 cast, Lyndon was proclaimed the winner. Stevenson immediately charged Lyndon with illegal ballot-stuffing, and the Texas Secretary of State was enjoined from placing Lyndon's name on the general election ballot.

Just a few days before the KTBC party, two U.S. Senate investigators arrived in Texas. Fourteen subpoenas were issued to officers in Jim Hogg, Starr, Duval, Zapata (Zapata County, Crystal City, home of Popeye the Sailor Man) and Jim Wells Counties: yet only seven subpoenas were actually served. All the ballots and records in Duval County had already been destroyed, and some were missing in other counties. In the end, there was no real investigation. Crucial persons were not to be found; ballots from "Box 13," a large Mexican precinct, were burnt by South Texas election boss George B. Parr, who was later found murdered by a single shot.

An FBI investigation months after the election uncovered that 202 of Lyndon's South Texas supporters had voted in alphabetical order in the "Box 13" precinct.

I knew about this controversial election. Everyone in Texas did. Nevertheless, my father, a staunch and loyal Democrat, had said that Lyndon Johnson was the best candidate, no matter how he won.[1] I told Lyndon an

1 A Texan Looks at Lyndon: A Study in Illegitimate Power, by J. Evetts Haley, 1964, docu-

abridged version of my life, omitting the dark side of the four years of drunken brutality spent with my husband.

As Lyndon's hand circled my waist and then spun me around, I caught another fleeting glimpse of the two familiar-looking men sitting in a close huddle with Sid Richardson and Clint Murchison. I continued to stare at one of the men who had a bulldog-like face. Finally, something stirred my memory from the FBI "G-Man" series at the movie theaters when I was growing up in the Thirties.

"Isn't that J. Edgar Hoover sitting over there with Clyde Tolson?" I whispered innocently enough into Lyndon's ear.

His brow creased and he arched an eyebrow. "Little girls shouldn't have such big eyes and ears."

Lyndon's suspicious reaction to my naíve query only heightened my curiosity. I had read in the newspapers that the FBI was still investigating the voter fraud case filed recently against Lyndon. Were Hoover and Tolson only at the party to question Lyndon's friends and associates?

"Where's your mind, honey?" Lyndon asked, wishing I would get my thoughts back to what was important. "We've got better things to do." Then he looked into my eyes in a way that pierced my very soul. I felt sensual chills play through me. His eyes held both a touch of innocence that I found unable to resist, and at the same time, a sultry glow that did not disguise his desire for me. It was a deadly combination. I felt hot, flushed, wanton.

Our eyes locked on each other as he discreetly placed a key in the palm of my hand. "Go on up to my suite on the fourth floor and take yourself a long, hot bath," he said in a low, breathy tone. "I have to kiss a few oil men's nasty asses, then I'll come up and join you darling. First, I've got to talk to Abe Fortas." Fortas was one of Lyndon's most trusted advisors whom he later appointed to the Supreme Court, after getting LBJ off the hook in the "Box 13" scandal.

As he walked away, I stood dumbfounded, holding my breath as I listened to the thundering of my heart and looked around to see if Lady Bird was there or if anyone was watching us.

Moments later, I twisted the key in the lock of the mahogany door and swung it open ever so slightly. The hotel suite was exquisite, I thought, as I walked across the dark-stained plank flooring and onto a luxurious green wool rug. The textured walls were painted white and the ceiling was

---

ments the tremendous scandal of the stolen "Box 13" election, and it is mentioned in many other historical works.

beamed in dark walnut to match the floor. Two double-wide arched windows were shuttered from floor to ceiling in walnut louvers. There was a sitting room with a massive mahogany desk and a small smoking table. I then turned my attention to the four-poster bed, which, when pressed on, allowed my hand to completely disappear.

The bathroom's floor and walls were covered in forest green tiles with tiny gold flecks. On another wall was a three-way mirror, brass valet and French bombe chest for toiletries. On the far wall was a green marble five-foot wide tub fitted ornately with gold-plated faucet and handles. On the comer ledge sat three glass bottles filled with bubble bath, oil, and bath salts.

I didn't waste a minute in stripping off the long, soft, white silk dress while the tub filled with steamy water.

I had spent forty-five minutes abandoning myself to the water-soaping, rinsing, and shampooing-when Lyndon arrived at the suite.

My breath caught in my throat as he stood in the bathroom doorway gaping at me as my drunken husband often did when he wanted to rape me.

Suddenly my arms crossed over my breasts and tears sprang to my eyes. "Please don't look at me like that!" I pleaded.

He leaned forward and kissed my eyes and tasted my salty tears. Then he kissed my cheeks, ears, and nose.

"You've got it wrong," he whispered smoothly. "You're just so beautifully innocent."

Lyndon peeled off his clothes as well, and stepped gingerly into the bathtub opposite me. Cupping my face in his hands, he drew me to him. His lips were soft, cool and precious, I thought, as he placed tiny kisses on my own trembling lips. For a brief moment he gazed deeply into my eyes as if looking for an answer to a question I had not asked. When he closed his eyes and parted my lips with his tongue, I felt as if I were lost in a whirlpool. With deliberate slowness, he teased and tasted my lips and tongue. Lyndon's lustful kiss blazed through me with the fire of a thousand suns, withering my reserve and melting my resistance.

His torrid kiss invaded the secret recesses of my mind, unleashing all the passion I had feared was permanently locked away. With a wild desire and wantonness I hadn't believed possible, I kissed him back, hungering for every second that his lips covered mine. He was my master, and I arched my body into his, telling him with my kisses and body that 1 wanted him as much as he wanted me.

Lyndon's continuous kisses consumed me totally, shredding the last of my self-control and savagely severing the reins I had so often gripped to control myself.

I handed him the sponge, but he dropped it carelessly on the floor. When I reached for the soap, he grabbed my arm and pulled me toward him until my breasts touched his chest.

"This is what I wanted to do when I first laid my eyes on you three weeks ago."

Lyndon bent his head and when our lips met once more, he devoured me with a ferocity that turned me into liquid heat. My body simmered from one end to the other. Every inch of my being was eager for his touch. I was surprised by my own passion, and then surprised again.

Lyndon was trembling with agonizing anticipation as he rubbed my breasts and began running his hands over the silky terrain of my hips, thighs, and legs. I thought I would go insane.

Suddenly he stood up, scooped me into his arms and carried me soaking wet into the bedroom.

Lyndon said, "It's been torture waiting for you. I feel like a cattle rustler who has run with coyotes for weeks," he laughed, "and now I'm only inches from crossing the border."

I buried my face in the strength of his neck. My diminutive kisses must have felt like tiny droplets flung from a summer rain against his wet skin.

When he placed me on the bed and lay down beside me, he put his arm under my head and gathered me near. It seemed an end less intermission as we lay side by side listening to the other's heart pound, the sound of one another's passionate breathing, and reveling in the warmth of our mingled bodies.

"Never has a woman's body excited me like yours," Lyndon whispered hoarsely.

Finally, I was holding my lover's strong body that I had ached for during the past three weeks. I ran my fingers down his roughened skin and traced his mouth. Lyndon responded rapidly, eagerly. He was as thrilling in bed as he was in the public forum of politics energetic, powerful and commanding. He explored all the nuances of my body, awakening lustful desires I feared had died.

He gazed into my eyes, my unquestioning trust urging him to take me, and I felt nothing but wild pleasure as he entered me effortlessly. Together our ecstasy grew like a roaring tide, overpowering us in its intensity until ultimately my moans rose into an ecstatic cry.

Lyndon rolled onto his back taking me with him. I loved the possessive way he held me, keeping me glued against his flesh. He traced the outline of my cheekbone with a definitive finger, started to say something, stopped and pulled my head into his shoulder and fiercely hugged me. Never had I felt such wonder, joy, and fulfillment.

A cornucopia of mixed emotions flooded over me, combining with the lassitude and physical exhaustion of our lovemaking as I fell asleep in Lyndon's wondrous arms.

I awoke in the middle of the night, turned and smiled as Lyndon leaned on his elbow and with his other hand scribbled his name across my naked breasts. I touched his cheek and ran my fingers through his rumpled hair.

"I must leave you soon,my darling," he said."In the morning simply go downstairs and tell the concierge your name. Jesse has made arrangements for a car from the station to drive you back to the air port."

Suddenly I was very uncertain about everything. Did Lyndon regard me as little more than a cheap one-night plaything that he could return for a refund at the store the next day?

Seeing the questioning look in my eyes,he said,"I promise you that from this night forward,nothing on earth will ever keep us apart. I will always be there when you need me and I always keep my promises."

I smiled and gave a sigh of relief."We shall see about that."

Then he rolled me onto my back,stroking me with tantalizingly slow movements. My skin tingled as if being teased by the fluttering of hummingbird wings. He kissed my arm, the palm of my hand and then took each one of my fingers into his mouth and sucked slowly. "What do you want me to say?" he asked breathlessly as he continued playing with my body,eliciting responses that made him smile seductively at me.

"Lyndon,we've been close tonight and as intimate as two people can be,but you're a married man in the public's eye and to morrow you may ... "

There was no mistaking the urgent passion in his kiss."Today is today. Tomorrow is tomorrow."

Neither one of us had any way of knowing that tomorrow would last the next twenty-one years.

5

Minks, Flowers, and Loneliness

One morning Ray Glenn stopped by my office to inquire about the progress of an account that I was handling.

"By the way, Madeleine, my good friend, Fred Florence, called me the other day to see how you were doing," he said. "I told him you had taken to full marketing like a duck to water."

"Thank you, Mr. Glenn." I was honored that my former employer, Mr. Fred Florence, the president of Republic National Bank of Dallas-one of the country's largest because of its oil financing program-had taken a personal interest in my success.

"How did you and Fred meet? I know you worked for him, but he seems to know you personally." Mr. Glenn asked, as he sat down in the chair across from my desk.

I explained that when I was a student at Dallas' W.H. Adamson High School, Mr. Florence had initiated a unique introductory pro gram to banking in all the Dallas-area schools. Every Tuesday was "Banking Day" and a student could bank an amount as small as a dime. (That's when a dime was really worth ten cents.)After passing several tests, I was selected by the principal, H.A. Allen, to serve as an administrative assistant to aid other students in making their weekly deposits.

Adamson had just celebrated their 100th anniversary of education, and the Speaker of the House of Representatives in Washing ton, Jim Wright, attended and spoke to the student body. Wright was a 1939 graduate of Adamson High School. One afternoon, Mr. Florence, a dynamic executive, was visiting the school and promised to provide me with a $90 a-month starting position with Republic National Bank when I graduated in a few weeks.

Florence, who had begun his own banking career at age 17 in Rusk, Texas, advanced me in the departments of transit, routing, book keeping-eventually every area of the bank-to teach me Republic's overall operation. Within six months I was promoted to teller.

It was in the teller booth that I first witnessed racism. A white military officer in the Eighth Service Command had walked into the bank lobby with his black wife to open an account. An officer of the bank abruptly rose from his desk and approached the military man, politely informing him that Republic National Bank was a Southern bank and did not wish to do business with "their kind." I was appalled at this open display of racial hatred. Here was a young man who was proudly serving in the armed forces of our country, who could not even open a checking account at the Republic National Bank because his wife was black. My family had raised me not to judge people by the color of their skin, but by what was in their hearts. My father used to say, "Madeleine, if God Almighty is no respecter of color, as the Good Book reads, how can I be?"

As in all jobs, there were decisions and policies that I personally could not subscribe to. But to advance to higher levels of position and pay, I had to keep my opinions to myself.

Florence came up to me one day at my teller booth and told me about an excellent opportunity for advancement at his good friend's advertising agency. In those days women didn't have many opportunities. They did not enjoy equal rights nor equal wages.

"Madeleine, I would love to keep you at the bank forever," he said. "But you've got the intelligence, personality, looks and aggressiveness to really succeed and go places at Ray Glenn's agency. I'm just not selfish enough to hold you back." I took his advice and made an appointment with Mr. Glenn.

"So there's no one else to blame for me being here but Mr.

Florence," I said as Mr. Glenn rose to his feet during our meeting.

He took my hand in both of his. "Thank goodness for Fred Florence, Madeleine. I'm glad to have you aboard."

I often compared these two highly respected businessmen, both diehard capitalists. They were so much alike, yet so different. Neither smoked nor drank and both exercised good health and moral habits.

Mr. Florence would roll up his sleeves and sweat with the other fifty employees of the bank when he saw a work overload. He routed checks, operated bookkeeping machines, and, on the first of every month, assisted in mailing statements to the bank's customers which in pre-computer days were done by hand. Mr. Florence was always the first to arrive at the bank in the morning and the last to leave in the afternoon. He certainly did not keep the proverbial "banker's hours" as many of his peers did at other Dallas banks.

Mr. Glenn, on the other hand, would arrive at the office at nine A.M. and leave at three P.M. Instead of laboring with the other ad agency employees, he would sit in his "ivory tower" office and direct us like an orchestra conductor.

Working at Glenn Advertising Agency required midnight oil, salesmanship of the highest order, deep keel, guts, thrust, and the ability to work in a continuous state of anxiety. It was popularly believed that advertising attracted neurotics who were naturally prone to anxiety. I never believed that, but what happened in agencies was enough to induce anxiety among the calmest people.

Mr. Glenn had his worries: Is such-and-such client going to fire you? Is a valuable partner going to quit? Will you make a hash of the new business presentation on Thursday?

Copywriters, such as Bob Ahola, also lived with fear. Will he have a big idea before Tuesday morning, and will the client buy it? Will it sell the product?A copywriter never sat down at his typewriter without thinking, "this time I am going to fail."

And then there were account executives like me. Although I was Media Director, I functioned as an Account Executive. We rep resented the agency to the client, and the client to the agency. When the agency erred, the client held the account executive responsible. When the client failed clumsily, the agency blamed the account executive.

Nevertheless, the atmosphere at Glenn was extraordinarily stimulating. It was a psychological hothouse. We were never bored because Ward Wilcox made work amusing. He used to say, "Miss Madeleine, when people are having fun, they produce good advertising." He killed grimness with laughter and encouraged exuberance.

What kind of paragon was this man who managed our successful agency? Mr. Wilcox, a World War II Marine, was enthusiastic, intellectually honest with the guts to face tough decisions, and resilient in adversity. He was not a bully but a natural charmer who encouraged communications upwards and was a good listener, a decent person, and, as we say in Texas, a man "you could ride the river with." One of the most agreeable benefits about working at Glenn Advertising Agency was that all the accounts were in different industries. In the morning we discussed the problems and opportunities of a client who made chili. In the afternoon it might be a bank, an airline, or a manufacturer of potato chips. But we paid a price for this variety.

Every time we saw a client, we had to be sufficiently briefed on his business to give relevant advice.

Agencies were breeding grounds for professional rivalry and back-stabbing. I knew of one major agency in town that had two chairmen, two presidents, two managing directors, and four vice-presidents. One would think that nobody would take such nonsense seriously, but they did. Giving out titles reminded me of Louis XIV: "Every time I give someone a title, I make a hundred people angry and one person ungrateful."

Later, in the mid 50's, after our agency's move into Mr. Florence's new bank building, Glenn signed a new account: one-half of the Lone Star Brewing Company. Wilcox's solicitation and proposals finally paid off. I set my self up to becoming the best-informed person in the agency on the account. I read books on the brewing and distilling of alcoholic beverages. I read trade journals in the field and spent Friday and Saturday nights in liquor stores, talking to customers. I visited the brewery and research laboratories in San Antonio and, yes, tasted the wares on occasion.

My workload increased so heavily that Glenn moved me into a spacious new office, complete with my own personal secretary. Jan West, a blond, medium-height beauty was a total perfectionist. However, it took the combined talents of both of us (not to mention long hours of overtime) to handle the heavy work and ever-pressing dead lines.

Most of the labor that Jan and I did was routine agency client public relations. But, our golden opportunity came, and we rose to the occasion. Mr. Glenn asked the agency to submit policy papers on my former employer, Republic National Bank, which, under President Fred Florence's direction, had a combined surplus and capital figure of $55 million. The other account executives put in adequate papers of five or six pages, but Jan and I took the trouble to assemble every conceivable statistic, and after working day and night for three weeks, came up with an analysis which covered over a hundred pages. The following week, after well-written and delivered presentations by Mr. Wilcox to the bank's different committees, Glenn Advertising, Inc. secured Republic National Bank as a new and valuable client, mostly thanks to Jan and me.

Our work was exciting. Some young men and women were attracted by the travel, the whirlwind of social parties, and other entertainment that was attached to the work of an account executive. They soon found that lunching in expensive restaurants was no fun if one had to explain declining share-of-market while eating smoked salmon. Riding the circuit of test markets could be a nightmare. But as my own reputation with Glenn

Advertising grew, my name began appearing on many impressive social registers in the state of Texas. Seemingly, each day or two, I would receive a formal invitation in the mail that would top the parties of Washington's social hostess, Perle Mesta. From newspaper and hotel tycoon Jesse Jones' parties at the Lamar Hotel in Houston (home-and second home-to some of the wealthiest men in history) to the glamorous parties hosted by Harry Jersig, president of Lone Star Brewing Company, and the Menger Hotel in San Antonio, I was always in attendance (with dancing shoes on).

The Lamar Hotel was built in 1927 by Jesse Jones, the owner of the Houston Chronicle, who lived in a suite on its 16th floor for three decades. The hotel was an elegant retreat for the wealthy. Eighty-eight of the 350 rooms and suites had been sold to rich businessmen. It catered to people who wanted to stay where it was quiet, and where there was no one around.

H.L. Hunt, the Dallas oil billionaire, often telephoned Jeanne Dixon, internationally known seer, not that he was superstitious, but he believed in the value of her predictions. He often said, "I can smell oil, but she knows where the deep fields are!" He, too, stayed at the Lamar when he was in Houston. He was fond of sitting in the lobby in tattered clothes, either reading the newspaper or playing poker, with one eye cocked to note if anyone richer than himself showed up. After he left the White House, Lyndon regularly stayed at the hotel. A special suite was built for his Secret Service agents.

Members of the 8F group, the political powerhouse of Texas, including the Brown & Root brothers, H.L. Hunt, Clint Murchison, Sid Richardson, and Judge Roy Hofheinz were all getting very rich, and they did not hesitate to display their opulence-their ladies' mink coats, diamonds, huge ranches, and Cadillacs.

Sid Richardson owned a fleet of Cadillacs, one in every town and in every city he traveled. Sid loved living in hotels and then traveling frequently to his island to hunt and fish. Lyndon would laugh and say, "In Texas they don't ask what kind of car you're going to buy. T hey only ask, 'What color?' However, H.L. Hunt ignored his riches and continued to dress like a bum. He drove faded, early-model jalopies.

In spite of my new-found high society living, my heart and ears waited patiently for a telephone call from Jesse telling me Lyndon was in Austin or Houston or San Antonio and wanted to see me. But Lyndon's burdensome duties as a new U.S. Senator kept him in Washington more often. The trips to Texas were becoming less frequent.

Lyndon, now at home in our nation's capital as Texas' fresh man Senator, had a deep desire to keep his campaign commitments and began spending long, endless, tiresome hours digging, planning, and researching government files. He was always on top of the oil situation and corresponded often with Clint Murchison, who predicted Lyndon would be the next president.

While observing the unwritten rule that freshmen senators should be seen and not heard, Lyndon was introduced to all the other senators of importance by Mr. Sam. He became good friends with Senate veteran Richard Russell, a bachelor from Georgia, and chair man of the powerful Armed Services Committee. Lyndon often told me he liked Senator Russell for being a workaholic and for his love of the South which he so diligently served. A member of the Senate "inner circle," Lyndon later appointed Russell to the Warren Com mission.

I was desperately in love with Lyndon. Oh yes, I played all those torturous mind games, pretending that he only wanted my body, thinking I would never see him again. But as the trips to Austin and the Driskill Hotel continued (not to mention the regular delivery of flowers, fashionable designer clothes from Neiman-Marcus, and beautifully scented perfumes), I happily realized that Lyndon loved me, too, though perhaps not as much as I loved him.

I knew there was always the real possibility that I would never see Lyndon again, but it wouldn't be because he didn't love me. I wanted to enjoy him while I could. I wasn't using him as an escape or a respite from my life. I truly loved him. He was the life I might have had under different circumstances. The life I should have had. The life Lady Bird had.

One autumn morning at the office, Bea Miller buzzed my intercom announcing that I had a visitor in the lobby. I hesitated for a moment, then checked my calendar. Odd, I thought. I had no appointments for that day.

As I entered the lobby, a tall man dressed uniformly in black pants and jacket handed me a large beribboned box before abruptly leaving.

I shrugged my shoulders to Bea and walked back to my office where I tore into the box with little regard for the satin ribbons and expensive wrapping paper.

Inside was an exquisite, black full-length mink coat! I picked it up and held the soft fur to my tear-stained face. Inside one of its pockets was a small card that simply read, "Soon."

The entire advertising staff had crowded into my office by this time to satisfy their curiosity. One of the office secretaries asked if she could hold the coat in her arms for a moment or two. "Jeepers, Madeleine, how did you get such a gorgeous coat?"

I smiled and coyly answered, "I got my mink the same way minks get baby minks."

A few days later my office phone rang and my "hello" was greeted by a long silence. The connection sounded scratchy, as if it was long distance.

"Is this Madeleine?" Lyndon's voice made me tremble. "Yes."

"Is it all right to talk to you?" "Yes, of course. Where are you?"

"I'm in Austin for a couple of days. I've got to see you, Madeleine. I'm at KTBC now. I'll have Jesse make arrangements for you to be flown down this afternoon."

Just then Mr. Wilcox walked into my office.

"Well, of course, Jesse," I said in a businesslike voice. "I couldn't agree with you more. That account is very important. I'll take a plane out late this afternoon and we can go over the radio spots this evening and tomorrow morning."

Mr. Wilcox whispered, "You're busy. I'll talk to you later." He turned around and left my office.

"You sound so good, honey," Lyndon continued. "You have no idea how this makes me feel just hearing your voice. It gives me a hard-on. You'll be here tonight, won't you, to take care of it?"

"Yes, I promise."

I immediately telephoned my parents, telling them I had to take an overnight trip to Austin to conduct business with radio station KTBC. Mother agreed to take care of Jimmy. Being able to get away so easily did little to relieve my conscience. I hated having to lie to anyone, especially my always-loving Christian parents.

They were beginning to question the arrival of such gifts as flowers, perfume, clothes, and, especially, the mink coat. In addition, they expressed concern that my position at Glenn Advertising was not a "9-to-5" job and was keeping me away from home and son.

I had called my father by his first name, George, ever since I was old enough to speak, and he had never requested otherwise. He was named after George W. Truett of the internationally known First Baptist Church of downtown Dallas, known today as Criswell's Church. He warned me daily that "sin just didn't pay." I was con fused. What did sin have to do with my career which I dearly loved, and which provided a living for Jimmy and me?

George would caution me each day as I left for work. "Be careful, honey, sin is so easy to fall into, yet so hard to get out of." I must have carried around different types of genes from my God-fearing Catholic parents who had devoted their lives to attending their church and living by the Ten Commandments burned into stone so many years ago. George's philosophy was "Cast your bread upon the water and it will come back like a deluxe sandwich."

Just a few hours later I was about to open the door of the bath in Lyndon's suite wearing nothing but my spectacular mink coat and very high heels dyed to match when I took one last look in the mirror. Dressed appropriately for the part, ready, willing and able to properly thank Lyndon for the fur. I opened the door and pranced proudly into the bedroom. My breasts were bouncing against the heavy, liquid smooth silk lining and luxuriant powder soft fur causing wicked, delicious waves of fire to course through my body. I wanted him in my arms so badly my knees began to vibrate from the urgency. With a shriek, I cried out in wanton appeal for my lover and Lyndon leaped from the bed, lowered me, mink and all, in his arms to the floor. He then took me passionately-perhaps too passionately-as I discovered rug bums on my buttocks later.

After our wonderful lovemaking we lay in bed talking, touching, laughing and kissing. All the nightmares of the past few years with Glynn seemed to be little more than a bad dream. This was what love was supposed to be!

"Madeleine, are you happy?"

In this peaceful moment I tenderly kissed his lips. That was my answer.

"I have a feeling things are going to start moving very fast now that I'm in the Senate," he said. "I don't want the important things to get left behind. That's why I have to tell you how much I love you. I can't let it wait."

For a moment he couldn't find the right words to continue. Then he said, "Spend the night with me. We'll just lie in bed and talk. I have so much to say. I want to be with you. You are something special."

"You really think so?"

"You're very special. I want you to be part of my life, Madeleine."

Lyndon's words jarred me out of my dreamy fog. I couldn't be a part of anything. The only future I saw was a miserable attempt to lead a double life, one that relied upon deception at both ends.

"Sometimes I get the feeling you're going to disappear," I said, "that I'll never have you, that our moments together are so great because there aren't going to be many. Lyndon, I love you too, but you're married. W hat is there for us?"

Neither of us knew what to say: we were silent a long time. He was so close to my face, looking into my eyes. He kissed me and we held each other tightly, as if we were afraid if one let go, the other would disappear.

"I'm sorry," he said. "I know you think I'm a rotten son-of-a bitch as a husband. You want to know about Bird? No more lies, Madeleine. She's cold and there's little affection. She's not the type of woman who is there waiting for you at the end of a long, hard day. She's a money-and-power woman and our marriage was one of convenience. My Daddy told me. 'Son, you can make more money at the altar than you can in a lifetime of work.' So what the hell, I took his advice."

Jesse confided in me that Lyndon was determined to marry for money ever since his college days at San Marcos. Lyndon had courted two young women. Each-Carol Davis of San Marcos and Kitty Clyde Ross of Johnson City-had been the daughter of the rich est man in town. In 1934 he began courting a third young woman.

She was Claudia Alta Taylor of Karnack, Texas. Her nickname was "Lady Bird," which was given her at the age of two by a black nurse because she was "purty as a lady bird."

I gently touched Lyndon's face with my fingers, then opened my hands and pressed them to his cheek. I could feel my heart pounding through my palms.

"I do love you, Madeleine. Lets be together like this forever.

With you at my side, I can do anything."

I was petrified. It was the best moment of my life, and the worst. The inevitable explosion of contrasting emotions nearly ignited.

"No matter what happens," Lyndon continued, "I'll love you forever."

I'll never forget the way he looked at me with his big brown eyes, so gentle and loving. "Don't be afraid," Lyndon whispered. "You'll never want for anything."

Slowly he began caressing each part of my body. He playfully nibbled my lips as he stroked my face, neck, and breasts with his hands. We kissed passionately. Time and place melted away into some thing wonderful.

The following morning I lay back against the white satin pillow and looked toward the large bedroom window. Lyndon was standing naked against the glass, his hands spread wide on the ledge, en joying the scarlet sunrise.

I pulled the satin sheet up about my own naked body and willed Lyndon to tum around. He didn't move. I wanted him to come back to bed, but I didn't want to ask.

I changed my position against the pillow. I looked down at the innocent swelling of my breasts beneath the sheet and blushed. Was it obvious? Could anybody tell at a glance that I had been making love-wild, searing love? I pulled my fingers through my hair trying to determine how tangled it was.

There had been a Greta Garbo film about a queen who was trapped in a wayside inn with a man. He did not know that she was a queen, and as the snow separated them from the outside world, they stayed in a room and made love. The queen had wandered around their quarters touching the now familiar objects and consigning them to her memory. For she would never return to the room and she knew nothing with the man would ever be the same again.

I wondered what in Lyndon's hotel suite could be stored away in my memory. The dark-stained plank flooring and green wool rug? The textured walls that were painted white? The beamed ceiling that matched the dark walnut floor? Or the four-poster feather bed?

I knew Lyndon loved me and I loved him, but his political career was skyrocketing, and lengthy periods of separation would routinely occur. I remember reading somewhere that if a woman is given only a limited amount of time to spend with a man she loves, she endures the separation by constantly recalling and reliving every moment down to the finest detail.

Suddenly Lyndon threw open the double-wide arched windows and staring at the blazing sunrise, bellowed like a bull, "Goddamn, I love Texas in the morning!"

Lyndon's outburst shocked me back to reality and I looked over once more toward him at the opened windows. A shiver of wind, the first of the day, tugged at the curtains, and he turned and approached me.

I felt myself becoming hot and moist and was ashamed. I lowered my gaze. Lyndon took my chin in his hand and forced it up so that he could look into my eyes. I wanted him to kiss me. To embrace me and press me back into the satin pillows and hold me tight and make me forget everything-except the marvelous feeling that had consumed me the last time.

Lyndon leaned forward again. He looked into my eyes for several seconds and then abruptly kissed me with such passion that I expected to taste blood on my lips. His hard shoulders bore me down. I trembled beneath his hands as he cupped the soft skin of my inner thighs.

"I met a reformed cannibal one time," he said, lowering his mouth to my breast, "and he told me what part of the human body was the tastiest." His head moved to the area below my abdomen.

I was moaning softly as my hips undulated, nudging him to ward them. With hot, heavy breaths I asked, "What part? What part? What part?"

After our "love rendezvous," Lyndon told me about buying the old Martin homestead, close to his birthplace. He had always wanted to be a rancher and was like a little boy with a new toy. "Hell, it was so run-down that chickens could run their necks up through the floor of the old house. I grew up here on the Pedernales River, with family and cousins. I can identify with everything in the rolling hills, with beautiful wild flowers and wildlife. I bought the old place at a real bargain, only twenty thousand. You know, Madeleine, my old man rode the countryside the day I was born and told everyone a United States Senator had been born."

It was on this ranch that belonged to an aunt that his family had celebrated many reunions and holidays. He had played there as a child, building dreams that he would even be President one day. Eventually it became the LBJ Ranch. "Goddamn, it's a big achievement for someone who was born poor in the hill country."

Lyndon was exuberant and continued to talk about the ranch and how he was going to refurbish and develop it into a showplace. He amused me by telling me the same story, but often in a different context.

Lyndon developed the LBJ Ranch into a palatial showcase with a beautiful lake in front of the house. He built an over-sized swimming pool. Later he constructed a landing strip for jets (at government expense) and called it "The Johnson City Airport." He developed an elaborate ranching operation, raised purebred and prize Hereford cattle, and irrigated pastures. Costly fences and endless barns graced the land. He loved every second at the ranch and continued to pour money into its operation until his death. In addition to its charms, the ranch was also a tax benefit for the Johnson empire.

My daily routine included a fifteen or twenty minute break at Vick's Coffee Bar in downtown Dallas. There I would purchase up to ten Roi Tans for Mr. Wilcox. My "coffee cronies" included policemen on the beat; advertising executives; secretaries; an attorney whom I'll call Harvey Bollinger, whose father had been a bookkeeper for Chicago gangster, Al

Capone; as well as oilmen such as Clint Murchison, Sid Richardson, and H.L. Hunt.

Haroldson Lafayette Hunt stood almost six feet tall, weighed approximately 170 pounds, and always wore clothes that looked as if they had been purchased from the local thrift shop. Before I began attending social functions and learned he was the richest man in the world, I used to buy Mr. Hunt a cup of coffee every morning (which he almost never drank) not only because I thought he was homeless and couldn't afford a ten cent cup of coffee, but because he could charm the birds out of the trees. Believe it or not, he was almost excluded from patronizing Vick's because of his appearance.

The advertising executives would brag about their new clients, such as Dr. Pepper, but it was the titillating stories of gangsters, gamblers, wildcatters, and off-color sex stories told by Harvey Bollinger and H.L. Hunt that added color and excitement to our mornings.

We chided H.L. often about his multiple ladies and his three marriages. He loved pretty women. We all knew he had ties with Jack Ruby's girls (who at that time was simply known as a former AI Capone guy). One of Hunt's favorites was Lacy. She was beautiful and appeared to be what H.L. often ordered. I never knew if any of my cronies were patrons of Madame Nina De Loache who operated what was probably Dallas' only true brothel, an exclusive place near the John Birchers who lived in the luxurious Turtle Creek section of Dal las.

H.L. Hunt, a school dropout in the fifth grade, had gambled in Chicago for years, going way back to when he was a young hobo drifting across the country on his own. Later, he parlayed a $4,000 pot from a game into a successful oil business in El Dorado, Arkansas. His first drilling rig had cost him $50. H.L. Hunt learned to play poker from cotton planters on the mighty Mississippi. After he had hit it big in the oil business, he started traveling to gambling joints in Chicago more and more frequently. Because of the amounts of money he played for, as well as his skills at poker, he was treated respectfully by young AI Capone. Occasionally H.L. visited Capone's gambling emporium called the Four Deuces.

Although H.L. and Capone came from different backgrounds and different worlds light-years apart, they followed the same rules in life and business-their own peculiar code of honor, trust, and respect.

Yes, H.L. and Capone were more alike than either man would care to admit.

6

Dreams

One late December afternoon, I received a call at the office from Jesse Kellam. Lyndon was in Austin for the holidays and was anxious to see me. As usual, a ticket had been purchased for me aboard an early evening TTA flight and a KTBC mobile news unit would pick me up at the airport.

Even though it was the holiday season, I was depressed. Lyndon had always totally confided in me. He confessed his insecurities, fears, hopes, and dreams. "I'm a goddamn open book for you, honey," he would say. "All you have to do is tum the pages. Oh, how I love the way you tum my pages!" But I had deceived him, misled him. He didn't know the real Madeleine Brown. He didn't know about the four years of hell I had gone through living with Glynn. He didn't even know about my little Jimmy. Now it was past time that Lyndon be told the truth about everything.

Hours later I opened the mahogany door of his suite with my own key. He stood on the other side of the room and I ran to him. We kissed passionately and frantically, laughing and crying at the same time. I felt so wonderful again. I fought to keep my emotions in check, but when he pulled back to kiss me, he stopped, startled by my tears. "Damn, darling, what's all this? Did you miss me that much?"

"Yes! Yes! Yes!" I said, choking with tears.

"I love you, my red-headed honey," Lyndon said as he took my hand and led me to the bedroom.

We made love and talked late into the night. I told him more about my life, telling him the truth about my years with Glynn. I couldn't go on. Through my tears I caught a glimpse of his face. The lamp reflected in his watery eyes. His breathing became quick and his anger was rising over the abusive way I had been treated. He shot off the bed and slammed his fists into the wall.

"Where in the fucking hell is this chicken-shit bastard that beats up on my redheaded lady?" he shouted, hitting the wall again and again. "Where is he? We'll just see how the son-of-a-bitch can handle someone who is his own size. I'll kill the bastard!" Then he sat down on the side of the bed and hugged me close in his arms.

"Now you belong to me," he said, holding me tighter, "and no son-of-a-bitch is going to hurt you ever again."

I dropped another bomb. "Lyndon, I haven't told you everything. "

"There's more?" He asked it with such incredulity. If l weren't so upset, I probably would have laughed.

"It's not real bad, or at least not to me. I don't know what you'll think."

"What?"

"I, uh, Lyndon, I have a son by my husband."

Lyndon closed his eyes as if in pain. The anguish I felt seeing his expression cut deeper.

"A son, huh?"

We were silent for a while. Lyndon was considering the matter carefully. Suddenly he brightened.

"Oh, what the hell! I love boys. How old is he?"

"Jimmy is almost two. He's a handsome, good-looking boy and I love him deeply."

Lyndon was quiet again. He wrinkled his forehead and thought some more.

"Nothing is going to change, is it?" I asked.

"Not on my part," he said. "I'll always love you. You're part of me no matter where I go or what I do."

Finally spent and exhausted after endless orgasms, we fell asleep holding onto each other.

The next morning, after we dressed, Lyndon received a phone call in the suite.

"I'm sorry, darling," he apologized, "but all the news unit vehicles are tied up. Jesse is having a car brought around for you to drive back to the airport."

I gave him a light kiss on the lips. "Lyndon, it's no big deal. I don't mind."

" Are you sure?"

"Honestly, I don't mind at all."

Lyndon escorted me out of the hotel and into the parking lot.

After spotting the car that I was supposed to "drive back to the airport," I stopped, then spun around to face Lyndon.

He flashed a mischievous grin and said, "Don't bother stop ping at the airport. Just drive the damn thing on back to Dallas."

The car was a new white, two-door Ford coupe with wire wheel covers and a red ribbon across the steering wheel that read, "Merry Christmas, Madeleine."

"It's mine?" I asked, catching my breath.

Lyndon nodded. "All yours, Madeleine. My Christmas present to you."

We both looked around the parking lot to see if anyone was watching, the fear of discovery uppermost in our thoughts. I pulled him to me and kissed him long and hard.

He lingered only a few more minutes in the parking lot, as I thoroughly examined the car, then began walking back toward the hotel.

"Merry Christmas, my love, " he said. "Jesse will be in touch with you the next time I'm in Austin."

I blew him a kiss with my hand and then drove the car toward the outskirts of town. It was early morning and the drive was pleas ant, the deer munching greedily on roadside forage. I quietly admired the arching hillsides and rolling countryside while I rehearsed an explanation to my parents as to how a girl making $375 per month, with a baby to feed, could afford a new car.

The one hundred ninety-eight miles from Austin to Dallas seemed like a thousand, even though I was driving seventy miles per hour.

Finally, I hit upon a believable lie. Glenn Advertising had just obtained the Lone Star Brewing Company account, and in addition, I was required to spend time at the Fort Worth Lone Star Beer Distributor office twice a week. Why not say it was a company car? It certainly made sense to me.

After arriving back home in Dallas, however, my father said he had never seen a company so benevolent toward its employees.

"I've worked for Dallas Power and Light for thirty years, and I just got a company car five years ago," he said skeptically. I shrugged my shoulders. "George, times are changing." He arched a quizzical eyebrow. "Yes, they certainly are."

7

Lonely Life

The late evening sun blazed harshly across the capitol. It moved slowly through the evening spectrum-yellow to orange to the red of the Texas soil-finally to darkness. The devilish wind became silent. I was attending a private Democratic party at a wealthy Texan's home nestled in the hills surrounding Lake Travis in Austin. Lady Bird and Lyndon were in attendance. As everyone danced and drank outside on the patio, the white banks of the hillside pool (into which a few drunken party-goers had already fallen) shimmered like an ivory balcony in the moonlight, and the house's party lights twinkled across the water like stars in a black rippling sky.

I was very uncomfortable with Lady Bird present. When she excused herself around midnight, my heart filled with joy, and I anxiously dashed back to the Driskill to await my love. Even though I was in the comfort of a beautiful hotel room, that essence of heavy heat filled the air leaving me sweaty and sticky. I told myself, "Madeleine, this won't do!" Lyndon would soon be here and I couldn't let him find me damp and untouchable. I opened my suitcase and pulled out the long, red lacy negligee that revealed much more than it covered, laid it across the bed and went in to take a bath.

As I lay in the tub of cool water, hot fevered thoughts of my lover inflamed my flesh and made my nipples ache. The cool water squeezed upon them from the washcloth did nothing to ease that ache. Only Lyndon's lips would dispel the taut hardness gripping them.

Wrapping the towel around me sarong-style, I left the bath and entered the bedroom to get dressed, which caused me to giggle in mirth. After all Lyndon would quickly strip me anyway, so why bother with the negligee? It was only because I liked to see the expression on his face when he first saw me in seductive things. His eyes would expand and show a complete white ring, eyebrows quickly flicked up and down and his chest expanded as he tried to catch his breath. Yes! Any woman's heart would be uplifted by such looks from her lover. With sensuous delight I slipped into my beautiful red nightgown, silky smooth and form fitting. I whirled around in front of the mirror for a critical look and stopped dead in my tracks. There was no way the reflection I saw in the glass was me: an elegantly beautiful, sexy, seductive and supremely confident woman stared back at me. Who was she? Where did she come from? Why was she here? What was her name?

I stood suspended in time – divorced from reality-caught up in a fantasy world where kings and queens shouted my name, princes sought my hand and court jesters danced around me throwing red roses at my feet. It was so real, I could even smell the roses and actually hear the crinkle of the jesters' costumes as they danced wildly. From far away I heard my name spoken softly, "Madeleine, Madeleine, Madeleine ..."

I turned in slow motion. Lyndon was standing there, arms cradling what must have been five dozen roses and nervously crumpling the green, florist paper that protected the long stems. Well! That explained the rose smell and jester noise.

Swiftly, smoothly, Lyndon covered the few feet between us and tenderly laid the flowers in my outstretched arms with his spoken words, "Red roses for my beautiful redheaded lady."

Beautiful as they were and as pleased as I was, I only wanted him in my arms. My heart swelled full of tenderness when I saw the look of love flood his face. His hurried solicitations and caring manner was carried out by strewing red roses all about my feet. Easily, I slipped back into fantasy (were there not roses strewn at my feet?). My king was calling out my name and taking my hand tenderly kissing the palm. I could actually see all this unfolding before me as if I was the director on a movie set. Perhaps I had, according to metaphysical teachings, an "out-of-body experience," but then, in my eyes, every experience with Lyndon was an out-of-body experience.

All night I watched from my vantage point the tableau spread before me. Two lovers vigorously locked in the pleasures of the flesh. An erotic movie, if you will, of great beauty and elegance framed in guttural grunts, cries, screams and moans.

How could there be any connection between the noises and language of passion with the beautiful wonder that it created? And even more wonderful were the moments after the passion had passed ...The holding, the kissing, the touching and caressing of the hair on my forehead, the champagne in fine, fluted crystal, and the scattered, fragrant rose petals from the childhood game of "He Loves Me, He Loves Me Not" (Lyndon always ended on "Loves Me")-all these left me feeling cherished. These loving moments made my life complete. The morning sun would come up and I would be thrust back into my dark secrecy and my fantasy would be put on hold. However, at daybreak, with a wrapped gift in his arms, Lyndon gently kissed me awake and we spent the morning together.

Few of the people who came in contact with Lyndon ever fully understood the man. His family, his friends, his political associates, the members of his Senate staff and especially me-each of us had his or her piece of the Lyndon Johnson puzzle. But no one ever really put the puzzle completely together.

John Connally once said of Lyndon: "There is no adjective to describe him. He was cruel and kind, generous and greedy, sensitive and insensitive, crafty and naive, ruthless and thoughtful, simple in many ways, yet extremely complex, caring and totally uncaring; he could overwhelm people with kindness and turn around and be cruel and petty towards those same people: he knew how to use people in politics in a way nobody else could that I know of. As a matter of fact, it would take every adjective in the dictionary to describe him." Even I would struggle to truly understand him. More dis concerting than anything else was that every new perspective seemed only to blur the portrait.

As I readied myself to return to Dallas, Lyndon said, "Here, honey, I think you deserve a pussy award for all that wild fucking!"

Inside was a beautiful doll wearing a gold and white swimsuit with high heels. Emblazoned in gold on a diagonal white sash were the words "MISS PUSSY GALORE!" After I laughed and expressed my appreciation, Lyndon went to the window, as he had numerous times before and once more bellowed like a bull, "Goddamn, I love Texas in the morning!"

Around seven that morning, Lyndon arranged for Jesse to drive me back to the Austin airport for my flight back to Dallas.

With a heavy heart, I climbed the dimpled metal stairs into the steel-gray airplane-it was like walking to the gallows. I looked back and saw Jesse standing at the gate. He waved slowly.

I waved back, then turned and entered the plane. Inside, the cabin and seats were dull gray. The plane was as dismal as the lonely life to which I was returning. I'd been so happy with Lyndon the night before and now the airplane, humming a funeral-like dirge, was taking me away.

I sat down in the gray seat next to the window and looked down into my arms. There was my award from Lyndon. Even as tacky and as vulgar as it was, I couldn't help laughing all the way to Dallas. I still treasure the award and memory after all these years.

I didn't hear from Lyndon for over a month until one day at the office a dozen red roses were discovered. The card read, "I Miss You!"

Lyndon called two days later from Washington, saying he was between committee meetings. He sounded out of breath as if he had run from somewhere and had only a minute or two to talk.

"I just got the urge to tell you that I love you. You don't mind, do you, darling?"

"I never mind," I said. "You know that."

"Our love is forever, Madeleine. Nothing else matters." "Lyndon, I' m in Dallas and Lady Bird travels so much with

KTBC business," I said slowly. "Do you ever feel like being with someone else?"

Lyndon's response was neither romantic nor diplomatic. Female manipulation did not bring out the best in him. "Don't give me any of that bullshit," was his abrupt, caustic reply.

• • •

I had recently heard rumors that Lyndon had taken one of his Senate secretaries to a social affair in Washington and introduced her as "his girl."

At our next rendezvous, I confronted Lyndon who angrily defended himself, "Aw bullshit! There could be a thousand women around and you would be the only one for me," he insisted. " Always believe that, Madeleine. You will forever be first in my life and I'll always be here for you."

He didn't call as often during the next month. His Senate career rocketed. There were articles about him everywhere, in Time, Newsweek, Life, all the major magazines.

In July 1950-after Lyndon had uncovered a lot of waste and corruption in the military's preparation for the Korean War-Senator Russell appointed him chairman of the Preparedness Investigating Sub committee of the Senate Armed Services Committee.

Almost overnight the subcommittee became headline news, with Lyndon relentlessly quizzing witness after witness about price gouging by tin producers, waste of manpower, and scandals involving misuse of military surplus.

The nagging paid off. In the Army he found supply sergeants issuing golf clubs, expert pilots acting as post-exchange officers, illegal slot machines at an air base, trained tank mechanics assigned to reserve units that had no tanks, and empty barracks at one army base while at another installation hundreds of soldiers lived in packing crates and mule sheds.

Even back home in Texas, Lyndon's investigators learned that a farmer had bought $1,200,000 worth of surplus airplane parts for

$6.89 and then sold them back to the government for $63,000.

Eventually, Lyndon's subcommittee (whose total operating expenses were $275,000) saved the U.S. Government more than five billion dollars.

Seeing him on television and hearing his voice on the radio made me miss him even more. I was so happy for him, but I wondered if he were changing. Had all the publicity and power gone to his head? Was he taken in by sudden fame?Would he still enjoy the simplicity of our love? I had a horrible feeling that I wouldn't see him again. His prominent career would make it harder to hide our love.

8

Love Child

The next couple of weeks were a daze. Every morning I began with a feeling of dizziness and nausea. I felt bloated, but brushed it off as a stomach flu. Then, one morning, I found myself almost doubled over with pain. I made an appointment with the doctor who had delivered Jimmy. I was overwhelmed with fear. After the humiliating examination with my feet in stirrups and my legs spread apart, Dr. Langston asked me to step into his office.

As he sat at his desk studying the results of my examination, I glanced at the framed photographs, medals, and newspaper clippings from his Navy days during World War II, displayed prominently on the walls. Behind him, rain lashed at the windows.

"Madeleine, you're two months pregnant." He smiled a slow, weary smile. He was a friend of our family and was keenly aware of my husband's institutionalization. He also knew my husband had undergone a vasectomy in the fall of 1949, performed by Dr. Bryant Baker of Dallas.

I said nothing. My body stiffened, my hands began trembling. I became dizzy and nearly collapsed on the floor when he told me I was pregnant! Dear God, what more could happen?Was this my punishment for being with Lyndon? I was confused, depressed, shocked, and sick. Ladies didn't have contraception in those days. The "pill" was unknown.

I started crying. "Please, please help me, Dr. Langston! I can't have this baby!"

He shook his head. "No, Madeleine, I'm sorry. I can't help.

You know Texas law forbids abortions."

I knew that Dr. Imogene Mayfield, a friend of Jack Ruby's, reportedly lost her license because she was performing abortions and dispensing illegal drugs. I also knew there were women in Oak Cliff (not licensed physicians) who performed abortions. One was an acquaintance of our family. A young girl with whom I had gone to school had bled to death in her office from causes reported to be a "folding table and a dirty knife," according to investigators. No, abortion was not the answer.

Shockwaves pounded me. This was the one child I should have truly celebrated. A child born out of love, fathered by the man I truly loved. Instead, Lyndon's career was at a critical stage. He couldn't survive the scandal of my pregnancy.

As Dr. Langston continued to explain the different stages of pregnancy, scheduling my follow-up appointments, I sat quietly, fighting back the tears. What would I do next? How could I tell Lyndon? With his incredible temper, what would he say and do? How would he respond?

Then my parents' smiling faces came to mind. They were so beautiful, so loving. What would they say?

Through a blur of tears, I somehow made my way out of Dr. Langston's office. The rain had subsided and the May heat coupled with the humidity produced overwhelming nausea. I leaned on his outside office door to catch my breath. Recovering, I ran to the car, opened the door, and struggled to get the key into the ignition. I was crying so hard I could barely see. I backed out and headed home.

"Why, God, why am I being punished?" I screamed. "Why?" My only sin was loving Lyndon. It's not fair!

Blinded by my anguish and pain, I nearly blacked out. I man aged to make my way to Kiest Park, a lush, wooded recreation area in the city where I could be alone. I kicked off my shoes to feel the grass under my feet and make sure I was still whole. I walked along the nature trail, crossing streams of water, drinking in the contrasting colors of the trees and daffodils, irises, beautiful Texas wild flowers, wine cups, bluebonnets, Indian blankets, and cornflowers.

This would be a nice place to die, I thought. I don't want to live any more. I have nothing to live for. Then I thought of my son. I wouldn't take my life. I loved my boy, Jimmy, too much. I had never spent much time with him, but I was working long hours to make a future for both of us. We were more than a family. I was young when he was born and he brought so much excitement and pleasure to my parents' lives.[As the youngest child, George always referred to me as the "fall crop." I had two older sisters and a brother. And, they all married into the same family. My two sisters married the Duke brothers and my brother married their sister. The Dukes and former Texas Governor, John Connally, are cousins.]

I stood holding my arms outstretched over my head, gripping my fingers so tightly my nails dug into my palms. Then I fell to my knees, unleashing more tears. I pounded the ground with my fists. God, what am I going to do? Finally I collapsed beside a stream on the cool grass.

The sun rays with their particles of light reflecting on the water had a soothing, almost hypnotizing effect. As so often happens when life gets depressing and burdensome, we begin reliving the happy, innocent and carefree moments when we were younger ...

George, my father, was a handsome man with coal black hair and steel blue eyes. He was a gentle, sincere, Christian man, who became something of a legend in his time as he strove to make our small (but ultra-conservative) Oak Cliff community, Trinity Heights, a better place in which to live and raise a family.

George loved to fly. We would go to Love Field every Sunday and take demo-rides. He earned his pilot license, and would take me with him to the Clearview Airport on Hampton and Illinois across from the now famous and historical Austin Cook's Bar-B-Q. Dallas Police Officer J.D. Tippit, who lost his life the same day as John F. Kennedy, worked there part-time. Rumors have circulated that he was having an affair with one of the waitresses and a supposedly jealous lover, not Lee Harvey Oswald, took his life. It is believed she even had a son by him.

George's father, John C., was a tall, strapping 6'4", two-hundred-pound railroad executive with equally black hair and blue eyes. His small and trim wife, Arlevia, was the sister of John L. Bowen, a good friend and business associate of Texas billionaire, Sid Richardson.

My grandparents, whose ancestral roots could be traced back to the Scottish royal family of Duncan, had two homes: one in Denton, Texas, where my grandfather's two slender, beautiful redheaded sisters, Billye and Pauline, attended college, and the other in scenic East Texas among pine trees so tall they seemed to touch the heavens.

T he fields of East Texas were graced with cattle, watermelons, peanuts, sugar cane, tobacco, and pumping oil wells with gas flares that burned like giant candles lighting up the sky. I delighted in visiting my grandparents, where, as the youngest grandchild for four teen years, I received preferential treatment. I learned to throw horse shoes and shoot pistols, rifles and shotguns. (Years later I would even outshoot Lyndon Johnson, who was an excellent marksman.) Every Christmas my Uncle Chester would dress up and play Santa Claus for me. Our home was festive with food, music, lots of packages, and a beautifully decorated tree.

My aunts, Billye and Pauline, with college boyfriends, would come by the house in rumble seat automobiles with their radios turning out the tunes, and I would yearn to go with them. T he fun-loving, wild side of me cried out to be let loose.

My mother, Mary Priscilla, was beautiful, petite, and frail as a China doll. She had big brown eyes and jet black hair. Her redheaded mother, Laura Tipps, was a descendant of the family that established the Ben Franklin Stove Company outside of Memphis, Tennessee. My grandfather, Joe G. Lee, a tall, slender, black-haired man with the pronounced characteristics of his Indian blood, was closely related to the heroic Confederate General Robert E. Lee.

Miss Laurie (as my grandmother was known) once caught my grandfather in a whorehouse in the "red-light district" of Greenville, Texas and beat him repeatedly with a buggy whip in the middle of the street. To this day, the avenue is designated as Lee Street in memory of that infamous night.

Miss Laurie and Granddaddy Lee lived in Josephine, Texas, in Collin County, a short distance from Greenville, proudly known at the time for the "blackest land and the whitest people." In more brutish times there was once a sign in Collin County that read: "THE SUN HAS RISEN, THE SUN HAS SET, BUT NOT ON A NIGGER Y ET."

I always looked forward to our Josephine weekend because we could visit my mother's only brother, Uncle Bill Lee, his beautiful brunette wife, Aunt Prudie, their children, and also my "little black friends" who lived on the cotton farm. They taught me to play marbles, fly kites, and make mud pies, an art lost by today's children. They knew and shared every secret of the barnyard that was off limits to us. And every now and then we would go skinny-dipping in the pond.

Grandfather, at our very formal noon meal, would sit at the head of a huge Duncan Phyfe table, preparing everyone's plate and passing them around. No one talked or ever left a spoonful of food on their plates. Everyone always said, "Excuse me."

Granddad, a great story teller, in his deep bass voice, would call out. "Now, young ones, I'll tell you a story soon as I listen to the WBAP's stock market. You may play outside." He always reminded us not to go near the water wells or the Delco Plant that generated electricity for the cotton farm.

After listening to the stock market report on the radio, he would call us into his large personal sitting room, where no one entered without an invitation. It was immaculately clean and dust free. His beautiful Victorian tiger oak rocker sat in the middle of the room. From there he could look out and monitor the activities of his "hired hands." The radio, with its big horn speaker, sat on one end of his big desk. There was a decorative coal-burning potbelly stove and a brown leather davenport that converted into a bed for his afternoon nap. It was a cardinal rule that everyone in the household take an hour's nap or rest. On the back wall was an old-time telephone with a hand crank on a party line connecting everyone in the small town, and, of course, Gen. Robert E. Lee's oil painting. Granddad's jet black Stetson hat and a Colt .45 revolver hung high on the wall.

Miss Laurie provided us with a beautiful handmade colorful quilt, padded with cotton from the farm. With my cousins Mary Jo, Betty Sue, and Jimmy, we would lie down in front of him and then Granddad would start his great story. Jim, his yellow canary, would perch upon his shoulder. He often brushed the formula "color-back" on his wavy hair or groomed his mustache as we all intently watched and listened. Sometimes he told us about Wild West frontier days, gold rushes, Indians-the great chiefs Sitting Bull, Cochise, Crazy Horse, and Red Cloud-Gypsies, KKK, crimes that the Dallas police and law officers ignored, and tent medicine shows.

When he told us about Dallas' bandit queen, Belle Starr, who had lost her life in unfriendly Indian territory at the tum of the century, he would take out his snow white linen handkerchief and blot tears from his enormous dark brown eyes. We knew Granddad was a lover of "juices" and cards, so it is reasonable to believe he knew Belle Starr personally.

His greatest story was about a devoted Christian named Patillo Higgins who took his Baptist Sunday School Class on a picnic near some springs on a hill called Spindletop in scenic East Texas. The rainbow colors in the water and the smell there convinced Higgins the earth contained oil. He finally raised enough money to drill, and in January, 1901, 'the Big Un' came in and the world has never been the same. Granddad said, "Oil is power! Cotton would clothe us. The land would feed us, but nothing surpasses the universal power of oil." He would point west to Dallas for us to see the red double-faced flying horse of Mobil Oil's Pegasus on top of Dallas' Magnolia Building, which we still honor and love today.

My grandfather Lee was a cotton broker who farmed the black land. He was not a church-going man, but he was a kind and fair gentleman who loved all people, regardless of color. He tearfully told the story about the time it rained and a white racist rode by in a wagon, splashing mud on the black children who had been forced to walk to school. But my grandfather told his hired help to hitch up a team of mules and a wagon and make sure that the black children had a ride to school the same as the whites. Granddaddy Lee liked to move around a lot. My grandmother would say, "A rolling stone gathers no moss." And he would reply, "A dumed 'ole settin' hen doesn't get fat."

My grandmother was different. She was the one who man aged the sizeable cotton farm with the aid of three black families who lived on the property. Grandmother treated them like her own family as they labored picking cotton, canning vegetables, and curing sausage, ham and bacon with smoke house expertise.

My grandparents lived in Sam Rayburn's district. He and grand father were good friends over the years. These two southern gentle men would sit on my grandparents' forty-foot front porch with its majestic Corinthian columns telling exaggerated Indian yams and Civil War stories, reassuring each other that "the South would rise again!" Each was a heavy smoker and my cousins and I would roll their Prince Albert cigarettes with a manual roller (Mr. Sam smoked two packs a day until his death in 1961.)

Those were Prohibition days, but that fact never prevented these two men from drinking straight whiskey from a gallon jug on the porch. Their laughter would drown out the noise from the barnyard.

"Mighty good tastin' white lightnin',"Mr. Sam would say. The contents in that jug were always closely guarded in a back closet of the house. I would stay awake at night, trying to figure out a way to get into that closet and see what genie was in the jug that made these two old men so happy. Mr. Sam drank a small glass of bourbon spiced with honey every morning.

I knew it was time for Mr. Sam to leave when he would tell my grandfather: "See the red barn over there? Any jackass can kick it down, but a carpenter has to build it. I'm going to go back to Washington and kick the barns down!"

I often wondered if Mr. Sam harbored more than friendship toward my grandmother. After my grandfather died in 1934, Mr. Sam continued to come and visit her and she would cook for him-South em fried chicken (Mr. Sam's favorite, prepared a special way), cream gravy, fresh vegetables from the garden, and homemade ice cream. I would like to share this ol' Texas recipe and the preparations. The special way that my grandmother prepared Mr. Sam's chicken printed below:

FRIED CHICKEN A LA SAM RAYBURN
2 young chickens
4 C. flour
4 heaping T. lard Salt Pepper to taste

> Cut chicken in pieces. Dredge in flour and sprinkle with salt and pepper. Heat lard in an iron skillet. Drop in chicken pieces and cook in sizzling lard until golden brown on each side. Then lower fire, put lid on skillet, and let chicken steam until tender. Serve on hot platter, accompanied by "a bowl of gravy," prepared as follows:
>
> After removing chicken from skillet, stir grease to loosen flour and chicken particles left in pan. Add two tablespoons flour and stir until mixture is smooth. Then slowly add cold water (or, if you want a white gravy, add milk or cream) and continue stirring until mixture is consistency you like. Let boil up two or three times, stir again thoroughly, and then remove from fire.

Gentle scenes from my life with my grandparents played in all corners of my mind, but the harsh reality of my pregnancy began pushing and shoving for some resolution. The good images were replaced by a surrealistic vision of my parents' agonized, teary-eyed faces. Finally, I desperately struggled to maintain my composure. The reminiscing had renewed me. My mind was working clearly again. I would talk to George-my gentle, strong father. I didn't know how I would tell him, but he would have all the answers. Somehow, he always did.

It was almost dark when I arrived home. Mother had already gone to her bedroom and George was happily content to sit in his overstuffed reading chair in the den, intrigued by the test pattern on our new television set. We were the first house on the block to own one. Neighbors would come by just to see this strange and remark able phenomenon. TV in the South was not common until long after World War II.

I was determined to tell him the truth. "George, I need to talk to you." He could tell by the expression on my face that it was a serious problem.

"What? W hat's the matter?" His blue eyes were wide, demanding, and full of fear. He braced himself.

"I'm pregnant," I said, holding back the tears, my whole body trembling.

He was silent for a moment. Confused, he started to say some thing. Nothing came out. He buried his face in his hands.

"He's a married man," I continued. "I didn't know if you would understand, if you would hate me."

He stood up from the chair, which creaked. "Madeleine, come here." he said, hugging me. "I love you. You're my daughter, my own flesh and blood, and nothing can change that."

Instead of comforting me, the words stirred my guilt. I was trapped, forced to hurt the best friend I ever had-my father.

Tears welled up in his eyes and he took his handkerchief from his hip pocket and dried both our faces.

"Are you absolutely sure?" he asked. "Dr. Langston confirmed it today."

George broke away and began pacing the room. He frowned. I could almost hear the wheels spinning in his head. "I've got to think how we're going to handle this."

In those days, especially in Bible Belt Texas, when young unwed girls became pregnant their families would send them away in shame and disgrace.

I could see the pain in his heart. I had only seen it once before when I wanted to get away from home and disobeyed his earnest pleas not to marry into the Brown family. My wedding to PFC James Glynn Brown created mass hysteria throughout the Oak Cliff section of Dallas because my respectable, but prudish, parents were still of the Victorian opinion that they should choose their children's mates.

Of course it didn't calm the situation when a story circulated that George would shoot any clergyman who would perform the ceremony. The church was filled to capacity as people jammed every pew to witness this event which, of course, never happened.

During the course of the next two days, my father went to talk to Dr. Langston and our parish priest, Father James Becker. Although my mother was hysterical, George would come home from work and sit in his easy chair, staring blankly into space or quietly reading the family Bible.

I was petrified the evening my parents abruptly summoned me to the living room. They greeted me warmly and told me to sit down. I tried to stay calm as they dictated "ground rules" for the remaining seven months of my pregnancy. First, they would not send me away. I would take a leave of absence, or quit my job at Glenn Advertising. Second, I would withdraw completely from society, including church services. (This requirement was rather agreeable, especially since my knees had callouses from the altar and confessional.) Third, I could not make or receive personal telephone calls. Fourth, I would steadfastly remain secluded in our home. Fifth, I would be allowed two more weeks to "get my business affairs in order."

My parents were ashamed. They didn't want anyone to know that I had betrayed and humiliated our family name. My own shame was unbearable. I broke down and cried often.

Later the next day, Jesse called my office. Speaking obliquely, he offered some work-related excuse for me to come to Austin. Catching a plane within the hour, I was met at the airport by Paul Bolton, news director of KTBC, and driven to the Driskill, where I made my way to Lyndon's fourth floor suite.

In the elevator I rehearsed lines like, "Lyndon, you don't have to be here for me. I understand. Things just weren't meant to be. It was wonderful and I'll never forget you, but you must go on with your life. Good-bye, my love."

I took a deep breath, took one final sweep with the brush through my hair. Then my heart nearly stopped as I opened the door to his suite. He stood looking at me for what must have been twenty seconds. He didn't say a word. Oh my God, he knows, I thought. Slowly he started smiling, then broke into a laugh. He dashed over, picked me up, and twirled me around.

"You look great, Lyndon. Like the big, famous Texas Senator that you are!"

"Yeah, can you believe it? Not bad for a poor boy from the Hill Country."

"Are you feeling all right?"

"I'm okay. Just a bit tired. I don't have time to think. Senator Russell's committee keeps my ass dragging noon and night."

We didn't talk for a long time after that. He held me tightly and kissed me on each side of the neck. I kissed his chest. The two month separation built our desire to a fever pitch. Instead of the changes pulling us apart, our love making was even better than it had been. We were so intent on being together. We had to embrace for several hours. Neither of us had any sexual inhibitions.

Afterward, Lyndon relaxed. He could be himself with me. He didn't have to worry about his political image.

"I remember the first night we danced, Madeleine. Goddamn, you were beautiful and sexy in that black dress. I love the way you dance, but I want you to dance only with me."

I kissed him deeply.

"If I couldn't keep seeing you, I think I'd die. Even when you're not with me, I feel you are with me and that keeps me going, Why don't you come to Washington and be with me?"

We both knew the answer. It didn't need discussion.

I stiffened when he embraced me again and he sensed some thing was wrong. I was determined to tell him what had happened the last time we were together.

Whenever I tried to talk, he would kiss me in mid-sentence and stifle my words. He was in a playful mood.

My eyes filled with tears.

"W hat's wrong, darling? W hat's wrong? I'm your Sandow, aren't I? Where's my fig leaf?" Lyndon was teasing and laughing. (Sandow was a male model who had posed nude for women and he was a kind of sexual idol. A fig leaf would not cover him; neither would it cover Lyndon.)

"I'm pregnant!" The confession unleashed more tears. " Are you sure?"

"I've been to the doctor. I'm two months along."

His face twisted up in anger. "You goddamn dumb Dora! How could you be so fucking stupid?" He screamed, pounding the head board of the bed with his fists. Lyndon often called women "Dumb Dora" when he was angry with them. The phrase originated from a comic strip.

The edge in his voice frightened me. "How do you know it's mine?" "Because you've been the only one."

"Are you sure you haven't been sleeping around on me? Are you sure you haven't had cattin' shoes on?"

"No, Lyndon," I said. "You're the only one. "I'm sorry. It just happened."

"Then you can just happen to get a goddamn abortion." His voice had become low and deep.

I swallowed hard. "I'm not endangering my life or that of the baby's. I'm having this baby, Lyndon, with or without you."

His anger drained as fast as it erupted.

"You're some lady, Madeleine," he said tenderly. "Don't ever change." He pulled me to him and kissed me. "I'm sorry I yelled at you. Hell, it's not your fault. It takes two to tango."

I was still crying, but they were tears of relief.

"Don't worry," he said, hugging me. "I'll have Jesse contact a lawyer friend of mine in Dallas who owes me his balls on a silver platter. He'll make damn sure you never want for anything."

I turned and looked at him lovingly and put my hand on his. I told him about the exiled seclusion my parents had arranged for me.

"Did you tell them who the father was?"

"Of course not," I answered. "They only know he's a married man."

"That's goddamn good,because if this bullshit somehow leaks out ... I'll arrange it so that this lawyer, Jerome Ragsdale, takes the fall for your pregnancy. Do you understand me,Madeleine?"

My body was shaking like a leaf in a windstorm as he began ranting and raving again.

"Do you know what kind of goddamn scandal this would cause me?" He was screaming."I'm just now getting over that fucking 'Box 13' shit and have all the Texas oil people backing me for President now,and I'm not about to sit here and let the press hang me out to dry because I couldn't keep my pants on!"

He reached over the bed and grabbed a porcelain lamp from the nightstand. He held it in both hands,then smashed it on the floor where it shattered into tiny pieces.

"I promise you,Madeleine Brown," he said,waving his finger in my face, "if you know what's good for you, you'll cooperate with Ragsdale or your ass will be in a hell of a lot of trouble."

Tears streaked my face."Dear God," I prayed."No more. No more."

"Will I ever see you again?" I asked meekly, trying to douse his fiery temper.

Lyndon eased up,putting his arms around me. "Soon,darling. Soon."

Jesse informed me later not to expect too much fatherly concern from Lyndon. When Lady Bird had her miscarriages and when his daughter, Luci,was born in 1947, Lyndon was elsewhere,playing dominoes while his wife was in labor.

Back in Dallas, I requested and was granted a leave of absence from Glenn Advertising."Please don't ask any questions, Mr. Wilcox," I pleaded.

At home I had lied to my father that the company was selling me the white Ford coupe so I wouldn't be without transportation.

"I don't care," George said,staring at the nightly news on the television."You won't be driving it anyway. It's going to stay parked in the garage."

The TV anchorman was announcing that the "Big Four" were meeting in Paris and America's Secretary of State, Dean Acheson, would be attending a diplomatic conference in an attempt to keep the cold war from getting hotter. I frowned at the television set. I had my own "hot" war going on. My quiet, gentle and loving home had be come a battlefront of tears and hysteria.

My thoughts were interrupted by a knock at the front door. "Don't even think of answering it, Madeleine," George ordered, as he got out of his easy chair.

A tall man dressed in a dark suit, lizard boots and a Stetson stood on the front porch. "Let me introduce myself-Jerome T. Ragsdale. I'm the attorney who has been retained to handle your daughter's legal matters regarding her pregnancy." He smiled. "Mind if I come in and talk to you about it?"

George opened the screen door and Mr. Ragsdale stepped in, beaming a wide smile at all of us as he extended his hand. Although I had no voice in discussing the terms of the agreement, it seemed fair and equitable. I would receive $200 cash per week for living expenses, which would be increased to $500 upon birth; a raft of joint charge cards with the accounts listed in the names of Jerome T. Ragsdale and

Madeleine Duncan Brown; a new six-room house; a live-in maid to assist in the care of the baby; and, in addition, all bills were to be presented to Mr. Ragsdale for payment. W hen he left, he said he'd come by the house weekly to see that my needs were taken care of.

It was hard to believe that I would be locked up in my own house for seven months. Could I cope with it? I didn't have any choice. I got myself into this mess: now I'd just have to see it through.

Inside I ached because I knew the pain my pregnancy was bringing my parents. I knew the sorrow and confusion it was causing, and the disappointment. I knew they loved me, but I also knew they felt humiliated by me. And what could I say to them? Would "I'm sorry" make any difference now? Would it ease the pain, the shame they must have been feeling? I felt like such a fool for letting my life slip away. I cried for many days, thinking how I was hurting them.

Weeks passed. Sleep was a trap. I had a pathetic routine. I would arise at the last possible moment in the morning. Then I would be sprawled back on my bed after lunch until the afternoon soap op eras came on the radio: "Portia Faces Life," "Stella Dallas," and "Ma Perkins." I would return to my bed after an early supper, sleeping until perhaps seven o'clock. Then I might spend an hour or two reading before dozing off for the night.

While marveling at my ability to sleep so much, I saw that my strength was being sapped with each passing day. My walk slowed, my shoulders began to stoop and seldom did my sallow face reveal any emotion. When released from my "house arrest," I wondered if l would ever regain the ambition needed to cope with everyday problems of life, let alone a job and the family responsibilities of raising two children.

Eventually, I simply lay in my bed, if not sleeping, staring in a trance at the ceiling. I spent hours on menial tasks like sewing and polishing my mother's sterling silver over and over. "Building time" was what it was called in prison, the technique prisoners used to pass their hollow days.

Walking slowly was part of my new everyday life; shuffling about as if acting out a melodrama in slow motion. Like an invasion of locusts, the empty hours ate away at my very being. Soon there was total disorientation: staring at the clock, its hands never moving, losing track of time and place.

Once every week or so, George would allow me to ride with him down to the Trinity River bottoms to take hot food to the home less who lived in makeshift cardboard shelters. I hated all the misery and poverty. Then it was back to our home where I drifted aimlessly and slowly around the house and the garden in the backyard. I just seemed to be floating ever so slowly, the expression on my face must have been foolish, as all of my emotions blended into one depressing, sandy haze.

During the latter weeks of my pregnancy, sleep was fitful. I was up and down, constantly shuffling in the darkness. Several nights I awoke totally disoriented, thinking it was all a bad dream. At night, the full extent of what it really meant to be locked up in the house settled upon me. I felt completely closed in and fearfully alone.

I endured the long, dark days and nights, reliving memories of Lyndon-our moments, every word he said, every embrace, every kiss. He never called directly (although Jesse would contact me every few days), but in any given week I would receive a dozen red roses from KTBC, KWTX, or any one of the other radio stations within the Johnsons' communications network. The uplifting beauty of the flowers would always erase some of the heartaches and remind me of Lyndon. Everything reminded me of Lyndon. One of the cards from Jesse read:

"What is impossible?
It's likejoy after sorrow. Rainbows after storms. Woundshealed.
Forgiveness after wrong.
Fresh, genuine hope ...once abandoned.
We miss you, Madeleine. See you soon."

9

All Alone With Our Son

Meanwhile, the North Korean Communist forces, outfitted with Soviet-made weapons and equipment, crossed the 38th parallel to invade South Korea. President Truman reversed American Far East em policy, and ordered U.S. ships and warplanes to the battle zone. General Douglas MacArthur was ordered to push back the Communists, but the American and South Korean troops were totally unprepared and also outnumbered. They could not repel "the Communist hordes." On the opposite side, the North Korean troops were well trained and equipped. The cold war was showing the possibility of becoming the hottest kind of shooting war. And I was still pregnant and had four months to go before my own private war would end.

Adversity in the Democratic party greased the road to national prominence for Lyndon. By the 1950 election, the Truman ad ministration was already bogged down in Korea. An array of civil rights and welfare proposals was dead. Lyndon observed with inter est that the Senate majority leader, Scott Lucas, Democrat of Illinois, lost heavily to Republican Everett Dirksen. Francis Myers of Pennsylvania, Democratic whip of the Senate, was also defeated.

True, being Whip was not to have power, but it was a position that could be the next step to power, and Lyndon was always aware of the next step ... perhaps even the next dozen steps. Mr. Sam Rayburn was right along with Lyndon making sure his "protege" was making the right steps.

My own anguish was so strong I couldn't sleep or eat. I was so young, although I felt so old. My only recourse was my faith in God. He would show me the way. He wouldn't desert me. I asked Him to forgive me for bearing a child out of wedlock. As time passed, I gradually felt assured that God understood, and would bless the child despite the circumstances.

During one of my scheduled examinations, Dr. Langston in formed me that my baby would probably be born at Christmas, the birthday of the Christ child. What would Lyndon want, a boy or a girl – or did he care at all? What should its name be if it was a boy, a little boy with Lyndon's face and his crooked grin?

The days dragged. Those last few weeks before a child is born are the worst. I felt bloated and uncomfortable, and wanted only to get it over with. Finally, on December 27 I opened my eyes groggily and saw a nurse standing over my hospital bed.

"My baby?"

"He's fine. Would you like to see him?" I nodded.

She brought him to me. He was beautiful. He opened his eyes. In that brief instance where lifetime impressions are made, I could clearly see Lyndon's eyes in his. His dark hair, little face, chin, big feet-he was every inch his father. How Lyndon would have loved him. I cried and held him in my arms. Alone.

Little did I realize I would be alone throughout Steven's life.

The next day, Mr. Ragsdale relayed Lyndon's desire not to share in the naming of our baby boy. His name would be Steven Mark, in honor of the two Christian saints. Dr. Langston, in an effort to spare my family any further embarrassment, listed James Glynn Brown on the birth certificate as this baby's father.

My parents entered my hospital room with strained smiles on their faces. They remarked how handsome and healthy-looking Steven Mark was. His petite bed in the nursery was next to the newborn son of SMU's star football player, Kyle Rote. Seemingly, everyone in the hospital was excited about his birth. Photographers for the Dallas sports pages were busily snapping his picture. Yet I could say nothing about the birth of Senator Lyndon B. Johnson's son.

Less than a week later, Lyndon was easily elected Majority W hip of the Senate. No one had ever risen to that position in so short a time. George commented that all the power in Washington was in the hands of Texas' own Mr. Sam Rayburn, and Lyndon Johnson was a good student.

10

Big Deals and Big Money

I went to sleep early on New Year's Eve so I wouldn't have to face the pain of entering 1951 alone. In the quiet of the darkened hospital, my thoughts constantly turned to Lyndon. Why hadn't he called?Why did he not want to give his only son a name?Wherever he was, wouldn't some inner feeling weaken his stubborn heart? But he would not come. He could not come. There was no way he could dutifully take his place beside me. I was a young woman separated from her "husband" even though one of her two children was his! The shining new image of the legislative magician of the Senate that he had cultivated would be gone, his political career washed away in scandal. I couldn't ask that of him. Not for myself. Not for our son. Maybe one day the sacrifice wouldn't be so great. The fame had to pass. It could not last forever. I would be patient.

Steven and I were released from the hospital a couple of days later and I returned to home and was aimless. I wanted to go back to my job at Glenn Advertising to get on with my life and move forward. "Go to work?" George asked incredulously. "Absolutely not.

You'll stay home and take care of your baby like a mother is sup posed to. A woman's place is in the home." How horrible, I thought.

I really didn't know much about motherhood since George and mother had always taken care of little Jimmy while I was working. With the nanny that Mr. Ragsdale would hire, it seemed to me that Steven could be properly attended to. He was such a quiet baby and didn't require any special care. But George was intent on my staying home with my children like all the other mothers in the neighborhood.

Fortunately,during one of Mr. Ragsdale's weekly visits,I en listed his aid in persuading George to change his mind. First,he promised George that he would hire a new live-in nanny. At first,George stood firm,saying,"I don't care if there are a dozen maids. A woman's place is to stay home and take care of her family." Eventually,George relented and agreed that I could return to work,but with little over time.

Dale Turner,a slender black beauty with a contagious smile was immediately hired by Mr. Ragsdale as our live-in nanny. She was happily devoted to Jimmy and his baby brother and they came to love her as well.

Steven's eyes,lips,face,and outrageously large ears- every thing resembled Lyndon. Even the shape of his hands and feet were identical to his father's. I saw Lyndon in so many of his expressions. I wanted to shout, "Lyndon, I want to see you!" I waged a constant battle against the urge to try to contact him. Although Dale did not know who Steven's father was,she must have seen the detached look in my eyes.

"There is a saying,Miss Madeleine," she began."Once you love and the love dies,it goes back into the heart and returns in the form of tears to wash away the hurt."

Dale was always trying to lift my spirits. She would say,"You white ladies need to learn a lesson from us black ladies,have you a spare man around ...and if he doesn't have any money,ask him to use a lay-away-plan."

"God never gives us burdens we can't carry." But when would the burdens end? "Start over," Dale advised. "Don't wait,forget the past,you've got a lot of life yet."

In a blur of activity,I returned to my job at Glenn Advertising where,thank God,very few questions were asked. Mr. Wilcox gave me a heart-warming "welcome back " and walked me to my office where a desk-load of paperwork awaited my attention."Now go in there and tackle the work. It'll be like skinning a cat," he added. Certainly, the work would take my mind off my problems.

The new medium, television, was sweeping the nation. Movie theaters were rapidly closing where network TV had been established. Glenn Advertising's clients were also reshaping their budgets where the markets supported the TV medium.

Mr. Wilcox stopped by my office and asked, "Miss Madeleine, I know you can split a hair figuring the client's budgets, but how are you at figuring the cost per thousand when we do not have all the TV market figures?" Mr. Wilcox asked.

"I keep checking with Joe Belden Associates (marketing ex perts) and the Department of Commerce," I answered, "to retrieve all their available information. In addition, I research the retail stores to see how many television sets are being sold. When do you think Austin is going on-line?"

"Mr. Roberts of KRLD was in the office last week and said Lady Bird had applied for a TV license with the FCC." (With KTBC flourishing,

Lady Bird, who had, up to this point, personally held the license to her station, decided to incorporate and applied to the FCC for permission to do so. When permission was granted, she "sold" her personal ownership to the newly created Texas Broadcasting Corporation, allowing only two shares to go "outside" and one of those was to Jesse Kellam. Lyndon owned none of it outright, but was inextricably involved because of Texas' community property law.)

Then, with television just beginning to move west, the FCC began a study to determine which cities should be allocated TV channels, and how many. The study continued for four years, at the conclusion of which the FCC published its findings, complete with maps. How many stations a particular city was allowed depended on its population as of the 1950 census, and Austin, with only 132,450 inhabitants, was thereby limited to one.

As it happened, there was on file with the FCC only one application for a television station in Austin. The application was from Lady Bird Johnson.

The question of why, as the years went on, Austin should continue to have only one television station carrying the major networks, was one that persisted right up until the station was finally sold in 1972. Although Austin was not far from San Antonio, which had three, there are other cities of similar size with two or three.

My pulse quickened and a streak of guilt ran through me when I heard the very mention of Lady Bird's name. How would she react if she knew that her husband and I were lovers? Even more importantly, what would she say and do if she knew that I had just given birth to his only son?

"In the meantime," Ward Wilcox continued, interrupting my thoughts, "keep all radio schedules pumped up to cover our clients' needs. By the way, Miss Madeleine, make sure that the slug ads (small directory listings) for the Brown and Root Company are placed. Sena tor Johnson keeps providing his old buddies, Herman and George, with government contracts for construction and they are our political connection. So take care of them, Miss Madeleine. Brown and Root places their advertising direct," Mr. Wilcox said.

George and Herman Brown of the Brown and Root Company were brothers who started a contracting firm in the 1920s in partner ship with Herman's brother-in-law, Dan Root, who died shortly thereafter. Of all the Texas wheeler-dealers whom Lyndon had been close to, George and Herman Brown were the dominant figures. (Herman and his wife lived in a tent, much to the dismay of the Roots, because the company was in a state of bankruptcy until Lyndon, President Roosevelt, and Austin attorney, Alvin Wirtz, began paving the way with government contracts).

When Lyndon ran for the Senate in 1941, and again in the 1948 elections,Brown and Root, having greatly expanded their operations primarily on government contracts, really laid the cash on their candidate's line. Clint Murchison did likewise, as did some of the other members of the 8F group! Marvelous expansion and success were understandable. With ready access to the best Washington sources, with advance information on proposed public works from which to estimate and figure, and with ready and telling influence when the contracts were let, they were in an excellent position to skim off the gravy, and did-especially at "cost plus." Progressing from local operations around Austin, the world became their client. To most Texans, there was really little that was criminal or unethical about it. It was open federal policy, and preferential treatment had become public policy. Brown and Root prospered. T he brothers had unbroken participation in government ventures, and they built, in the entire period of Lyndon's political career, roads, dams, bridges, ships, tanks, railroads, tunnels, ocean and navigation locks, offshore drilling rigs, air bases, pipelines, and atomic energy plants.

George and Herman Brown's private plane was always at Lyndon's disposal. He was a frequent guest of George Brown's Middleburg estate. How did George and Herman Brown so handily finance Lyndon's campaigns? Columnist Drew Pearson on March 26 and 27, 1956, dipped into the devastating records of the Internal Revenue Service investigators (which he had somehow acquired) and disclosed what I had known for years. The records of the IRS showed that the handiest device Brown and Root "used to finance the Johnson campaign was to make out checks to employees of Victoria Gravel Company," one of their subsidiaries, who in tum cashed them, and contributed the money for campaign purposes.

As an instance, a check for $5,000 was made out to J.O. Corwin, Jr., of Victoria Gravel, and charged off as a business expense. Corwin apparently cashed the check in Lyndon's home town of Austin, and later, under oath, admitted that he had mailed half of it to Lyndon's campaign headquarters.

In similar fashion, a check for $2,500, issued to another Victoria employee, Randolph Mills, was deposited in his own bank. The same day he withdrew the same amount, which was given to J. Frank Jungman, Lyndon's Houston campaign manager. In tum, as the IRS records showed,

Jungman deposited it in the Second National Bank in Houston for the Lyndon Johnson Club.

IRS agents found that Brown and Root, through Victoria Gravel, had issued checks in the amounts of $5,000 on May 26, and two more for $3,000 and $4, 500 on June 7, 1941 to Edgar Monteith, a Houston attorney. He seems to have "distributed" $10,000 of this "as a profit" between himself and his law partner, A.W. Baring, who then repaid the amount to Monteith, who in tum supported the Johnson effort by writing checks to pay for radio time, printing, and other campaign expenses. W hen asked specifically about the matter, Lyndon told the IRS that he "had never heard of Monteith," much less of his financial support, though Monteith was the brother of a former Houston mayor.

The most interesting disclosures were the oddly-timed bonuses that Brown and Root's books showed had been paid to its officials, and then how these tax deductible windfalls had been used. They found that L .H. Durst, their purchasing agent, was paid two bonuses of $3,500 and $2,000; W.M. Powell, vice president, $4,000; Carl Burkhart, office manager, $5,000; D.B. Young, secretary (for shop ping) $30,000. But these "bonuses" were not given toward the end of the year-in keeping with the usual business practice, but between March 28 and May 20, 194 1, which just happened to fall in the very middle of the hot Johnson-0'Daniel senatorial campaign. These "bonuses" tallied almost to the penny with the amounts these same executives contributed to Lyndon's campaign.

Diversifying, like most American mega-businesses, Brown and Root came to own hotels, oil and gas production, real estate and office buildings (KTBC had its offices in the Brown Building in Austin until the station moved to a street level comer of the Driskill Ho tel, another Brown and Root property). Sid Richardson, Clint Murchison, H.L Hunt, and other oil oligarchy people, likewise prospering, were purchasing railroads, food plants, race tracks, and huge oil storage tanks. Considering the history of the Driskill Hotel, per haps it is ironic and appropriate that Brown and Root owned the property. Jesse Lincoln Driskill built the hotel after a long arduous cattle drive in 1886, bringing fresh meat to a protein-starved region that hadn't recovered from the Civil War and unscrupulous Yankee carpetbaggers. The once vast American herds of buffalo had been decimated to near extinction along with the fierce Comanche and Apache Indians, leaving scattered roving tribes struggling to survive because our-government had issued blankets infested with deadly smallpox. They were valiantly making a last stand in parts of Texas, their hopes and dreams, their proud Indian heritage ground into the dust under the heels of broken government treaties, greed, and Mani fest Destiny.

A man of vision, Jesse Driskill, saw the lucrative business opportunity of a fine hotel in accommodating poor Austin, and in 1889 he opened the Romanesque Revival Driskill Hotel, four stories of luxury-majestic capped columns, a beautifully arched entrance way and a separate entrance on Boise d'Arc Street for women (so they wouldn't be exposed to the bar and high-spirited boisterous men with their love of fine liquor, poker, and cigars). T he main entrance was on Brazos Street, claiming one of the highest arched entrances in Texas. T he hotel was a veritable oasis of refinement, culture, and comfort amid the raw, crude, and coarse Texas capitol on the Colorado River.

11

Shattered Dreams

In the afternoon following my conversation with Mr. Wilcox, Jesse Kellam called to see how I was doing. It was nice to have someone like Jesse to confide in. We talked a little about Lyndon. His comments were a bit confusing, at first supportive and then more realistic. "I just want him to see our baby boy," I pleaded with Jesse, "to see how he looks like his father."

"Easy now, Madeleine. Be patient and everything will work out. You'll see Mr. Johnson soon enough. Just don't hurt yourself by holding onto the past."

Jesse didn't realize it, but he had twisted the knife in my heart another tum. It was over. He was telling me to let go. I had to let Lyndon go.

Each new account of Lyndon's continued success made him appear more distant. I stopped reading newspaper and magazine articles about him. I changed the station when I heard his voice on the radio. I tried to ignore his existence, and almost convinced myself it was possible.

I had hit rock bottom-unwanted-rejected-my dreams shattered. Lyndon didn't want me anymore, but I still loved him.

That evening, I went to church and knelt for over an hour, asking God to give me strength and to take the pain away. I prayed that Lyndon would be happy and pleaded with God to erase my guilt concerning Steven. He would never know his father now.

Finally, months after Steven Mark was born, Jesse called one morning at the office and said Lyndon was anxious to see me.

"Can I bring our son, Jesse?"

"I'm afraid not, Madeleine. He's on a tight schedule and you're going to have to meet him at the Lamar Hotel in Houston."

When I arrived at Hobby Airport, a limousine was waiting for me, and the same tall, dark, handsome chauffeur, with a great wide grin on his face, whom I had met before, motioned to me.

"Hey, what's wrong with you?" he asked. "Are you all right?

You're shaking like a leaf."

I said, "I'm fine. I just had a rough ride on Trans Texas." I was trying to ignore my anxiety, knowing quite well my emotional and physical reactions were caused by the thought of getting to see Lyndon.

When we arrived at the Lamar Hotel, he had to help me from the supple brown leather seat of the limousine.

" Are you sure you're all right?"

I managed a smile and said, "Sure. "

As I walked through the elegant lobby of the Lamar Hotel, I noticed H.L. Hunt and Clint Murchison playing gin rummy while the hotel's owner, Jesse Jones, and Judge Roy Hofheinz sat on a nearby couch, smoking cigars.

H.L. was dressed in his usual attire, an ill-matching baggy suit and white socks, puffing on the ever-present cigar. (Later he broke that habit and became a total health fanatic.) He broke out a fresh deck of cards and the two men played for a dollar a point. H.L. took Clint quickly for $800 in the first game, and as they began a second, I took a seat beside Jesse and the Judge. Some of the Big Texas regular Members of the 8F Suite of the Lamar Hotel, were leisurely sitting around the lobby with their ears tuned to pick up information about the newest Texas oil gusher blowing in.

After the customary hugs and kisses. Jesse asked me what I was doing in Houston.

"I have advertising business here," I answered, knowing full well that the Brown and Root Company occupied an entire floor in the hotel.

"I need my checkbook," said Clint when it was apparent he had lost the second game as well.

"Clint, where's your buddy, Sid Richardson?" I asked. "I thought you all ran everywhere together."

Clint never looked up from the card game. "He's out in La Jolla at the race track with Hoover and Tolson."

"Hoover and Tolson are playing house together," the Judge whispered wickedly in my ear.

Clint had built a summer cottage for the FBI director and his assistant behind Clint's hotel in La Jolla where they entertained their Hollywood friends. After Governor James Allred banned horse racing in Texas in 1936, Clint and Sid (natural-born capitalists) later purchased the Del Mar Race Track, which attracted some of the wealthiest people from Texas, as well as other parts of the world. When anyone would ask Clint what horse was the best bet, he would smile and quip, "The one with the longest tail. "

"You sure Sid isn't out there raising money for Eisenhower to run for President?" H.L. asked between puffs on his cigar.

Sid had recently played bridge with the popular war hero on a train in Colorado and was committed to Ike's pursuit of the presidency. Sid was a very strange person. His office was in his hat and he never had a secretary.

"General Douglas MacArthur is my number one choice for President of the United States," H.L. said as he dealt the cards to Clint and himself. President Truman had recently fired the general for insubordination, and MacArthur's politics were most closely aligned with H.L.'s.

"No," H.L. continued speechifying, "Eisenhower is clearly not the man of destiny to lead America during these crucial hours of its life-and-death struggle against international Communism."

"Do you honestly think MacArthur's got a chance of getting the nomination?" Jesse asked.

"I've never contributed anything to a candidate unless I thought he had an awfully good chance of winning," H.L. replied.

When they added up the points, H.L. had won $1,100 more for a total of $1,900.

Clint stood to knot his tie and put on his jacket, when H.L. leaned over and pinned a button on Clint's lapel. The button read,

"GENERAL DOUGLAS MACARTHUR FOR PRESIDENT."

Later, at Flag Pole Hill near his Mt. Vernon home, H.L. joined the other SF men, announcing his full support of Ike in front of a record-breaking crowd of 3,000 people.

As pre-arranged by Jesse Kellam, I checked into the suite adjacent to Lyndon's: lush carpet, beautiful draperies, a silky apricot bedspread, a breathtaking bathroom with bronze faucets, and even a telephone! The window overlooked a lovely cluster of vines that were in full bloom. The setting was certainly seductive. I had to stay calm. My mind flashed back over the past year. How many nights had I tossed and turned in bed dreaming of being in his arms, kissing him, holding him, making love to him again?

A light knock at the door caused my heart to stop. On the other side of the door stood the only man I had ever loved. I slowly opened it. For an instant I just stood there, gaping. Finally, coming to my senses, I noticed he was staring just as intently at me. He made the first move, coming in and closing the door behind him without taking his eyes from mine. He grabbed me and pulled me to him. We held each other so tightly, afraid that if one let go, the other would disappear. I could feel his body trembling – or was it mine? He slowly re leased me without letting me out of his reach. His eyes were tearing. He lifted up his hands and ran them through my hair, then came close again. I could hear him inhaling deeply, taking in the fragrance of the French perfume he had once purchased for me from Neiman-Marcus. As he did, he squeezed me tighter, his thank-you for my having worn it.

"Its good to see you, Lyndon," I said, breaking the ice. "I missed you so much."

"My redheaded lady," he whispered.

He walked over to the bed and sat down on the edge. He clutched both my hands as he spoke.

"I thought I'd never see you again. I had Jesse send you roses every week. Did you get them? I wanted you to know that no matter how busy I was, I never forgot that you were going through hell and that I was thinking about you. " He sounded so emotional. I thought he was going to start crying. "I missed you so much. I wanted to be with you, right by your side, where I was supposed to be. I know you needed me, Madeleine. Please, please understand my position."

I put my hand to his mouth. "Shhhhh, you don't have to ex plain. I brought you some photographs of your son, Steven Mark." I reached into my purse and handed him the pictures.

He stared at each one over and over again. Tears were rolling down his cheeks. "I know you thought I didn't care. But my every thought was on you and our son. Goddamn, if things could only be different!"

Lyndon was anguished. T here had to be something else wrong, but I didn't want to put him through it.

"You don't have to explain."

"Yes, I do. I'm so damn tired and run down. I work all night reading transcripts and writing questions to ask at the next day's hearing on MacArthur. I haven't slept in three days, but I think it's paying off. All the public emotion for the arrogant son-of-a-bitch seems to have subsided." He paused and rubbed his forehead. "Besides, I'm still continuing the hearings of my Defense Preparedness Subcommittee. I feel like the most popular whore at Miss Mona's Chicken Ranch." (T his was located in LaGrange, Texas and it was considered the Texas A & M University's playground. Here seniors introduced "real life" to the freshmen.)

I massaged his shoulders. "W hat's really bothering you, Lyndon?"

"I'm so goddamn upset over my sister, Josefa." He turned and looked me straight in the eyes, unblinking. "You remember what I tell you, Madeleine: You hear nothing, say nothing, and don't ever repeat a goddamn thing."

Lyndon confided in me that his younger sister, Josefa, had been having an affair during 1949 and 1950 in the Washington, D.C. area with Malcolm E. "Mac" Wallace, a former University of Texas student body president who was working as an economist for the Agriculture Department. He was generally known as "Lyndon's boy" (a hatchet man like Jesse Kellam). Lyndon said Josefa, at the time, was getting a divorce, and had just been released from a Washington area alcoholic rehabilitation center.

During 1951, though, Lyndon said, Josefa had stopped dating Wallace. In Washington she began a relationship with John Douglas Kinser, a thirty-three-year-old popular Austin golf professional. Kinser owned Butler Park, a scenic spot across the Colorado River from the center of Austin, where he operated the Pitch and Putt Golf Course. Kinser, according to Lyndon, began dating Josefa hoping to get a federal small-business loan, a typical Texas back scratching deal-a variation on the classic "It isn't what you know, its who you know."

One mid-afternoon, thirty-year-old Mac Wallace drove up to the Pitch and Putt course, walked in on "Doug" Kinser at the keeper's house and shot him dead. Wallace fled, but was caught, indicted for murder with "malice aforethought." He was released on $30,000 (later reduced to $10,00) bond arranged by Lyndon through a William E.

Carroll.

"Goddamn, Madeleine, can you believe this fuckhead Wallace?" Lyndon was pacing the floor now and waving his hands for expression. "No one loves to drink and fuck more than me, but shit, I wouldn't kill anyone over a piece of ass. The world's full of ass!"

He sat back down on the bed beside me and loosened his neck tie. "Hell, I've got friends in Austin who owe me favors. I'm going to call in my markers for Wallace's trial. Madeleine, I can't have this bullshit embarrassing my family."

Ten years later when Lyndon was Vice President under John Kennedy, Mac Wallace helped negotiate Billie Sol Estes' cotton allotment along with Cliff Carter and the former governor of Minnesota, Orville Freeman-secretary of Agriculture. Soon Wallace was suspected as the trigger man in Henry Marshall's death and Billie Sol much later testified to this. Marshall was the Agriculture administrator who turned against Billie Sol and Lyndon in 1961. Had not Marshall and the others not been killed, Lyndon would have been forced out of office right then, but the rest of us had no idea what was really going on. I was beginning to learn: Fix a murder trial! I trembled at the power this man wielded in Texas. But, as every woman knows, power is an aphrodisiac. I was uncontrollably excited, sexually aroused by this powerful man. And, since my tubes had been tied after Steven's birth (upon the advice of my doctor as a result of various medical complications), fear of pregnancy was no longer a factor, and I was ready.

He looked at me with a strange desire mirrored in his dark brown eyes. After being so close, so intimate with the man, anything out of the ordinary was quickly perceived. Even though Lyndon had always been a vigorous, strong lover, I was shocked by his roughness that night and pleased by his eagerness as he frantically stripped my gown from my body and flung me like a rag doll on the bed. He towered over me exuding a magnificent animal vitality. My eyes traveled the length of his body. Chest heaving and nostrils flaring, he made me think of a prize stallion primed and waiting impatiently to service the mare. Looking down at me, he said in an excited, husky voice, "I'm going to rope, throw and brand you because if any other son-of a-bitch dares to look at your bare ass, he'll know for sure he's rustling LBJ's pussy."

Adding action to his words as I lay there naked and exposed, he reached up with both hands and in one savage jerk ripped his shirt open. The popped buttons of his garment made sharp staccato counterpoints as they struck the wall and rained down upon the bed. The tied tie was still draped around his neck, lying against his bare chest. The soft hairs began curling around its edges attempting to capture the silk as it rose and fell with Lyndon's deep breathing. I looked deeply into his eyes. A dark raging desire blazed in their depths. With shaking hands my lover slid the knot away from his neck and drew it over his head. He held the tie suspended over me as a hangman holds the noose ready for its victim. The macabre image released hormones of fear when Lyndon lowered the tie, tracing it across my nipples. I screamed with primordial release.

Lyndon fell upon me savagely, yet at the same time strangely tender, pinning my arm beneath his leg. I gasped in sharp denial as Lyndon roughly positioned my hand at the bedpost above my head and quickly tied my wrist with the hangman's noose tie. Then, leaping up like a crazed wild man, he snatched my expensive, newly purchased Neiman-Marcus hose from the dresser and secured my right leg to the bed. Slithering wickedly, he crawled onto the bed between my spread legs, slid his hard naked body on top of me, and suddenly grabbed my free arm in his powerful hands and tied it to the other bedpost, leaving me bound and defenseless on the bed, except for my left leg which was helplessly free.

The whole scene was so bizarre that forbidden, hidden desires slashed through me. I was so hot, so wet, so needy of his lovemaking that crazy, ugly animal gasps, moans, groans and cries escaped my lips. I tore at my bonds for freedom in hot frustration so I could devour my master. In a hoarse, ragged voice I screamed out, "Take me, Lyndon. Take me!"

In sudden submission, my captor lowered his face slowly, softly, seductively to my fevered flesh, his wide tongue delicately licking and tasting my sweet juices.

As Lyndon rose above me, I opened my legs for him and he sank into me. Inevitably we were pressing tightly against each other in frenzied motion.

Some time later, as we lay in bed, Lyndon's face pillowed against my breasts, we discussed emotionally, but realistically, Lyndon's parental responsibilities to his son. We cried and laughed and kissed until completely exhausted. Then we drifted off to sleep.

12

Power Play

The summer's blistering heat was over and we welcomed the beauty of the colorful fall as the trees grew bare. The earth was a sea of fallen leaves around the new six-room house that Lyndon had Mr. Ragsdale purchase for the boys and me. Dale continued to live with us, effectively acting as a surrogate mother to Jimmy and Steven while my workload at Glenn Advertising kept me at the office for ten to twelve hours a day. My heart ached when I thought how neither boy would ever know what it was like to be part of a real family.

Steven was growing into an extraordinary child. His motor skills were advanced. He had begun walking at ten months old. Each day I would admire his growth and say to myself, "Look what his father is missing."

On the morning of Steven's first birthday, I received a call from Jesse Kellam at the office. "Mr. Johnson can't see Steven right now in person, Madeleine. But he's arranged that his birthday can be seen on Channel Four in Dallas."

"On TV!" I asked, disbelieving what I was hearing. "Are you kidding me, Jesse?"

"I've taken care of all the details. A caterer will provide a cake and refreshments. Just be at the TV station with Steven by two P.M."

The city of Dallas, and especially my suburban community of Oak Cliff, were astonished that a baby, my baby, had his first birthday on the then new medium of television.

The opening shot of the program, in fact, was of Steven nursing his baby bottle. The master of ceremonies laughed and said, "Here's one guest who has brought his own bottle!"

Later that day, Jesse stated that Lyndon had requested a film clip for his own private showing in Washington.

"Jesse, how did Lyndon arrange Steven's first birthday on television?" I innocently asked. "If Steven were the mayor's son or the TV station owner's boy, I could understand. But I'm just Madeleine Brown, a girl from Oak Cliff with a baby boy whose father is ... "

Jesse interrupted."A very powerful United States Senator from Texas. And don't ever forget that, Madeleine Brown. Always remember who Steven's father is."

The next week, Steven's father was on the cover of Newsweek magazine.

Three months later, Mac Wallace, the crazy South Texas killer, was brought into the 98th District Court of Travis County before Judge Charles A. Betts, with John Cofer (Lyndon's lawyer during the "Box 13" voter fraud case in 1948), as attorney for Wallace's defense.

District Attorney Robert J. Long, another ally of Lyndon's, prosecuted Wallace without showing a motive, although he described it as "a near perfect murder " (Wallace was apprehended with a bloody shirt on, and in his possession was found a cartridge of the same caliber as was used in the Kinser murder).

Wallace did not take the stand. No evidence was presented to suggest cause or extenuating circumstances. Cofer simply filed a one page motion for an instructed verdict, pleading that there was no evidence upon which the State could "legally base a judgment of guilty."

Long said nothing whatever in rebuttal. There were less than two hours of testimony, shut off so abruptly it left the packed court room with jaws ajar. Long urged the jury (D.L Johnson, one of the jurors, was the first cousin and good friend of lawyer Gus Lanier, who during the trial sat at the defense table for Wallace) to "punish Wallace in whatever degree you can bring upon."

Thus, after one of the briefest and most perfunctory trials on record-even for Texas-of a prominent murder case, the jury nonetheless found that Wallace was, as charged, guilty "of murder with malice aforethought. "

Wallace's punishment was a five-year suspended sentence for murder in the first degree! Anyone familiar with the justice system in Texas, particularly in the 1950s, knew a conviction for premeditated murder meant the death penalty was mandatory. A suspended sentence for such a crime was unheard of.

I asked Lyndon from time to time if Mac Wallace was related to Texas Governor Maw Ferguson. After Ferguson was elected governor in 1933, she opened the doors of Huntsville State Prison and let everyone out. The joke in Texas was, "If you make a mistake, just say, 'Oh, pardon me!'"

Maw, which was an acronym from her maiden name of Miriam Amanda Wallace, was born into a very wealthy family of Bell County.

She lost the election in 1936 to Fort Worth's "Lightcrust Dough" W. Lee "Pappy" O'Daniels, who later defeated Lyndon in the early 40s race for Senator. W. Lee "Pappy," as Texans called him, coined the phrase "Please pass the biscuits, Pappy!" He headed up Burris Mills, a bakery, in Fort Worth. I remember when Maw Ferguson was dying in 1961, and Lyndon rushed to her bedside and sang her campaign song, "Put on Your Old Gray Bonnet."

I did know Lyndon had strong ties to Maw. He often com pared her to his own mother, Rebekah. They both were like the Rock of Gibraltar, according to Lyndon.

One day after Lyndon had placed memorial flowers on her grave in the state cemetery in Austin, he told me Maw's tombstone epitaph read:
LIFE'S RACE WELL RUN
LIFE'S WORK WELL DONE
LIFE'S VICTORY WON
NOW COMETH REST.

Maw Wallace will always be symbolic amongTexans. Unfortunately, so will the name, Malcolm E. Wallace, who left a trail of bloody murders. To many of us he is still a prime suspect in President Kennedy's assassination. Even though Mac Wallace died some ten years later in Pittsburg, Texas, victim of a hit-and-run accident, I never determined if he was related to Maw Ferguson.

Many years later, I met with U.S. Marshal Clint Peoples to discuss Malcolm Wallace because I had witnessed Mac practicing at the Dallas Gun Club. Clint had investigated Wallace's death for years. He was planning to break the case open with proof that Wallace was one of the shooters behind the picket fence overlooking Dealey Plaza. Unfortunately, Clint's untimely death under mysterious circumstances prevented this announcement from ever being made. It is a fact, how ever, that a Wallace Plumbing truck was at the scene of the assassination in Dealey Plaza.

Clint's car was run off the road shortly before he was to meet with me and some associates. His car was hit by a truck and he was killed. It is said that his wrists showed marks from handcuffs.

Clint Peoples had been a famous Texas Ranger in the old days who investigated a string of deaths in the Billie Sol Estes scandals after Lyndon became Vice President. All of the men had carbon monoxide in their bodies, although Henry Marshall had five bullets in him as well. Each was officially declared a suicide. Only in Texas do we have suicides with five bullets in them.

Wallace told Lyndon's associates and Billie Sol Estes later that he had caught Marshall in a lonely place on the road and was gassing him with a hose from the exhaust when a stranger came along in the distance. Wallace then shot Marshall five times and got away, thus saving Lyndon's bacon.

Years later, Clint became the Chief U.S. Marshall of Dallas (before he retired to Waco), and he took Billie Sol Estes before a grand jury where he told the real story, and the suicide so long before was changed to murder. The grand jury had been asked to hear the issue because Marshall's family had retained a lawyer, Phil Banks, of Bryan, Texas to try to get the old verdict changed. Banks was a class mate of Lyndon's and my son Steven in 1973.

No matter how you cut it, lawman Clint Peoples was a great hero out of the old West. He wasn't afraid of Lyndon at all, either.

13

Wheelers and Dealers

In November the Democrats lost decisively. Eisenhower won the presidency in a minor landslide, and the Republicans, by a one-vote margin, gained control of the Senate.

Disaster for the Democrats somehow resulted in opportunity for Lyndon. Since Democrat Ernest McFarland of Arizona had lost to Republican Barry Goldwater, the post of minority leader of the Sen ate was now open.

A few days later Lyndon was elected at a caucus of his fellow Democrats to assume the leadership, after having served only four years as a Senator.

As minority leader, Lyndon was to gain the gratitude of Eisenhower for his active cooperation with the Republican branch on legislative matters, along with the scarcely disguised dislike and dis trust of many liberals in his own party who believed he was too conservative, and was carrying bipartisanship too far.

Lyndon was said by many to have been the most proficient of anyone who ever held the post. Without resorting to bombast or open exhibitions of punishment or reward, he adroitly convinced tempera mental and independent-minded senators to see things his way. Actually, his bag man, a former Senate page, paid off the Senators. This became the third of three massive scandals that would have brought Lyndon down at the end of 1963 and caused his resignation, had not John Kennedy been assassinated.

I remember one conversation when Lyndon told me that he held a second trust deed for fifty thousand dollars on another powerful senator's home. When a routine investigation of financial affairs almost exposed the loan, Lyndon called in his marker. He went to see the senator and demanded payment, in full, on the loan before the incriminating document proved bribery. Technically, Lyndon was off the hook, but the senator lost his home.

At Glenn Advertising's weekly creative conference, Mr. Wilcox was outwardly excited about the results of the recent election. "Things are going to start moving for America again. Dwight D. Eisenhower is a 'middle-of-the-road' kind of guy who is above the mud-slinging of politics. People in America and all over the world hold Ike in high regard. Some of the oil giants are watching him carefully and most of them approve. Dick Nixon is the one who gets along with Clint and Sid. They like his national policies."

"I didn't know you were a Republican, Mr. Wilcox," I said. "Hell, I'm whatever our client is," he replied with a wide grin, the ever-present Roi Tan cigar dangling out of the comer of his mouth. Then he handed me two small gold pins. "When you are with a Re publican client, wear the elephant. When you are with a Democrat client, wear the jackass. Always be whatever our client is!"

After the meeting Mr. Wilcox asked me to stay after all the others had left the conference room.

"Get your secretary (Jan West) on the phone," he politely re quested. "I want to meet H.L. Hunt at the Adolphus Hotel's Variety Club, or better still, Louie's Oyster Bar. I'm going to give him a chance to win some of his money back."

"You beat H.L. at cards?"

"Just once," Mr. Wilcox smiled. "He usually cheats better than me!"

"Can you beat the notorious card shark, Judge Hofheinz?" "He and H.L. both play a mean hand of poker. The best guy with a deck of cards, though, is ol' Sid Richardson. But I don't see him very often because he stays out in California to relieve his asthma."

Sid Richardson was a paragon of the Texas good-ol' -boy very rich oilman. With equal ease, he negotiated for leases while drinking buttermilk with Baptist ranchers and traded properties with fellow oilmen while downing more potent beverages. He met my uncle Johnny Bowen while drinking buttermilk. Though a shrewd businessman, Sid liked to convey the impression that he was just plain folks. "Luck," he once remarked, "helped me every day of my life. And I'd rather be lucky than smart, cause a lot of smart people ain't eatin' regular."

Despite this self-effacing observation. Sid's success had far less to do with luck than with an uncanny ability to seize and exploit the peculiar opportunities of time and place-in this instance of Winkler County in the mid-Thirties-and to do a lot with a little bit of money. Sid Richardson's success was not just luck. He and Clint Murchison, real gamblers at heart, together pumped "hot" oil (and anything else they wanted to do), totally against government regulations. Many lawsuits were killed, and most often Sid and Clint came out smelling like roses. Ingrained in the being of both men was love of the soil, the woodlands, cattle, peaches, fishing, plus respect for the cotton, rail road and oil industries.

In 1932, Sid Richardson, a strong supporter and a long-time friend of President Roosevelt, had become an independent oilman of the wildcat promoter variety. He and Clint grew up in Athens, Texas. Clint's family were bankers and Sid's family included a keeper of a saloon and a share-cropper of a large peach orchard. He had made several small fortunes in developing and trading properties and lost them down dry holes. However, he managed to hold onto producing properties in Ward County that yielded a modest income. Sid stretched that income as far as possible. He used secondhand equipment, like many a poor-boy operator, and what he could not buy on credit, he borrowed. When other operators paid workers twice a month, Sid paid once a month, and sometimes he paid workers in groceries he had obtained on credit. For all this, he got along well with his hands, kidding them and cadging sandwiches from their lunch boxes at the rig.

In raising capital, Sid augmented production income by borrowing on any asset a lender would accept as security for a loan. The daughter of a rancher from whom he leased many eventually productive acres noted, "My abstracts are full of liens against Sid Richardson." At Vick's Coffee Bar, once I had asked Sid why he didn't marry the rancher's daughter who held the liens against his property and he replied, "All women are looking for a place to land and I'm all fogged in."

By the mid-1930's, however, Sid Richardson and Clint Murchison had succeeded in arousing the interest of Nathan Adams' First National Bank of Dallas and other large lenders in their ventures. John J. McCloy, a financial ally of Clint's and Sid's, was the longtime chairman of the Chase Bank of Manhattan, New York, be cause of his loyalty to the oilmen. (When Lyndon formed the Warren Commission after the assassination, he chose McCloy to serve with Earl Warren, Gerald Ford, Allan W. Dulles and others. McCloy's selection by Lyndon was at Clint Murchison's insistence.) This development was in large part a result of pro-ration, with regulated production and stable prices. Banks and other lenders began to look more favorably on settled production as security for loans. Because pro ration was strictly followed in the pipeline-short Permian Basin, Sid was able to obtain larger loans from Nathan Adams' First National Bank of Dallas on his production.

They were also able to attract private lenders like prominent publisher Charles E. Marsh. As the scale of his operations grew and Sid moved into the intermediate rank of independents, he found that his financial needs took him to banks in Chicago (headquarters for organized crime, which controlled the money supply at that time), Boston, and New York. Like their smaller Texas counterparts, these banks viewed oil as less speculative after statewide control of production was assured by the Texas Railroad Commission. Richardson thus tailored this strategy to take advantage of new conditions.

On the basis of his earlier success in Ward County, Sidnego started a 240-acre farmout from Gulf-Skelly, Tidal, and the owners of minerals under other Winkler County leases. He improved this holding by gaining an additional contribution of acreage from Shell with the right to purchase additional leases from companies carving up acreage from the Keystone Cattle Company and the J.B. Walton ranch. After reaching these agreements, Sid marshalled resources for his test well. Like most independents, he relied on his suppliers to provide credit, which customarily was extended for ninety days with mechanics' liens on equipment taken as security. With a small stake of his own and even more borrowed from others, Sid drilled his well. It came in for 250 barrels a day. With a well completed by Gulf a week earlier, this discovery of new productive sand opened the way for extensive development in the prolific Keystone field. T he discovery well completed, Sid exercised his options on acreage and acquired additional leases, accumulating twenty-one separate leases in the field. Generous farmouts, shrewd dealing, and adequate financial backing, as well as the luck he was fond of citing, put Sid Richardson on the high road of success. By the end of 1940, he had producing wells all over West Texas in Keystone, Slaughter, South Ward and Scarborough. With a multitude of producing wells in three contiguous counties, Sid Richardson had put bean jobs far behind him. And thus he turned his interest to the broadcasting field, becoming one of the executives of the Texas State Network. He shared broadcasting interests with President Roosevelt's son, Elliott, and Lady Bird as well.

Jan's voice on the intercom interrupted the conversation. "Mr. Wilcox, I have Mr. Hunt on the phone. He wants to know what time to meet you at Louie's Oyster Bar?" He said. "R.L. Thornton (president of Mercantile Bank), and Earle Cabell will join you." Cabell's family owned the Cabell Dairy in Oak Cliff. Earle Cabell was Mayor of Dallas when JFK was killed there, and hated Kennedy. His brother had been the Deputy Director of the CIA until Kennedy had fired him for his role in the Bay of Pigs.

Mr. Wilcox said, "You know about Bob Thornton, he is one big doer who had humble beginnings. He will tell how he picked 500 pounds of cotton a day, toyed with being a candy salesman, owning a book store, but ventured into banking at the age of 36. His Mercantile is the base of our today's BankOne. He built the first skyscraper (with four big clocks on it) for his Mercantile Bank, though it is now vacant and overshadowed by newer skyscrapers. Many of the oil giants, H.L. Hunt, B.F. Phillips, Lu Egan and lots of attorneys, including Jerome T. Ragsdale, kept offices there."

"Tell him I'll be there in thirty minutes or less," he answered, depressing the intercom button. "There isn't a better or luckier oil man in the country than H.L. Hunt," Mr. Wilcox said, turning his attention back to me. "I really believe he misses the old days when he was actually out in the oil fields. H.L. was known as the Midas of Muleshoe County because he could smell oil in the ground. It's hard to believe that H.L. Hunt was a school dropout in the fifth grade. His natural ability overwhelmed people."

Later H.L. had become a public figure for the first time in his life. Issues of both Fortune and Life ran articles on America's super rich, identifying H.L. as the richest man in the country. The magazines estimated H.L.'s income to be one million dollars a week and his total assets to be from 400-700 million. According to Mr. Wilcox and some of my own rich Texas friends, these figures were a shade on the conservative side. To determine the exact extent of H.L. Bunt's fortunes would have required a regiment of accountants and statisticians (these were pre-computer days), as his vast empire-in addition to some of the largest oil reserves in the world-included the Far East, vast tracts of land in Texas, Louisiana, Arkansas, Florida, Mississippi, Montana, Wyoming, North Dakota and probably a few other states H.L. had forgotten.

Recently H.L. had put up the money to create a publishing division to print and distribute anti-Communist pamphlets and a monthly magazine called Facts Forum News. He also produced a similar-styled network of radio and television programs named Life Line. T his was aired on more than three hundred and fifty radio stations and eighty television stations across the country.

"Why don't you get some of his advertising dollars?" I asked Mr. Wilcox.

"Hell, he's too tight! He's probably got the first dime he ever earned. I just like to shoot the bullshit with him and find out what's going on in the oil industry. You know our client, Republic Bank, has an oil department and we must include a good budget for the oil publications. Now he's teaching his boys the business. Have you met either one of them?"

"Yes, sir," I nodded. "I've met Bunker and Herbert and their lovely companions at social functions."

"Too bad, Miss Madeleine," Mr. Wilcox continued, chomping on his cigar, "that you can't nail down one of the 'Texas Giants' for a husband. They can feed the world with what they've got and have enough left over to float a battleship."

As he stood up from the conference table and walked toward the door, I thought to myself, if he only knew the truth about Lyndon, Steven and me.

"If H.L. and I gamble too late, you leave by 5:00 P.M. today. Just make sure all the contracts for Lone Star Brewery are in order and call Gene Sommerhauser (President of Marketing for Lone Star). T he three of us need to meet and update the media file. You know the big bash at the brewery is coming up soon." T hen, with a jaunty wave, he was off to gamble with the richest man in the world.

T he Lone Star Media Party was the social event of the year in Texas. I smiled to myself as I thought that no military operation had ever been planned with as much detail – or contained such confusion. I knew that at this very moment there were trucks stretched down the entrance drive of the brewery as workmen unloaded and began to set up a dance floor and a bandstand, their drummers drumrolling a call to arms. There'd be another platoon, out of sight around the building exterior, repainting the walls and manicuring the landscape.

Media representatives from radio, television, newspaper, magazine, outdoor, and direct mail, along with the Lone Star distributors, would be served Texas-styled barbecue and Lone Star Beer, of course, which would flow like rampaging Texas rivers. At one Lone Star Media Party in the 1960s, other advertising executives had toasted me as the "Mary Wells of the South," a real compliment, since Mary Wells was known as "the best" in the ad business up North.

In attendance, also, would be the wheelers-and-dealers, movers-and-shakers of Texas politics and business: Jesse Kellam, Lee Glasco (WACO Radio), Buddy Bostick (KW TX-TV Waco), Jim Brown (KONO TV, San Antonio), Judge Roy Hofheinz, Sid Richardson, Herman and George Brown, Billie Sol Estes, and the Lone Star President Harry Jersig, and his son-in-law, Charles Kuiper, and all the Lone Star distributors. If Lyndon would be attending, he would be practicing his "Johnson Treatment." He would talk business and twist arms and call in favors for every Texan invited to the big bash. But Lyndon never attended the media parties, no matter how grand. As a Senator, he "would feel like fresh meat for a flock of hungry vultures."

Besides, Lyndon was too busy campaigning for the '54 election during 1953. T here were many candidates who were reported to be ready to run against him, including a rumor that Texas Governor Alan Shivers might enter the race.

There was a strong consensus that Lyndon would be beaten in '54, and when he wasn't in Washington, he went through Texas like a whirlwind. It was later estimated that he shook at least one quarter million hands and made two or three speeches a day.

As he did during his Texas campaign tour, Lyndon called me sporadically from Washington. But he typically spent fifteen hours a day in the Senate Chambers, cloakrooms, and offices when in session.

During those years, Lyndon, always a powerhouse, moved so fast and so furiously and with such blinding effect that, it was re ported, when someone once asked a page boy if he had seen Lyndon, the youth replied: "I haven't seen anything but a burning bush."

14

Small World or Set-Up?

The same day that I had met with Mr. Wilcox, I had gone shopping at Neiman-Marcus downtown during my afternoon break. As I was coming out of the store, I literally bumped into Mr. Ragsdale and a squat man with slick dark hair who looked somewhat like film star Edward G. Robinson.

Mr. Ragsdale was dressed in his usual tailored western suit, Justin boots, and a pearl Stetson that would have been worth a month's pay for me.

"Madeleine Brown, this is Jack Ruby," he said, introducing me to the other man, who politely shook my hand. "He owns the Carousel Club, which is where we're heading now to have a couple of drinks. Would you care to join us?"

"I appreciate the offer." I said declining the invitation, "but I really need to get back to the office. I would love to take a rain check, though."

Mr. Ruby smiled and said, "Miss Brown, you've got class. Please come by the club any time at your convenience. Just knock on the door. The club is open to the public after 7:30p.m. As my honored guest, your drinks will be on the house."

Over the course of the next few years, I often saw these two men walking together on Commerce Street or in the King and University clubs. Occasionally, I spotted them huddled with H.L. Hunt (H.L. and Mr. Ragsdale both officed in the Mercantile Bank Building) where they seemed to be involved in intense negotiations, with oversized briefcases constantly at their sides.

Ten years later, Mr. Ruby, a fifty-two-year-old underworld figure and owner of the Carousel Club (a striptease joint), would murder ex-marine Lee Harvey Oswald on live television. The event, as the world knows, took place in the basement of the Dallas City Jail under the watchful eyes of the Dallas Police just two days after Oswald had allegedly assassinated President John F. Kennedy. Ruby was well known in the police department.

When the police searched Mr. Ruby, they found two Facts Forum radio scripts in his jacket pocket.

"Where did you get these?" they asked.

"In a sample package of HLH food (HLH Foods was H.L. Hunt's health food company) at the Texas Products Show a few weeks ago," he answered.

In their routine interrogation of Ruby, the police also discovered that he had visited the offices of Lamar Hunt (another of H.L.'s sons), a short while before Kennedy's assassination. Why he was there was never made public. While awaiting a new trial, defended by San Francisco's famous Melvin Belli, Jack Ruby was diagnosed by Dr. Jack Barnett as having cancer of the pancreas. He died at Parkland Hospital in Dallas on January 2, 1967, and his body was returned for burial to his native city of Chicago.

No one has ever proven in a court of law or anywhere else for that matter, that there was any kind of direct link between Lee Harvey Oswald, Jack Ruby and the ultra-conservative oil billionaire, H.L. Hunt, who were seen together. But the questions remain and the doubts will always be there. I personally saw Lee Harvey Oswald or his look alike at the Carousel Club. John Curington, H.L. Hunt's assistant, has admitted to me that he saw Ruby, Oswald, George DeMohrenschildt, and H.L. Hunt together on various occasions.

Later that afternoon, while Mr. Wilcox continued to play cards with H.L., I left the office at 5:30p.m., much earlier than usual, and drove to the Dallas Gun Club where I often shot a round of skeet or trap. Trapshooting from different angles at clay pigeons was a form of relaxation for me, a way to unwind from a stressful and frustrating job with too many responsibilities.

We formed teams of four: Fred Alford, who was in a wheel chair, his lovely wife, Oleta, owners of Alford's Refrigeration Co., and a tall, broad-shouldered man with dark hair, mustache and matinee-idol good looks. He was obviously impressed by my ability to shoot twenty-five straight pigeons.

"That's a good-looking set of stacked barrels and the lovely young lady holding it is no slouch with a gun either," he observed.

"Thank you," I replied, obviously blushing. "It's a Charles Daly. Have you always been a Winchester man?"

"Yeah, ma'am. I've been an appreciator of Winchester pump shotguns for longer than I care to remember."

"I haven't seen you here before. Are you a new member?" "No. I just get to come here about once a week because of the traveling involved with my job. I'm a field representative for Pneumatic Tube System," he added matter-of-factly.

"It sure sounds impressive."

"My boss decided it was cheaper to give me an impressive title instead of a raise!" he laughed. "Seriously, though, we make the tubes that transfer your check and cash at the drive-in facilities at your bank."

"It sounds impressive anyway, Mr.-?"

"I'm sorry," he apologized, extending his hand. "West. C.G. West, and yours?"

"Madeleine Brown."

"And what do you do, Miss Brown, besides shoot the pants off of me?"

"I'm an account executive at an advertising agency."

"Oh, now that does sound 'Big Time.' So what does an ac count executive do?"

"I mostly figure and analyze budgets and direct the clients' full marketing plans, purchase media advertising time for our clients and travel a great deal to radio and television stations around the state."

"I have a good friend who is a general manager of a radio station in Austin which is owned by Senator Johnson."

"You mean Jesse Kellam at KTBC?" I asked.

"Yeah, that's him," he replied. "Do you know Jesse?"

"Jesse and I not only know each other, but we're real good friends. We do a lot of business together. How do you two know each other?" I asked with raised eyebrows.

"I'm a staunch Democrat from way back and so is Jesse. That's how!"

"It's such a small world sometimes."

"Well, since we have mutual friends and interests, we should get together more often, " he proposed. "Do you play golf too. Miss Brown? It is Miss Brown, isn't it?"

"Yes, it is," I smiled. "And I usually shoot in the upper eighties, in golf, that is."

It was a pleasant conversation and we talked for a few more minutes before exchanging telephone numbers.

"The next time I'm in town," he said as he packed his Winchester in its case, "I'll be sure and call you for a few holes of golf." As I drove home, I wondered if C.G. West was related to Wesley West, the wealthy oilman and rancher from Llano County, Texas, who, according to the newspapers, had recently given the most lavishly ornate party for the state's richest citizens. Texas was still gossiping about the "most glamorous gala of the century." Ultra-rich party-goers had private airplanes lined up in "combat formation" while limousines transported guests to this wild, colorful bash.

When I arrived home, the telephone was ringing. It was my Uncle Johnny and Aunt Della Bowen of Colorado City, Texas. T hey had struck a new gusher of oil in Texas' famed Permian Basin and, of course, wanted to share their elation with me. They had never had children and, consequently, took a special interest in me.

"You and the boys come and stay a week with us," Aunt Della pleaded. T hey were being honored in a gala dedication for their more than generous donations to the Baptist Foundation, the Buckner Boys' Ranch in Burnet, Texas, and other orphans' homes.

"I'll see if I can take off from work," I answered, knowing there was no possible way that I could take any vacation time with the Lone Star Brewery Media Party just around the comer.

I remember when I was a child and all the family went to the Colorado City Baptist Church for services because Uncle Johnny and Aunt Della had donated a sizeable pipe organ. Afterwards, at their home, where the servants had placed the crystal, silver and china for the family dinner, there was a knock on the back door interrupting the mealtime blessing by Uncle Johnny. My grandma, Arlevia Duncan, sat quietly as Aunt Della shooed away a beggar asking for only a taste of food. I noticed tears beginning to well in my grandmother's eyes.

"What's wrong, Grandma?" I asked.

"Christ comes in many ways," she replied, "and that could have been Him. But Della turned him away hungry."

My grandmother was so brokenhearted that watching her cry through dinner made me lose my appetite, too.

Aunt Della was a school teacher who had married John L. Bowen, another school teacher and Grandmother Duncan's brother. She was disinherited by her wealthy banker family (Royce City, Texas) for "marrying below her means." Her father, to spite his daughter, gave her what he believed to be a worthless piece of land in Colorado City, Texas. But this was the magic land of Sid Richardson and Clint Murchison, and, as poetic justice would have it, my aunt and uncle struck oil and immediately became multi-millionaires. They netted over $5,000 a day during the Depression.

As Puritans, they first gave ten percent of their earnings in tithes to the Baptist Church, the next ten percent to themselves and to pay bills, and the balance back to the Lord. They never wheeled and dealed like fellow oil tycoon Sid Richardson. It was very disturbing to me when I called the Baptist Foundation for a copy of Uncle Johnny's oil photograph to learn it no longer hung in the Burnet Boys' Ranch. Someone had disposed of it and the only way the devoted Baptist will be remembered is by his place in this book. Bless this good man and his spirit. The First Baptist Church's Elders in Colorado City and members of the Baptist Foundation fought over his coffin about who would pay for the $25 slab of concrete going over his grave. I was appalled over their lack of graciousness-he had left both foundations millions of dollars.

Prior to his death in 1962, Uncle Johnny sent all his legal heirs a $100 check to see what they would do with the money. Everyone tried to second guess him and deposited their checks in the bank. But Uncle Johnny's heart's desire was for each of the heirs to donate their check to an orphanage or the Buckner Boys' Ranch where he had built the Bowen Cottage. The sizeable trust fund left in his will was given exclusively to the Baptist Foundation and the Buckner Boys' Ranch. Needless to say, the bequests in his will left several relatives with very, very sad faces, not to mention empty pockets.

Clint Murchison, also benevolent in giving large contributions to orphanages and boys' homes, would often say, "Money makes strange bed partners. People should spread it like manure . This would make everyone happy." Clint donated profits from the Del Mar Race Track to Boys' Inc. to help cure delinquency, while simultaneously alleviating some of his tax burdens.

15

Pay to Play

A few weeks later, I was in San Antonio, home of the Alamo, to attend the Lone Star Brewery Media Party. Our maid and nanny, Dale Turner, who had become more like a surrogate mother to the boys, stayed with them at the historic Menger Hotel in an exquisite suite just a few rooms away from Lyndon's. Although he would not be attending the media party, he was in San Antonio campaigning for re election and Jesse had made suitable hotel arrangements convenient for an intimate rendezvous between us.

Guests began arrving early in the evening at the brewery. Black and Mexican waiters moved among them with trays of drinks, while the orchestra played soft background music. Jerome Ragsdale was in attendance, dressed in his best western tuxedo. He made certain to stay out of range of any grease that might spatter from the barbecue pit, where a whole steer turned, basting slowly on a massive iron spit. Harry Jersig was motioning to a waiter to baste the steer some more and watched the Mexican swab dark and bloody-looking sauce over the sizzling meat. Buddy Bostick was standing tall, holding in his belly. He strutted with his arm around a beautiful redhead, whose identity, unlike her body, was never revealed. Her nipples were barely concealed in a low-cut sequined dress. I stood looking at Buddy watching the play of his hand over the hip of the lady in question and the upward mobility of that hand along her rib cage close to her conical breast.

Billie Sol Estes, the new King of Texas Wheeler Dealers, was moving across the brewery like a seasoned politician, shaking hands with everyone and twisting influential arms. He had been introduced to Lyndon and the inner circle of friends by Clifton Carter, an attorney from Smithville, Texas. He and Mr. Ragsdale grew up in this small community, not far from Austin. Carter went on to Washington and became a "hatchet man" for Lyndon. Mr. Ragsdale remained in Texas and worked with Jesse Kellam.

I remembered an incident shortly after Lyndon had introduced me to Billie Sol Estes at a Democratic social function in Austin. Billie Sol had promised Lyndon a $500,000 contribution, but had been slow in sending it. Lyndon called before dawn one morning, "W here the hell is that cash?" he bellowed from our suite at the Driskill.

"Lyndon, do you know what time it is?" Billie Sol replied. "Hell, I didn't call you to find out what time it is! I called you to find out where the hell that cash is. I want you to get out to the fucking airport and get that goddamn cash on its way now!"

Billie Sol went on to become one of my best friends through the years. Once he told me, "Madeleine, you know as well as I do that Lyndon would do anything for you that he could-if you paid him enough. "

The hosts, Lone Star Brewery's handsome and silver-haired President, Harry Jersig, his daughter and son-in-law, Mr. and Mrs. Charlie Kuiper, and Vice President, Mr. and Mrs. Gene Sommerhauser, and Mr. and Mrs. Floyd Sneider, moved across the dance floor saying hello to guests they knew, stopping to meet and speak with those they didn't.

After making my required appearance and mingling with all the other guests for two hours (Mr. Wilcox was present), I hurried back to the Menger Hotel for my prearranged meeting with Lyndon. He greeted me with a bear hug and a smile and said. "Honey,

I can only give you fifteen minutes of my valuable time, but nobody can begrudge us a little session together."

"You're on!" I said as I took his hand and led him to the bed. "A little time with you, Lyndon, is yum yum yummie!"

We always delighted in each other's body, loving and being loved. That lasted a long time.

"My redheaded lady," he whispered into my ear. "Lyndon, you look-"

"Tired," he said. "Go ahead and say it. I look it and feel it, Madeleine. But you-ah, you look like you're glowing as bright as the Texas sun in the morning."

"And you're still trying to be a poet," I laughed. "I wish we could be together more often, but you're such an important national figure now, and probably your every move is watched by the press." "Fuck the press," Lyndon grunted. "If a man can't do a little of what he's not supposed to, he ain't much of a man. Hell, our country is so outdated. Why can't we do like the Chinese and fuck all the women we want and populate the world like the good Lord wanted us to? What's so goddamn wrong with that? In this fucking Victorian society, we've become stalemated by fucking only one woman."

Entering me, Lyndon breathed, "Damn, I'll never have enough of you."

"Don't," I said, moving to meet his body. "Don't ever have enough." Sandow, my Sandow!

16

Love and Forgiveness

The next-day in Dallas, I stopped by my parents' home for a brief visit on the way home from the office. George was standing on the front porch when I drove up the driveway. I watched my father's face, but couldn't read it.

"I want to talk to you a moment, Madeleine." There was nothing to read in my father's voice either. Most times I could grasp what he was thinking, knew instinctively what he wanted done. Right now, everything was out of kilter.

"I'm buying a house in the Cedar Crest area that will be big enough for all of us, including Dale."

"What are you trying to say, George?" I asked frowning.

"I want you and the boys to move in with your mother and me," he said, his voice sharp. "Jimmy and Steven need to have the right Christian upbringing, which you are not providing for them. If you insist on continuing with your present lifestyle, that's your business. You can still have your freedom to come and go as you like, but your mother and I want to raise the boys. Is that asking too much?"

"Forget it, George," I replied. "It won't work. I know you have good intentions, but it just won't work. So forget it."

"But, Madeleine-"

"Case closed, George. We're all not going to live together as one big happy family. It's just not practical. It just won't work."

George hung his head low, obviously disappointed with my reaction. "I'm on vacation all this week. Will you at least bring Steven by tomorrow and let him spend the day with me while his brother is in school?"

I smiled. "Of course, George."

Early the next morning George was in his rocking chair on the porch as I parked my car and walked toward the house with Steven in my arms.

"Our business is not done, Madeleine." George began lecturing me once again. "I really want you and the boys to move into this house I'm buying. I know we'll all be happy together like we used to be before you got into trouble and shamed our family's name. This is our last chance to start all over again. Please, Madeleine, please listen to what I'm saying."

Sitting Steven in his lap, I turned and blew my father a kiss across the palm of my hand. "We're not having this conversation again, George." I argued as I walked toward the car. "I'm raising the boys just fine without your interference, and that's final. F-1-N-A-L!"

Later in the day, with his beloved grandson on his lap, while he rocked in his chair on the front porch, George felt as if the sun had come down very close to his head. The air before his eyes filled with dancing golden specks, and with a wave of his hand, he warned Steven away. The excruciating blows inside his body made him choke for air and every beat of his heart was agony. Suddenly, he felt he was trying to breathe in a vacuum, the very air denying oxygen.

George pitched forward onto the porch and was very still. Steven raced inside the house to get his grandmother and aunt (my sister was living next door at the time). They found George face down, fists clenched. Mother knelt beside him, holding his hand, while my sister called for an ambulance.

With great effort, George opened his eyes to see his wife's tears. The massive stroke had turned his ruddy face almost blue.

The ambulance rushed him to St. Paul Hospital where he was immediately examined by some of the best neurosurgeons in the country. They informed us that George had suffered a total and debilitating stroke, paralyzing the right side of his body. He would never be able to speak again or have control of his bodily functions. They said he would not live long (how wrong they were!).

In his room, I stayed beside him. When I put a cool hand on his forehead, George looked up at me with unfocused eyes. He tried to speak, but it was only the whisper of a moan.

I tried to keep from breaking down, but failed. I looked into his eyes with tears spilling down my cheeks. I felt so utterly guilty and responsible for what had happened to him. If I only hadn't caused him to get upset.

"I'm sorry, George," my voice faltered. I paused a moment, then continued softly. "We could have all lived together, but I was so stubborn. I know now that you only wanted the best for me and the boys. " I put my arm around his shoulders and pressed him against me. My head sank down against him and I whispered into his ear. "I love you so very much, George. I always have and I always will. Please, please forgive me."

17

LBJ's Brush With Death

In the 1954 congressional elections, Lyndon easily won re-election. With President Dwight Eisenhower at the reins, the 48-47 Republican majority in the Senate was exactly reversed and at the age of forty-seven, Lyndon took his front row center aisle seat as the young est majority leader in the history of the Senate. However, on July 1, 1955, hard-working Lyndon very nearly burned himself out when he suffered a life-threatening heart attack on the way to his old friend George Brown's estate in Middleburg, Virginia. He nearly died as he was being rushed to Bethesda Naval Hospital. His chances of survival were considered no better than fifty-fifty.

Jesse Kellam called me on July 5 to wish me a happy birthday, inquiring about Lyndon's condition, and in turn, informed me that he had in his possession a copy of Lyndon's will. He urged me not to worry because Steven and I had been discreetly, but substantially, provided for.

I felt like the weight of the world was on my very shoulders. First my father's paralyzing stroke, and now Lyndon's potentially fatal heart attack. The only two men whom I ever really loved and cared for had both been struck down. (My divorce from James Glynn, who was still institutionalized, had recently been uneventfully finalized). Please don't cry, I told myself. There is nothing I can't handle. We need grief in life so our hearts will know what happiness is.

The same day, Earle Clements, Democratic Whip of the Sen ate, interrupted his campaign for re-election to return to Washington to read a statement to the Senate as dictated by Dr. James Cain, Lyndon's personal physician. "Senator Lyndon B. Johnson has had a myocardial infarction of a moderately severe character. He was quite critically ill immediately following the attack, but his recovery has been satisfactory. He should be able to return to the Senate in January."

Lyndon was not a good patient, as he had a tendency to throw fits of temper and abuse the staff. He was discharged on August 7, to the relief of many of those at Bethesda Hospital, and appeared to enjoy a complete recovery.

On August 27, his forty-seventh birthday, Lyndon flew home to his ranch in the Texas Hill Country where he was born and raised ("Where people know if you're sick and care if you're dying," as he put it) and was met at the airport by his mother, Rebekah, and Josefa, his sister.

One month later, President Eisenhower also suffered a heart attack while on one of his frequent golfing vacations in Denver. He was taken to the hospital while a staff of eight leading physicians was summoned. The doctors reported that the attack was "moderate." In October, Eisenhower began directing government policy, with Richard Nixon, from his hospital suite. He returned to his desk in December.

Meanwhile, in Dallas, my father lay paralyzed in his bedroom at home, attended by his companion, Mildred Teel, and two neighborhood registered nurses, Mrs. Vess and Mrs. Belise, and the Dallas Power and Light nurses, Margaret Johnston and Frances Dennehy.

Each day when Lyndon woke up to savor another Texas morning, George would stare out of his bedroom window, unblinking, at the sunbeams dancing in the yard.

He was as far removed from the world as anyone could be.

Lyndon's massive heart attack ("about as bad as a man can have and still live," as he described it), put him on the sidelines for six months, but, as Jesse said, "He recovered like one of his political campaigns."

He gave up the chili dishes he favored and also his three-pack a-day cigarette habit, trimmed down from 220 to 180 pounds and cut his normal working day. In addition, he moved into a more normal family relationship with Steven. Lyndon called me often to ask about him, seemingly more interested in his son's welfare.

Steven was growing up fast. Even at an early age he displayed characteristics of his father. He would approach me every once in a while to say that he wanted to buy something from one of the neighborhood stores located on the busy, but humble, Saner Avenue, but didn't quite have enough money. There were many small neighbor hood stores, including Spann's Drug Store, Binion's Grocery Store, Gardner's Grocery, Stalling Grocery, and Hopkin's Variety Store. Of course, I would always give him funds, unaware that he was putting the same sad story to his grandmother, aunt, Dale and Mildred. Just like Lyndon, he was a true capitalist.

Out at the LBJ ranch, where it was quiet and still, Lyndon was aware of his heart attack's effect on his political career. During those long four months remaining in 1955, his mind was constantly working, knowing full well that his whole career was at stake. He was in close contact with all the oil giants-and J. Edgar Hoover, who continued to run a one-man government within the government.

Lyndon called me from Jesse's office at KTBC. "Bird thinks if I stay in the Senate, it will shorten my life. Madeleine, do you think I should resign?"

"I don't think you should retire from politics," I told him. "Politics has been your life. It's what you know and love." Lyndon asked everyone his or her opinion so no one person could be flattered more than another.

"Goddamn it, I told Jesse you would point me in the right direction, Madeleine. I just can't see myself sitting in a rocking chair on my porch at the ranch. "

Jesse confided in me later that after Lyndon talked the situation over with me, he began to recuperate and get better, stronger, and more cheerful. He no longer suffered bouts of depression and hopelessness. In January, 1956, Lyndon returned to his Senate post, his energy renewed.

18

Variety is the Spice of Life

Meanwhile, my father proved the neurosurgeons wrong by continuing to live far beyond their expectations. Still he lay paralyzed in his bed, oblivious to what was happening around him.

One morning, I sent my parents' companion, Mildred Teel, to the neighborhood "washateria" to launder George's sheets and pillowcases because our own washing machine was not working. Those were the days before disposable paper products.

Mildred, a loving, compassionate black woman with an effervescent personality and the cleanliness of a surgeon, was the epitome of dedication and loyalty to my invalid father.

"Do you think we can get all of George's bedding laundered today?" I asked her.

"Honey, give me a little money and the Lord," she replied, "and I can do anything."

Within minutes of leaving the house, Mildred was back with the dirty laundry.

"What happened?" I asked her. "Is the washateria closed?"

Tears were streaming down her smooth, black skin. "Only to me," she answered, pointing to her arm. "I'm black and I couldn't go in."

"We'll just see about that!" I fumed, grabbing Steven by the arm. With the bundles of laundry, I marched angrily with him and Mildred the short distance back to the washateria.

In the window was a prominently displayed cardboard sign that read: "WHITES ONLY." Although my hands trembled from suppressed anger, I reached for the sign and ripped it in half, throwing the pieces on the floor as a rather large woman pushed herself through the crowd of women washing their laundry. The movements of her massive frame were so vigorous that they created a breeze.

"She's not coming in here," she pointed at Mildred. The woman was a Gestapo type. Her mouth was hard and tight and she appeared devoid of lips. Her dark hair was short. She had no breasts and looked like a man.

"Who says?" I asked, my manner at once intimidating. "I do," she replied, staring at me suspiciously.

"Well, miss, you're wrong!" I glared, pointing my finger in her face. "My father's sick in bed with a stroke and we've got an important job to do. Now you either step back or I'll whip you from here to Sunday. It doesn't make a bit of difference to me."

Dumbfounded, the woman retreated. I helped Mildred load the washing machines with our bundles of laundry and then turned my attention to Steven.

I said, "I have to get back to your grandfather, so you stay here with Mildred. If that woman says anything-good, bad or indifferent-you be sure to come and get me and I' 11 take care of that Miss." Mildred has often repeated this story, pointing out that I was as skinny as a green bean and that Miss Gestapo could have made a pancake of me.

But that put an end to racial incidents, fortunately, and Mildred continued to use the washateria at intervals over the years. Looking back at that day, I know now that if my family hadn't been friends with McGowan, the owner, Mildred and I both would have been put in jail. At that time in Texas, and the South, breaking the "color laws" guaranteed a jail cell.

In 1957, Eisenhower sent federal troops to Little Rock, Arkansas to enforce school integration. Governor Orval E. Faubus ordered the Arkansas National Guard to bar black students from Central High School. He warned that rioting would break out if blacks were admitted to the school. Eisenhower tried to persuade Faubus to enforce the law and prevent rioting, but the President finally had to send troops to protect the black students.

T he news reports of the Arkansas school crisis had frightened even young Jimmy and Steven. One afternoon when they were riding with Mildred on a city bus, the driver scolded them for sitting in the "colored" section in the back with Mildred and ordered the boys to move to the front seats where "whites" sat. Jimmy and Steven were crying and trembling when they arrived home because they feared something horrible was going to happen to Mildred when they left her alone in the back of the bus.

Simultaneously, the continuing Senate debates over civil rights legislation were putting Lyndon's leadership to its most severe test. As never before, he was the central figure on the most divisive and quarrelsome issue disturbing the American people. When we met at the Driskill in the summer of 1957, civil rights were on the mind of both of us.

As Lyndon and I sat down beside each other on the soft, poster bed, I immediately began relating to him the unfortunate incidents at the washateria with Mildred and the boys on the bus. "You've got to do something. You're the leader of the Senate, and you can do some thing. Change the laws-whatever it takes-before there's another Civil War in this country and many good people get killed."

He put his arm around me and hugged me, "I'm glad you still haven't learned to mince your words."

I turned my face to him. Lyndon kissed my mouth softly. "You don't want to change me." I said.

"Oh, Madeleine, I've missed you." He closed his eyes and spoke in a murmur. He lay back, pulling me with him, so that I ended up leaning over him. "And don't worry, Madeleine," he continued, "I've warned the other Southern senators that a civil rights bill will go through this session, absolutely, no doubt about it."

"You make it sound like you've been working on this for sometime."

"Hell, I've already spent most of the winter and spring planning the stages toward the passage of a bill that everybody-well, the Democrats anyway-could live with. But the folks back here in Texas are pissed-off over any civil rights bill. I've received thousands of letters that read: 'WE ARE TOLD YOU ARE READY TO SELL OUT THE SOUTH. IS THIS TRUE?'"

"All I hear is Senator Johnson talking," I said. "But how does the Lyndon Johnson whom I know and love really feel about the civil rights of my friends like Mildred and Dale?"

"Mr. Sam tells it just like I tell it. 'God knows, I am one man that has no racial or religious prejudices. I want everybody to go to heaven on their own route.' So fuck all those lily-white bastards that keep sending me letters. You tell Mildred and Dale that Lyndon Johnson is going to make goddamn sure that no one treats them badly because of the color of their skin. You can count on it."

I kissed him lightly. His eyes seeming to undress me and devour me all at the same time. My eyes twinkled with a wanton invitation.

"Madeleine, you ready for something different?"

"You're on," I cried out impulsively.

With his innocent country-boyish grin he placed a satin sleeping mask over his eyes that was embroidered on one side with the words: "WAKE ME ONLY FOR SEX OR GOLF." At that time he had little interest in golf.

Standing in his birthday suit, he reached over into a brown grocery bag and removed a little black whip along with a string of pearls and a funny looking big peter. I gasped seeing all of this.

"What are you going to do to me?"

He grabbed me, gave me a bear hug so strong that my rib cage felt as if it had been ground into sand.

"You're so goddamn innocent. I guess that's what I love about you. But your body is so hot it's like a burning tumbleweed rolling on the desert. Hell, you make me come before I even get started," Lyndon said.

He began putting everything back in the bag and yelled, "Hey, be careful! I'm afraid your body heat will bum up all my toys before we get to use them!"

Shocked and excited, uncontrollable passion rocked me. "Take me now, Lyndon!" Neither of us could wait!

As we climaxed together, his orgasm flooded me like rolling rapids, and my body dropped into deep oblivion. I slowly removed the mask. Lyndon's eyes gazed into mine lovingly. I kissed him tenderly and then placed the mask over his eyes again so that he could get the mid-day rest he so desperately needed. A nap had even been prescribed by his doctors.

"What's the problem, Madeleine?" he asked. "Are you afraid that if I don't get a goddamn nap that I might kick the bucket while we're screwing?"

"Lyndon," I scolded, "don't talk like that. It's not funny." "Oh, hell, what a way to go! I can just see the Washington

Post headlines now: "SENATOR JOHNSON DIES WHILE FUCKING. AIDES SAY HE CAME AND WENT AT THE

SAME TIME!" Lyndon said, "You just wait, redheaded lady, I'm going to teach you the big time stuff that every red-blooded male dreams of doing."

I said, with bells still ringing in my ears, "I love you, Lyndon.

Sleep well," and then I closed my eyes.

19

CIVIL RIGHTS

On the touchy issue of civil rights, Lyndon finally had to a take a very public stand. Before 1957, he had consistently voted against all civil rights bills, including a much-debated Administration bill in 1956. Even after our conversation at the Driskill, he seemed much more involved in the politics of civil rights than in the moral issue at stake. But all along, he insisted that he was not prejudiced and that he wanted equal opportunities for blacks. He had supported this image by telling stories of rampant racism in the South that he personally found "insulting" to his proud Southern heritage.

In Houston, Southern Pacific Railroad had applied for a permit to build a railway station in the downtown area, but the city council vetoed the permit because "blacks and whites would have to stand on the platform together." But Lyndon's most oft-told story was of a trainload of Marines (my ex-husband, Glynn, among them), arriving in Dallas just after World War II. On board, all the military men, both black and white, were laughing and joking with each other until they crossed the border into Texas. T he conductor, with the assistance of the MPs, told the men that they were now in Texas and the blacks and whites could not intermingle. When the MPs tried to separate the men by races, they became belligerent and tied up the conductor and the MPs, and basically commandeered the train.

When the Union Pacific train pulled into the railroad station in Dallas, all the white Marines left the train with the black Marines on their shoulders. "We fought side by side in muddy foxholes around the world," one of the white Marines said, "and saved each others' lives as if we were blood brothers. We're not about to tum our backs on them now just because we are in America! It doesn't make any sense to me why a black man can go to war to risk his life for all Americans – of every color-and then return home to sit in the back of a bus or have to drink from a separate water fountain."

"Since we are all Americans," Lyndon told his colleagues, "we must stand side by side from the foxholes to the mountains."

Lyndon's heart attack had put a temporary damper on speculation that he was a leading contender for his party's presidential nomination. Speculation had arisen that Lyndon seemed to be trying to divest himself of the image that he was a segregationist.

Early in the 1950s, Lyndon had acted independently of his fellow Southerners when he refused to sign the "Southern Manifesto" that all other Senators from the South did sign, denouncing the Supreme Court decision on desegregation of public schools. Finally, by 1957, he was openly proud of having piloted through the Senate the first Civil Rights Bill since Reconstruction.

20

Flight of a Lifetime

In December, 1957, the Texas Democratic Party had scheduled an extravagant appreciation dinner for Lyndon at the Adolphus Hotel in Dallas to honor his outstanding achievements as the state's senior United States Senator, and to proclaim his candidacy for the Democratic nomination for President. Locally, oilmen Clint Murchison and H.L . Hunt, along with banker R.L . Thornton, and Earle Cabell, focused attention upon Lyndon. In essence, he was their power base. As usual, Jesse Kellam had called me at Glenn Advertising to inform me that Lyndon would want to spend some time with me in his suite afterward.

Unfortunately, a few days before the festive celebration, Mr. Glenn suffered a massive heart attack . As a member of Christian Science, a religious movement which believes in the power of Christian faith to heal sickness, Mr. Glenn disavowed any medical attention from doctors. The following day he died, and on December 11, the day of Lyndon's appreciation dinner, the employees of the agency attended a short memorial service at Restland Cemetery in Dallas where he was entombed in a stately mausoleum.

Immediately, business arrangements and contracts were initiated by Mr. Jersig and Lone Star Brewery to continue financing Mr. Glenn's successful advertising agency. Nevertheless, job security was threatened and chaos was the order of the day. Jesse called me at the office on the afternoon of Mr. Glenn's burial.

"I know you are in mourning at the agency, Madeleine," he apologized. "But life goes on, business goes on. I really think you need to be at the appreciation dinner tonight for the professional con tacts if for no other reason." He paused and then added, "Don't worry, Madeleine. Lyndon just will not have time to see you, but he agrees with me. If you want to really become a successful advertising executive, then you have to get out there and shake hands, kiss asses and smile-even though you do not feel like it."

It was at the Adolphus Hotel in 1948 that I first met then Congressman Lyndon Johnson. As I arrived at the carriage entry, a distinguished-looking doorman welcomed me with the same gracious charm that another one had given me almost ten years earlier.

Through the grand lobby of sumptuous objets d'art, the concierge escorted me to a separate mezzanine which housed the select Crystal he politely opened large ornate doors, kaleidoscopic images from that elegant evening in 1948 danced across my memory ...Lyndon gentlemanly kissing my hand and holding it in the palm of his,the band breaking into a rhythmic rendition of Cole Porter's "Anything Goes," Lyndon leading me to the dance floor, putting his arms around me and pressing his warm body next to mine. The tenderness in his voice that night,the passion in his eyes-it was all still there as my heart soared.

I looked at the crowd and tried to pick out Lyndon or even Jesse,and failed to find either. The ballroom was inundated with Democrats who had come to cheer Lyndon.

Finally,over the heads of the crowd,between moving figures, Jesse stood up at his table and motioned for me to come over and sit next to Lyndon's faithful political supporters and fund-raisers. At this table were Billie Sol Estes, Clifton Carter, Jerome T. Ragsdale, Lyndon's Dallas attorney and conduit for Steven's child support payments; and,of course,Jesse himself.

As the evening progressed,Billie Sol,the ever-generous Texas businessman, told me that, as a lay preacher, he helped build black and Latin American Church of Christ congregations in the desert town of Pecos. In tum, I told him that I gave up a great deal of my spare time as a den mother for Steven's group of Cub Scouts from St. George's Episcopal Church.

Suddenly, I felt a familiar feeling hand resting on my shoulder. "Who do we have here?" Lyndon asked Jesse coyly.

"Surely, Mr. Johnson, you remember Miss Brown from Glenn Advertising in Dallas?" Jesse continued the charade.

Acting embarrassed, Lyndon apologized. "Please forgive me, Miss Brown, I meet so many-"

"Please don't apologize," I interrupted. "You surely can't re member everyone you meet."

"Did you know that Miss Brown spends her spare time as a den mother for her son's Cub Scout troop?" Jesse asked him.

Lyndon looked genuinely surprised. "Is that so? Well then, Jesse, why don't you make appropriate arrangements for Miss Brown to fly to Austin with her Cub Scout troop for an all-expense paid tour of the Capitol?"

Jesse nodded. "Consider it done, Mr. Johnson."

Gently squeezing my shoulder, Lyndon said in a soft drawl, "Once again, please excuse my forgetfulness, Miss Brown. I promise next time to remember your lovely face."

I was about to reply when he asked Billie Sol, Clifton Carter and Jerome Ragsdale to meet with him privately in his suite.

A little over a month later, on January 25, 1958, Steven's Cub Scout Pack 40, Dens 1 and 2, flew aboard a Trans-Texas airplane to the State Capitol. Out of all those first-time fliers, I was the only one who became airsick. The flight was courtesy of United States Sena tor Lyndon B. Johnson.

Our group of seventeen 8-year-old boys was met at the Austin Airport at 8:30 A. M. by KTBC's roving news unit, "Red Rover," and its driver, Paul Bolton, as well as a police motorcycle escort and convertibles for the trip from the airport to the Capitol.

From 11:30 A.M. to 12:00 noon, the boys appeared on KTBC's television program "Now Dig This," and then they were treated to lunch in the spacious dining room of the Driskill Hotel.

Afterward, the group toured the Capitol Building and then were escorted to the Governor's Mansion. Jake Pickle, a long-time political confidant of Lyndon's and member of the Democratic Executive Committee in Austin (later a U.S. Congressman), arranged a meeting between Governor Price Daniel and the Cub Scouts. The Governor was attending a meeting of the Texas Press Association all day, but Jake worked out a meeting with the Governor and the boys just prior to his joining the Texas Press group.

An Austin business provided courtesy convertibles for our motorcade from the Capitol back to the airport, and upon arrival in Dal las, we were met by WFAA-TV Channel 8, who stated on the air that I, "had to be boy crazy to take seventeen boys to Austin" for a day. In addition, a photograph taken of the Cub Scouts and me, with a TTA plane in the background, appeared in newspapers throughout the country with a caption that read: "SCOUTING AROUND."

On January 31, I received a letter at Glenn Advertising from Jesse on KTBC Radio and Television stationery:

> Dear Mrs. Brown:
>
> One of the things the world needs most is mothers like you. Hearty congratulations to you for having had the insight and taken the time to give the membership of Den 1 & 2, Pack 40, St. George's

> Episcopal Church, what I know was an experience that will live in their memories.
>
> Thank you, too, for having given us the opportunity to work with you in such a worthwhile venture.
>
> Sincerely,
> J.C. Kellam General Manager

On February 10, I also received an official letter on State Democratic Executive Committee of Texas stationery, from Lyndon's good friend and political associate, Jake Pickle:

> Dear Mrs. Brown:
>
> I was a Boy Scout for some six years, and some of the most pleasant memories of my boyhood are those occasions when I made trips with other Scouts. Had I been given the opportunity to visit the governor of my state in the Mansion, I think it would definitely have been stamped indelibly on my mind. I'm sure that's the way those young boys felt when they were in Austin recently.
>
> They were a well-behaved and interesting group. I know the governor enjoyed having them, and you were most considerate in bringing the boys to Austin so they could see their Capitol City.
>
> It was a pleasure to have worked with you on this project. Let us hear from you again when we can be of service.
>
> Sincerely,
> J.J. Pickle

But not everyone shared the boys' elation over their field trip to Austin. The Cub Scouts' headquarters had been bombarded with grievances from other dens complaining that they were never allowed to take such exceptional and extravagant field trips. Several dens openly questioned whether I had any political influence in Austin. Eventually, the Cub Scouts' headquarters issued a scathing reprimand stating that I had not properly cleared the trip through their organization and had not requested the appropriate permission.

When I told Lyndon what the Cub Scouts' headquarters had officially said to me, he replied in his typical manner:

"Did Steven and the boys enjoy the trip?" he asked.

"Of course," I answered. "They'll be walking on air for months."

"Then who gives a shit what the Cub Scouts' headquarters say?!"

21

The Spirit Lives On

The vibrant, colorful fall and the deeply bone-piercing winter were part of a dark and sad year in 1958 for both Lyndon and me. Rebekah, his mother, lost her battle to the viciousness of lymphatic cancer, and on September 12 was buried beside Lyndon's father, Sam, under a beautiful oak tree. The family graveyard is beside the life-giving Pedernales River near the ranch. In my mind there was no doubt about Lyndon being her favorite child because she ruthlessly drove him to success after success, triumph after triumph.

We knew that George was also slipping away. On Christmas, 1958, my own beloved father's death came after suffering a paralyzing stroke four and one half years earlier. My beloved mother died on Christmas Day as well, in 1984, exactly twenty-six years later. I re member these two beautiful people daily and still see the fruits of their works. My own selfish ways were altered when, a few days prior to George's death, I opened the side door to my mother's kitchen and saw mounds of toys, groceries and clothes.

"What in heaven's name are all these things?" I asked.

Mother's big brown eyes sparkled and said, "They are for a needy family on Michigan Street."

In total grief, I replied. "Well, who cares if there is a needy family, Mother! What about George? We are not going to have him much longer. Our love and time should be with him."

Mother slowly took her handkerchief from her apron and dried her tear-filled eyes, saying, "Baby, darling (the name my mother always called me), please don't ever have a heart like that. You know if your dad was able there would be twice as much of everything for the poor. George went out searching for people who needed help."

I quickly closed my eyes remembering how I hated poverty and asked "the One upstairs" to forgive me. I kissed mother, then went to place a kiss on George's fevered brow. He was laboring to breathe. I added to my prayers, "Please, Lord, if it is your will, help George and please don't let him suffer any more. He has been such a wonderful, good person and the best father a child could have." I turned and began loading my automobile with the provisions for the needy family.

The day George was buried, the most unusual, gorgeous snow flakes, as large as saucers, fell, as the long funeral procession of friends blocked traffic for miles. All were gently taking him to his final resting place at Laurel Land (the same memorial park where Dallas Policeman J.D. Tippit is buried). Media people from all over Texas, especially the Johnson Broadcasting Network, sent over 400 memorials honoring my father. Today, his spirit remains alive in the community of Trinity Heights. Nobel Prize recipient Mother Teresa employed my father's old homestead near St. James Church as a shelter for the homeless and the hungry.

In 1959Texas real estate and oil tycoon, Sid Richardson, died and a memorial service was held on his private San Jose Island off the coast of Rockport, Texas, with The Reverend Billy Graham officiating. Later, his body was returned to Athens, Texas for burial.

Sid's partner from boyhood, Clint Murchison, survived ten years longer. His death came on June 20, 1969, thus ending the powerful force they had mustered in Washington, D.C. Both these men, who had become billionaires, contributed to the betterment of man kind. They were forever exploring the most powerful product of the world, "Black Gold."

Clint was responsible for the first transcontinental gas pipe lines across Canada and North Africa. His death came before the Australian gas lines he envisioned were completed.

Sid and Clint's million dollar deals were often made in five minutes or less, and written on the backs of envelopes.

They are buried close together in Athens, Texas. Ironically, their close friends, J. Edgar Hoover and Clyde Tolson are also buried near each other, as well.

Clint's favorite ranch in Mexico was called Acana Mariquita, where the campesinos called him El Jefe (the boss, or chief). They placed a sturdy wooden cross on the highest point of the mountain with the following inscription:

> Clint W. Murchison
> 11 Abril 1895-20 Junio 1969
> Nunca nos olvidaremos de el (We will never forget him)

In October of1959, Sam Rayburn scheduled a press conference in Dallas in which he announced that the "Johnson for President Committee" would open in Austin under the auspices of Governor Price Daniel and himself. Publicly, Lyndon ignored this move. *Pri*vately, Jesse Kellam began coordinating plans with Jack Valenti for me to work in the campaign placing radio and TV schedules. The very thought of handling such big schedules was exciting. I could never understand how Lyndon had so many loyal people working for him. He would curse one and all alike. Strangely, Lyndon bypassed Horace Busby, Walter Jenkins, and Bill Moyers to give full reins to Jack Valenti in his upcoming election campaign.

22

The Vice President

Lyndon's decision to seek the presidential nomination in 1960 was handled as cagily as most political decisions in his life. He allowed friends to mount an unofficial campaign for him as early as December, 1959, but withheld his own announcement until my birthday July 5, 1960-shortly before the opening of the 1960 convention. Jesse called and wished me a happy birthday. "Be sure to listen to Lyndon's speech on July 5th; it will be your Happiest Birthday!"

Many observers contended that he never seriously believed he could take the prize away from Senator John F. Kennedy, starting as late as he did in his attempt to win delegates. Kennedy went into the convention at Los Angeles with impressive primary victories, plus the solid results of hard work and sharp dealing with state conventions by his staff and most notably by his younger brother, Robert, whom Lyndon despised.

I asked Lyndon a few months later, "Why the wait, why the indecision about publicly announcing your candidacy?" He said that he was gravely concerned about all the international problems through out the world and first thought he would be more beneficial in serving his country in the Senate. There were three main issues of the campaign: first, Cuba; second, Quemoy and Matsu which China massively bombarded (there is reason to believe that-at least in the past-the CIA trained, equipped and financed Chinese Nationalist commando raids on the mainland which were launched from these offshore Is lands); and third, the question of whether President Eisenhower should have apologized to Khrushchev after the U-2 spy flight of Francis Gary Powers was shot down over the Soviet Union.

Lyndon believed that the Catholic issue would hurt Kennedy, preventing his nomination. Then the public would tum to Lyndon. That would bring about a free-for-all at the convention, he thought, between Senator Stuart Symington and Hubert Humphrey, and Lyndon would emerge as the nominee of the Democrats. He knew he had the support of Clint Murchison and Senator Knowland from California. Also in his comer was

H.L. Hunt and his top assistant, John Curington, who were in constant contact with Joseph Kennedy.

I received an anonymous phone call telling me that Kennedy had the nomination cinched before the completion of the first roll call because of the well-laid plans by Joseph Kennedy, John's father, and the Invisible Government. From the start of the 1960 campaign many were convinced that Cuba alone could be the deciding issue in the election and, in retrospect, it was one of the decisive factors in what proved to be the closest presidential election of modem times. Certainly, cloak-and-dagger tactics by the CIA played a dominant part on both sides, against Nixon and Kennedy alike.

Kennedy's selection of Lyndon as his running mate came as a distinct surprise. So did Lyndon's acceptance. His old friend, "Mr. Sam"Rayburn, who had placed his name in nomination to lead the ticket, tearfully pleaded in vain with him not to be "fool enough" to surrender his powerful Senate leadership in favor of the largely ceremonial position of Vice President, even though this office had control of the Invisible Government (the 54112 Group).[2]

It was common knowledge at the time that there was no love lost between Kennedy and Johnson, but Kennedy could obviously benefit from Lyndon's considerable presence on his ticket. As a Roman Catholic Easterner, Kennedy's position in the Southern Bible Belt, traditionally regarded as a bastion of anti-Catholicism, was not strong. He was also on shaky ground in the West. T he Lyndon Johnson image of a Texan, a Westerner, a bit of a conservative, would obviously be helpful. Certainly, no one could quibble about Lyndon's performance in the Senate.

Many years later John Curington told me that it was the joint decision of H.L. Hunt and Joseph Kennedy to place Lyndon on the ticket as Vice President.

Lyndon also understood that his whole political future, whether or not he and Kennedy won in November, depended on his ability to deliver the South to the Democrats. Immediately after the convention in Los Angeles, Jesse was optimistic because of the marketing expertise of the loyal and brilliant Jack Valenti in Houston. Jesse instructed me to begin purchasing blocks of broadcast advertising time for the Kennedy-Johnson campaign

2 See Bill Moyers, The Secret Government: The Constitution in Crisis, 1988, Seven Locks Press. Moyers, of course, worked closely with President Johnson; L. Fletcher Prouty, The Secret Team, New York: Prentice Hall 1973; David Wise and Thomas B. Ross, The Invisible Government, New York: Random House 1964, Vintage; Inside the Shadow Government, The Christie Institute, Washington, 1988. Another instrument of the secret or shadow government was the 40 Committee.

throughout the entire southwest region of the U.S. I began scheduling political rallies, with the "Big One" to be in the Wynnewood Shopping Center-the heart of Dallas' Bible Belt. All the big Democrats were invited-Judge Sarah T. Hughes, Mike McCool, Lew Sterrett and Henry Wade (Dallas' District Attorney). Bob Bobbitt, Lyndon's brother-in-law, had me secure big door prizes (fur coats, color televisions, etc.) for the occasion and tons of balloons, circulars, and campaign buttons.

After the death of Mr. Glenn, I had departed from the chaotic and insecure atmosphere of his company and joined the staff of George Bevel & Associates as an account executive. My new employers were elated, and impressed with the new presidential campaign account I had brought to their company. All advertising agencies are desirous of political connections.

In September, Kennedy and Johnson stole the show at the Alamo in San Antonio. Picketers were carrying signs that read: "THEY WANT THE BIBLE AND THE CONSTITUTION AND WE DON'T

WANT THE KREMLIN OR THE VATICAN." Lyndon countered by introducing Kennedy with his "Little ole war hero" speech: "And then that little ole Massachusetts boy took his little ole torpedo boat and rammed it into the side of a Japanese cruiser, and there wasn't nobody around askin' what religion he was. And when he was savin' those American boys in his crew, they didn't ask what church he be longed to."

Kennedy's speech, perfectly suited for the Alamo, said, among other things, that "side by side Bowie and Crockett died, McCafferty and Bailey and Corey, but no one knows whether they were Catholics or not. For there was no religious test at the Alamo."

The applause was gracious. Many, though not all, of the picketers put down their signs.

There was strong anti-Catholic feeling in Texas. H.L. Hunt bought radio time throughout the 1960 campaign and he himself would come on the air and make speeches about the Pope moving into the White House. Texas had not come around. The state might go one way, might go another. No one knew. We did know the Republican Party was growing by leaps and bounds in the South.

The ultra-conservative H.L. Hunt had been anti-Lyndon ever since the war when Lyndon voted against the Disney Bill which would have raised the ceiling price of oil. In 1948 H.L. had contributed heavily to Coke Stevenson's campaign against Lyndon. But by 1960, H.L.'s feelings about Lyndon had softened. First of all, Lyndon had never again voted "wrong" on oil. Second, Lyndon had proved himself a strong leader in the Congress. Hunt was sure Lyndon would be able to control what he viewed publicly as the ever-present threat of Communist subversion in the government. On the other hand, Kennedy was a Catholic and Catholicism was an anathema to H.L.

Jesse instructed me to intensify all broadcast schedules and print new campaign ads to run in Texas during the last week as Lyndon returned to his home state.

On November 4, just four days before the election, Lyndon carried the Democrats' campaign into Dallas. I witnessed the crowd of hecklers and demonstrators that built up outside the Adolphus Hotel. Lyndon turned down an offer by a hotel official for a change in plans for security reasons and said that he was "coming in the main en trance, wherever that is."

The Adolphus Hotel had served as a headquarters for Dallas Democrats through the 1960 campaign. One afternoon,while Steven and I were collecting campaign buttons and brochures,Lyndon's sister,Rebekah Bobbitt (her husband,Bob was a member of the managerial staff of KTBC) was going on about what a tall and handsome young man Steven was."He could pass for Lyndon's son," she bragged. My heart sank. I thought to myself,could she possibly know the truth?

Perle Mesta was there and she agreed."You're right,Rebekah, he does look like that hunk of a brother of yours." My heart rate increased until I thought I would pass out.

Lyndon dismissed police guards and he and Lady Bird plowed their way through the howling,chanting,jeering throng which waved signs reading: "LBJ SOLD OUT TO YANKEE SOCIALISTS," "SMILE JUDAS," "DOWN WITH LADY BIRD," and "REMEMBER DUVAL COUNTY AND BOX 13."

It took Lyndon and Lady Bird almost thirty minutes to inch their way through the Republican demonstrators to the Adolphus Hotel's Grand Ballroom where they were greeted by two thousand wildly cheering luncheon guests, but Lyndon's supporters were all deeply troubled by the angry throngs of people and their unkind re marks.

In his opening statement Lyndon told the crowd: "It makes me sad to know that we have people-attractive people,nice people who can be so frustrated and so discourteous and so desperate. I can't understand it. He who has any knowledge of our history has never seen the Republican Party rise to power and demonstrate it as it has today."

U.S. Attorney Barefoot Sanders and I had been with Lyndon and Lady Bird at KRLD-TV,Channel4,when he taped his statewide television speech for the next night. Lyndon said,"We were hissed at and spit upon ...in a mob scene that looked like some other country. It was hard to believe that this was happening in Dallas,Texas." Later, the same hostility happened to our U.N. Ambassador Adlai Stevenson when he came to Dallas and was jeered and spat upon.

Lyndon scared the cameramen and crew into total silence when he roared like a lion. "If you're against me, get the hell out of this studio. Did you hear me? Fuck the disloyal!"

Lyndon's outburst sent Channel 4's president and general man ager, Clyde Rembert, scuttling to his office while the rest of us remained still- and very quiet.

The incident triggered widespread response both pro and con for the demonstrators, and Lyndon himself quickly expanded the is sue in the last days of the campaign, looking for sympathy.

"God, forgive them for they know not what they do," Lyndon told crowds throughout the state on the final day of the campaign, and he predicted that the incident had cinched a Democratic victory in Texas.

Like Lyndon, Kennedy was a formidable campaigner, yet the Democratic ticket beat the Republican team of Richard Nixon and Henry Cabot Lodge by the smallest margin in this century. Of the sixty-nine million votes cast, the Democrats won by approximately 113,000 votes. T he Kennedy-Johnson ticket also barely carried Texas by slightly more than 46,000 votes, and many political observers later credited the incident at the Adolphus for winning Texas for the Democrats.

Lyndon's good fortune in being able to run for two offices at the same time in 1960 was made possible when the state legislature passed a law allowing him to do so. It was widely known as "Lyndon's Law," and when challenged in a Texas court, it was upheld. No matter what might happen in the election, Lyndon would not have been unemployed in November.

The Presidential inauguration was on January 20, 1961, but the Senate, as always, convened right after the new year. Lyndon was sworn in for his third term as Senator, and then, of course, resigned. When Lyndon vacated the Senate office, it became an opportunity for John Tower, and he remained in office for years. He and his daughter perished in a plane crash in the early summer of 1991. Many believe Senator Tower carried secrets regarding the J.F.K. assassination to the grave.

On January 20, 1961, Lyndon joined John Kennedy, Chief Justice Earl Warren, former President Harry Truman, outgoing President Eisenhower, Jackie Kennedy, and Lady Bird for the inauguration. Using a Bible given him by his mother, Rebekah, Lyndon was sworn in as the Vice President of the United States by "Mr. Sam." It was the first time a Speaker of the House had ever sworn in a Vice President, but it was generally agreed that it was appropriate, since Lyndon was Mr. Sam's pride and joy. Lyndon had taken the place of the son Mr. Sam never had.

My heart was saddened as I watched powerful Mr. Sam standing by Lyndon, taking a back seat in our government, accepting "left overs" from the political arena.

However, Lyndon was still the favorite son of the Texas oil boys. Often H.L. Hunt would sing Lyndon's praises, grinning, "The South will rise again." Steven's father proved himself a winner once more.

23

Missing Person

Perhaps to a greater degree than he expected, Lyndon lost most of his former power in the Senate. Immediately the jokes began circulating about vice presidential trips to attend state funerals. But Lyndon did play along with the formalities much better than I expected. He and Lady Bird even sold their old home where they had been neighbors with J. Edgar Hoover, and purchased a nearby mansion, The Elms, from Washington society hostess, Perle Mesta, and turned it into a small but well-staffed home. They entertained more formally and more lavishly than ever before. But Lyndon wanted more. He could never thrive on the mere surface glitter of power. He demanded the real thing! He carried a torch to become President, and everyone knew it.

Frustrated, Lyndon was often in a dark mood during those days and he would return to the tranquility of his beloved Texas, in the Hill Country, when an opportunity made itself available. I always thought it was because he could be with me. For relaxation, he loved homemade movies of animals mating, and when we made love, he would imitate the animals' bellows. "Goddamn, isn't this great?" On one particular weekend, Jesse had arranged for me to meet my "favorite person" at his suite in the Menger Hotel in San Antonio.

Whenever I traveled, Dale and the boys always accompanied me. They particularly loved San Antonio and the river boat ride which took us through the city. Before the Lone Star Brewery purchased the Buckhorn Saloon, they enjoyed an artist named Salinas who sketched Texas scenes while singing. One tune about Billie Sol included the lyrics "What a friend we have in Lyndon" and the boys would always exclaim, "We know, the Vice President."

Secret Service agents were everywhere, in the lobby, on the stairway, on the floor of Lyndon's suite, taking up an entire suite next to his, and other places unknown to me.

Obviously, Lyndon had notified them of my arrival because as I escorted Dale and the boys to their suite, which was a few doors away from

Lyndon's, they acted as stoic and oblivious to our appearance as the stone-faced guards of Buckingham Palace.

Lyndon's door opened and he walked swiftly to meet me half way, literally picking me up off the floor in an affectionate bear hug. Suddenly startled, his eyes caught something behind me. I quickly turned around and saw Dale and the boys removing their over night bags from the hallway and taking them inside their suite. As Steven started to say, "Hello, Mr. Vice President," Dale gently, but firmly, pushed him back into the room and smiled politely at Lyndon before closing the door.

"Goddamn it," he muttered.

"What's wrong?" I asked as we walked hand in hand back to his suite.

"I never wanted her to know who you were really meeting," he answered, shaking his head. "The less people know, the better off we are. I'll have Ragsdale replace her on Monday."

"No, Lyndon, Dale is like a mother to those boys," I pleaded. "Steven is ten and she's been with us ever since he was just a few weeks old. No, Lyndon, you can't just dismiss her like hired help. She's more than that-she's family."

"I'll think about it, Madeleine," he said unemotionally, as he opened the door to his suite. "But right now we've got to fuck in a hurry because Jack Benny's coming on TV!" Jack Benny was his favorite entertainer and nothing stopped him from seeing his show.

After another one of our passionate lovemaking interludes, Lyndon and I lay naked in the king-sized bed, arms and legs wrapped around each other. I fondled my Sandow, as much in love with him as ever. As we talked, it was painfully clear to me that Lyndon was disgruntled, if not disgusted, with being Vice President. It was an office he had never wanted. From his college days on, his loyal followers, such as Jesse Kellam, had seen his potential and, in the wake of his enormous ego and personal charisma, had predicted the presidency as a climax to his career.

"I want to be President," he would say over and over. "There's an old story," he began, the satin mask pulled up over his forehead, "about the mother who had two sons. One went to sea and the other became Vice President and neither was heard from again."

"Oh, come on now," I said, running my fingers through his hair, "it's not all that bad."

"Bullshit! I hear the goddamn jokes and stories. It's always been a favorite indoor sport in Washington to make fun of vice presidents and the constant insults from that goddamn Bobby Kennedy. He needs a noose around his neck-and someone is going to do it." Privately, I felt Lyndon was showing great discipline and strength. I think it was a major effort of self-control to fit his volcanic personality into the restraining role of vice president.

"The first thing when a man is elected vice president," he continued, "those sons-of-bitches in the press start asking, 'Well, what's happened to Lyndon, the Vice President? Where is Lyndon Johnson?' Fuck 'em!"

"I really wish you wouldn't be so bashful, Lyndon," I teased him. "You need to learn to let your true feelings out and quit bottling them up."

"You're a smart-ass, Madeleine Brown," he laughed. "I ought to tum you over and spank your bare bottom!"

"Oh, no, you don't," I replied, pulling up the sheet to my neck. "The hell I will; you love anything I dish out, now, don't you?" "Sandow, don't be so ugly, I love you."

"I love being around you, my redheaded lady," he said in a voice yearningly serious. "You make me laugh and forget all my goddamn problems. I can't get down here to Texas as much as I want to, so why don't you quit your advertising job and you and the boys move to Washington. I'll get you an impressive job in the press office or something and we can all see each other more often."

"I'm sorry, Lyndon," I apologized. "But since George died, my mother's heart has been giving her problems. She's bedfast so much of the time that I have to look after her and manage her business affairs. There's just no possible way I can pack up and move to Washington right now."

The familiar Lyndon Johnson temper began to erupt. His face twisted up in anger and went blood red. No one ever said "no" to Lyndon: "Goddamn it! I don't know why everyone always has to come before me. I offer you the chance of a lifetime and all you do is piss in my face!"

"But, Lyndon," I said, swallowing hard, "you, of all people, should understand family responsibilities."

"Don't fucking lecture me about family, Dumb Dora!" he screamed, waving his finger in my face like a madman. "I've got enough problems without putting up with an uncooperative woman!" Only those close to Lyndon knew how he could rant and rave one second while butter melted in his mouth the next.

As my eyes filled with tears, I quickly dressed and headed for the door, "I love you, Lyndon."

Still in bed, he rolled over on his side, turning his back toward me like a spoiled little boy.

With tears streaking down my face as I opened the door, I said, "I'll see you later."

Disdaining even to turn over, he muttered, "Tell Dale goodbye."

Sure enough, a few days later, Dale called me at my office and asked for the remainder of the afternoon off to take care of some personal business. I told her to take the boys to Mother's house (we lived just a few blocks away) so that Mildred could care for them until she returned.

But Dale never returned. Our maid for ten years, as well as being Jimmy's and Steven's surrogate mother, had disappeared with out a trace. The boys cried for days. I notified the police, telephoned her family and friends-all to no avail. To this day, I have not seen or heard from Dale Turner. Never.

I did continue to see and hear from Lyndon whenever he was in Texas. His anger toward me disappeared as quickly as it had erupted. We met several times in San Antonio and Houston, but most often at the Driskill in Austin.

Meanwhile, Steven was growing up with a gnawing uneasiness about his paternity. My ex in-laws, the Browns, always treated him less favorably than his brother, Jimmy. And if there was a father son event at school, Mr. Ragsdale, at Lyndon's urging, would some times stand in, but it was always business with Mr. Ragsdale and Steven sensed the coldness and calculation. He felt closer to me, thinking of me as his "best pal."

Steven often asked, "Is Mr. Ragsdale my father?"

"No, Steven. Some day I'll tell you about your father. Right now is not the time, but I know he loves and cares for you. It is impossible to explain now."

Once in a while, Steven and I would attend a political function together where Lyndon would be present. Steven always sensed there was a hidden something between Lyndon and me, saying, "Mother, he really likes us. He pats me on the head all the time."

On one occasion, Lyndon came up to him, placed his hand on his head and said, "Son, some day you're going to be in the White House!" I naively took that statement as a promise that one day Lyndon would acknowledge Steven as his son and help him have a political career of his own.

I genuinely believe that Lyndon would have tried to see Steven if my son hadn't begun to look so much like his father as he grew older. I never told Steven that Lyndon was his real father, then because I was afraid he'd make a slip of the tongue and ruin our secret arrangement, or perhaps create something much more serious.

Lyndon Johnson was not a man to leave tracks. We always met in hotel rooms. The flowers, gifts and money he sent were always from Jesse Kellam or KTBC. My credit cards were in the joint names of Madeleine Duncan Brown and Jerome T. Ragsdale, and my bills for living expenses were paid by his office. But Lyndon had become increasingly concerned about being found out. I received calls from Jesse praising me for being a "good girl," which I knew were reminders to keep my mouth shut. Although I never really knew what had happened to Dale, I had nevertheless begun to feel frightened at the sheer, unadulterated power and impulsiveness of my lover.

24

Paper Marriage

One weekend at the Driskill in 1961, Lyndon somberly met me at the door and after a passionate embrace we sat together on the sofa. "Madeleine, I've got a fucking big problem," he said slowly, taking my hand in his, "and you're the only one that can solve it." "What's the problem, Lyndon?" I asked.

"It's not 'what,' it's 'who.'"

"Then who is the problem?" I asked impatiently.

"It's that queer bastard, Hoover. Kennedy thinks of Hoover as a relic who has survived beyond his time, and he has," Lyndon continued. "He plans on making Hoover leave the FBI when he reaches the mandatory retirement age on New Year's Day, 1965. I just can't have this happen. I rely on Hoover a lot. He is my contact with the oil guys. 01' Clint owns Hoover-you know."

"So what's the problem?"

"Hoover knows I'm fucking around and it is causing heat in Washington and especially with Bird. He knows about you and Steven and he's calling in his marker," Lyndon said, lowering his head. "If I don't get Kennedy to waive his mandatory retirement, Hoover's threatening to go public about our relationship. I'd rather have Hoover inside the tent pissing out than outside pissing in."

I knew that Hoover's blackmail threat was intimidating Lyndon, an unlikely and uncomfortable position for the master intimidator himself.

"So I need your help, Madeleine." "What can I do, Lyndon?"

"I've talked it over with Jesse and Ragsdale and we think you should get married so it would take some of the heat off me. People, especially my Bird,don't suspect married women."

I started laughing."Married? Are you kidding me? W ho would I marry? I haven't been seeing anyone but you." (Lyndon's long-time aide and former Presidential Press Secretary George Reedy,wrote in his revealing memoir in 1983,Lyndon B. Johnson, that one of Lyndon's "favorites ... who held his attention longer than the rest and for whom he exhibited some really deep feelings was married off,prob ably because a continued relationship was incompatible with the Vice Presidency.")

"Jesse says you've been shooting skeet and playing golf with a friend of mine by the name of West. He would be a likely candidate."

"You people know everything that I do," I protested,not able to conceal my surprise."Besides,he's just a friend. We're not lovers or anything."

"I know that,Madeleine," he said matter-of-factly."It would strictly be a marriage for appearances' sake. He'll live in his house and you'll live in your house. There'll be no hanky-panky and we can continue to discreetly see each other."

"You make it sound like the man has already agreed to this arrangement,Lyndon!"

He nodded."He has. The only thing left undone is for you two to go down to the justice of the peace so I can get my balls out of Hoover's vise grip ...and soothe Bird's jangled nerves. At least it will please Edgar."

"How much did you pay Charles?" I asked courageously. "Every man has his price," he smiled."But when this bullshit is over,I'm going to make Hoover kiss my ass in Macy's window on the hottest day of the year and swear it smells like roses."

In a few weeks,Charles G. West (who later committed suicide),and I were married "on paper " in a very short,unceremonial civil service by a justice of the peace. Evidently our charade was successful in derailing Hoover's blackmail threats,as President Kennedy took immediate steps to make Lyndon the most active vice president in history.

Before Hoover reached the mandatory retirement age of seventy on January 1, 1965, President Lyndon Johnson staged a ceremony in the White House Rose Garden to announce his waiver of retirement: "J. Edgar Hoover is a hero to millions of decent citizens and an anathema to evil men. No other American, now or in our past, has served the cause of justice so faithfully and so well.

"J. Edgar Hoover has served the government since 1917. He has served nine presidents and this Sunday he celebrates his fortieth year as director of the FBI. Under his guiding hand, the FBI has be come the greatest investigative body in history.

"Edgar, the law says that you must retire next January when you reach your seventieth birthday and I know you wouldn't want to break the law. But the nation cannot afford to lose you. Therefore, by virtue of an act pursuant to the authority vested in the President, I have today signed an

Executive Order exempting you from compulsory retirement for an indefinite period of time."

I was sitting at my desk, trying to sort out my emotions over my ersatz marriage to C.G. West. My life had once more become a distortion of lies and heartaches. My wedding to Glynn would have been perfect had I received the approval of George and mother. Their strong religious convictions would not permit them to give their blessings because Glynn was not of our faith. But the wedding day itself was beautiful. Six bridesmaids and six groomsmen, flower girls throwing rose petals before me, my brother giving me away in marriage before an altar banked with white orchids and candles, Glynn and I kneeling to take our marriage vows. What could go wrong?

I was blotting tears when Jan asked if l could take Jesse's call on line two.

"Top of the morning to you. What brings you to Dallas, Jesse?" There was a long pause.

"Jesse, is there something wrong?"

He started to stutter, "You need to meet me at Love Field.

We'll have lunch."

"Tell me," I insisted. "There is something wrong with Lyndon, isn't there? It's his heart."

Jesse's only reply was, "I'll see you within the hour."

The drive to Love Field was beautiful. All the trees were in full green foliage, some spring flowers were still in bloom. We had an early spring, and the weather was pleasantly cool. While I was drinking in all of nature's beauty, my mind was in torment. My Sandow was ill! Oh please, Lord, don't let it happen!

Jesse's embrace was much stronger than usual. Kissing my hands, he began, "I'm sorry I have to tell you this. I know how hurt you will be."

The hostess sat us in a quiet comer of the restaurant so we would not be disturbed by the sound of incoming flights. Jesse kissed my hands again, clutching them, his face lowered almost to the level of the table. Looking up, he slowly said, "Edgar says there will be a wedding in a week or two. One of the secretaries is pregnant. Lyndon is the father!" Shock waves froze me.

"Jesse, please, tell me it isn't true!"

Helping me to rise from my seat, he gently nodded his head in the affirmative. "I'm sorry. I must go now. I'll be in touch."

In a total state of disbelief, my body wrenched in agony, I returned to my office. I had compassion for the girl, wondering how many tears would be shed, how many people would be affected.

President Kennedy sent Lyndon on missions to thirty-three countries during the thirty-five months he was Vice President! The primary intent was to keep him out of Washington. Most of Lyndon's chores were ceremonial, but not all. Lyndon might have reaped snickers by befriending a camel driver in Karachi, Pakistan, and entertaining him later in the United States, but he also flew to beleaguered West Berlin in August, 1961, to spread peace and hope in an unsettled world. Lyndon did want peace. When he returned from that trip, a very ill-looking Mr. Sam met him at the airport to welcome him home to America.

On Armistice Day, November 11th Mr. Sam's physician warned the press that the House Speaker's death was imminent, and at 6:20 A.M. on Thursday, November 16, 1961, Mr. Sam passed away quietly in his sleep. His death devastated his home town of Bonham, Texas. Miss Laurie wiped tears from her eyes acclaiming this was a great loss for everyone. I knew then she had experienced great feelings for Mr. Sam. (However, with Miss Laurie's strange, Victorian religious beliefs, one could only be married one time, a cardinal rule of the Bible Belt.)

After Mr. Sam's death, it was hard for Lyndon to come back to Texas. Every death was hard on him. I could see his grief. He was significantly more somber.

T hen on Christmas Day, 1961, Lyndon's sister, Josefa, an alcoholic, died of a cerebral hemorrhage at the age of forty-nine at her home in Fredericksburg, Texas, near the LBJ ranch.

25

The Vast Estes Empire

With magical ease (at least in Texas) the very name of Billie Sol Estes conjured up images of money, multiple murders and the madness of a witch hunt. How did such a basically kind, generous, religious and good man inflame the evil passions that ran amok in Texas and Washington, D.C.? Why were Billie Sol and his lovely family destroyed by powerful, devious men? The answers began unfolding along with "cloak and dagger" rumors that President Kennedy and Attorney General Robert Kennedy would dump Lyndon from the '64 ticket. Both the President and Attorney General saw an opportunity to publicly humiliate Lyndon forever when Billie Sol's financial entanglement involving the United States Agriculture Department caused the largest scandal in Texas history. Kennedy, seizing a golden opportunity, ordered an "investigation" (witch hunt) and the Justice Department sent in seventy-six FBI agents to investigate one millionaire.

Billie Sol, with only twenty-eight-thousand dollars in his pocket after moving to the dusty West Texas desert town of Pecos, had be come, in a ridiculously short time, one of the wealthiest men in the Lone Star state. With his cash on hand, Billie Sol bought cheap land. Then, by simple irrigation, he doubled its productivity, and hence its value. Pecos' farmers had tried irrigation before, but the high cost of electricity to run the pumps proved insurmountable. Yet, with singular elegance, Billie Sol located the nearest natural gas pipeline and formulated the plan to get it extended to the Pecos' area so that irrigation pumps could be driven by much less expensive natural gas.

Using his own natural management style and marketing ability, coupled with favoritism and resources from the U.S. Agriculture Department, his personal friendship and association with Lyndon and Cliff Carter, Jack Puterbaugh, and Orville Freeman, Billie Sol gained first-hand knowledge on the "inside" of government operations in the Cotton Allotment Program. Billie Sol skillfully used this information to achieve the best possible development of the West Texas desert soil. His drive, sincere manner, and imagination were his major as sets. Eventually he caused the deserts to bloom in fruitful abundance, fueling a massive shot of money into the Texas agricultural economy. The Jet Set called him the "King of the Texas Wheeler Dealers" and everyone respected him as a wizard of financial enterprise. He was a pillar of his church, the benefactor of people down on their luck-making sure the homeless had a roof over their heads, the hungry had a sack of groceries, and the children an education. Billie Sol was indeed, in character, much like my dear father George, our son Steven, and grandfather Lee, always displaying loving, tender care for all mankind, especially the needy.

Jesse told me that Lyndon had requested Billie Sol to meet with him at the Driskill along with Cliff Carter, Lyndon's hatchet man in Washington, Puterbaugh, and Freeman, in the early cold spring of 1961. As they were approaching an intersection near the Driskill, they came upon a blind beggar with outstretched hands holding a rusted tin cup. Billie Sol reached deep into his pocket and filled to overflowing the beggar's cup with sizeable bills. Jesse, in a disapproving voice said, "Hey, don't do that. He's richer than all of us together. He owns a big ranch in South Texas."

With his usual warm smile and fingers pointing to his eyes,

Billie Sol in a compassion-tinged voice exclaimed, "You're so very wrong, Jesse, he could have all the capital in the world and we all would be richer by far-we can see the sun, the moon, and the stars!"

On one occasion, before joining Lyndon in his suite, I met briefly with Jesse in his office where I negotiated a contract for our client, Southland Life Insurance Company. As I left his office, I caught a glimpse of Lyndon and Mac Wallace, heads together, in one of the KTBC executive suites. I would often see Lyndon, Cliff Carter, Mac Wallace, Jerome Ragsdale and Jesse Kellam together in the KTBC executive offices. Noting the cold look in Lyndon's eyes, sadness overcame me as I remembered the John Kinser murder on the golf course in Austin. My morbid curiosity was aroused about whose life and which political issue was at stake.

As I opened the door to Lyndon's suite, I found a note giving me instructions to "make myself comfortable" while I waited for his arrival. Lyndon seemed extremely tense when he arrived and perfunctorily said, "Shit, Madeleine, we don't have time to play with the string of pearls or any of our toys-but, when I return in a couple of weeks, we'll have one hell of a party."

Kiddingly I said, "Sandow, Jack Benny must be waiting for you."

However, our fast and furious fifteen minutes did absolute wonders for both of us. Lyndon left looking a relaxed, smiling and confident man.

Immediately after my Austin trip, Billie Sol's scandal began to mushroom. With slight-of-hand maneuvering, he had roped prosperous farmers in the Cotton Allotment Program and tank manufacturing companies into a complicated sale-and-lease-back arrangement so he could raise more capital for his snowballing enterprise. His own capital was exhausted, so he started using the farmer's credit to en able the tank companies to get mortgages from finance companies for a 10% fee.

Jesse told me he didn't understand why everyone in Washing ton was so upset. Sid Richardson, Clint Murchison, and H.L. Hunt were always wheeling and dealing along similar lines. Sid made his and Mr. Sam's protege, Robert Anderson (an aide to Eisenhower who was being groomed to be vice president), a millionaire, by a phony deal which permitted him to buy oil stock for a dollar a share and then sell it for a profit of almost a million dollars. H.L. and the others entertained us often about similar deals. No one ever got upset and certainly there wasn't a government investigation. However, when Henry Marshall, the U.S. Agriculture official, started investigating

Billie Sol, mayhem and murders started popping up overnight.

On June 3, 1961, Henry Marshall was found dead on a remote section of his farm near Franklin, Texas, shortly before his investigation became public. His death was ruled a suicide (without an autopsy-even though the family requested one), despite the fact that he had been shot in the torso five times with a single shot bolt action rifle. Clearly an improbable suicide, but a probable murder.

Meanwhile, I flew to Washington with my close friends, Earle and Dearie Cabell, to celebrate John Kennedy's glittering birthday on May 27, 1961. Plates were one thousand dollars apiece. And it turned out to be an Alice-in-Wonderland experience that I shall always re member.

After Mr. Sam's demise, Billie Sol got the word that his allotments had been canceled. He immediately contacted Clifton Carter and East Texas Senator Ralph Yarborough and then flew to Washing ton in early 1962. The outcome of that meeting was that the cancellation of Billie Sol's allotments was overturned and they were quickly reinstated.

It is still difficult to believe that almost a year later, Billie Sol was in jail in lieu of a half-a-million dollar bond; grand jury charges were prepared; suits and counter-quits were filed. Senator Yarborough and other politicians were anxiously scanning every news release: Lyndon was discreetly silent. Federal agricultural authorities began investigating whether the millions of bushels of government grain in Billie Sol's storage were intact.

Among the most important of the many-sided Billie Sol Estes enterprises was his anhydrous ammonia fertilizer business which, with rigorously competitive procedures, he was building into a virtual West Texas monopoly.

Robert E. Manuel, counsel for the minority Republicans on the House Subcommittee conducting the investigations, grew impatient with the closed hearings and cover-up procedures and "leaked" a 175-page Agriculture Department report on Billie Sol's cotton allotments. It incorporated the work of the late Henry Marshall, who was, the papers casually reported, shot to death while investigating Billie Sol's acquisition of extensive cotton allotments.

Manuel revealed that when Billie Sol was in Washington in January, he had pressured Carl J. Miller, an Agriculture Department employee, by invoking the names and influence of Lyndon and Clifton Carter. For such improper and embarrassing conduct, the Democratic dominated House committee at once fired Counsel Manuel.

But when Manuel "leaked" the sculpted Agriculture report with the results of Marshall's investigation, he fanned the fires of suspicion smoldering in Texas. Already many were asking: "Did Marshall really commit suicide?"

On the night of April 4, 1962, at the western end of Texas, a rancher came upon the body of George Krutilek in the sand hills near the town of Clint, slumped in his car with a hose from his exhaust stuck in the window. He had been dead for several days, and the El Paso County pathologist, Dr. Frederick Bornstein, held that he certainly did not die from carbon monoxide poisoning.

Krutilek was a forty-nine-year-old certified public accountant who had undergone grilling by FBI agents on April 2, the day after Billie Sol's arrest. T he investigation concerned the Billie Sol affair. Krutilek had worked for Estes and had been the recipient of his favors.

On May 18, 1962, at Bryan, Texas, District Judge John Barron ordered a grand jury probe into "the mystery death" of Henry Marshall, "to clear the clouds connecting this with the Billie Sol Estes case..." and indicated that Secretary of Agriculture Orville Freeman, former governor of Minnesota, would be called to testify, particularly in view of his public statement on May 7 that "much of Billie Sol's case was cloudy because many of the facts died with Marshall."

Marshall's body was exhumed, and for days pathologists, doc tors and scientists tested, sifted and analyzed the findings. They discovered enough carbon monoxide in Marshall's lungs to have incapacitated him, which was strange, since his body was not found in his pick-up truck. A blow on his head was likewise serious enough to have incapacitated him. The single shot bolt-action .22 caliber rifle, which he would have had to hold at arm's length, with the bolt operated by hand after each shot, was found at the scene. Five shots had entered the body from the front. One severed his aorta near the heart, another penetrated his liver and another had gone through his lung, any one of which could have been fatal.

For anyone who knows guns, the conclusion of murder was inescapable. But after almost two weeks, the Texas grand jury, impaneled with twelve "good men and true," ..."were unable to agree" on whether or not Marshall's death was a murder or a suicide. Billie Sol told me years later that he believed that someone was deliberately placed on the jury to "hang it," to prevent a forthright honest verdict. Whatever the reason, the verdict stunned the entire state of Texas as the Mac Wallace murder case in Austin had ten years earlier.

(In March of 1984, Clint Peoples, U.S. Marshal, encouraged Billie Sol to come forward after twenty-three years of wondering about Marshall's death. Billie Sol testified with immunity from prosecution before a grand jury that he had attended at least three meetings with Lyndon-. two in Washington and one at the Driskill Hotel-during which they discussed the need to "stop Marshall from disclosing Estes' fraudulent business dealings and his ties with Johnson." Billie Sol wanted to clear his conscience about Marshall's death, and named Malcolm "Mac" Wallace as the triggerman.)

Billie Sol's now desperate circumstances forced him to file for bankruptcy, causing a host of creditors and mortgagors to descend on the Federal Court in El Paso to file their claims. No one in power would help him. Bankruptcy proceedings were filed against Estes on April6 and he was adjudged bankrupt, July 13, 1962, after which J.C. Williamson moved at once to recover his properties. But trustee Harry Moore had already taken over in order to receive the monthly payments on government grain. He refused to surrender possession. Through Judge Tomason's court, Williamson pleaded in vain for relief, in keeping with his contract.

Significantly, this approach to Williamson seemed to have been one of the first steps by Morris Jaffe, Vice President Johnson's warm friend, to move in on the Estes empire. A year later, in June 1963, with J.C. Williamson practically converted to the conservative cause, his splendid installation at Plainview was taken over by Jaffe's American Grain Corporation at "what was against it"-a drastically reduced note for just over $418,000 at the Midland National Bank, Midland, Texas.

Meanwhile, Morris Jaffe took over-the newspaper generously said "bought"-the still vast and valuable Billie Sol Estes as sets. "The news" that Jaffe, a "San Antonio businessman," had offered $7 million for them broke in the summer of 1962, and it soon developed that the fine hand of Walter Heller-through his lawyers, Henry Strasburger of Dallas, and Greenberg and Schimberg of Chicago-was playing an important, if not dominant, role, as well it might, with seven million at stake and Commercial Solvents in the favorable position of holding a lien on the principal assets. Thus, Commercial Solvents was a key party in the business. This turned out to be prudent and progressive. With the support of these two big outfits (Walter Heller and Commercial Solvents) and with hidden political influence to spare, Jaffe took possession of Billie Sol's assets, thousands of acres of the best Pecos irrigated land, ranch holdings, and the multi million dollar grain complex.

The conclusion is inescapable that the Johnson-controlled political machine in Texas designedly set the stage for Jaffe's take-over, as the cleanup was without financial risk.

The selection of the Austin firm of Cofer and Cofer to represent Billie Sol's defense was at the insistence of Lyndon. The subsequent mishandling of the defense by John Cofer, Billie Sol believes, was more the result of Cofer's efforts to protect Lyndon.

Cofer was a long-term confidant and representative of Lyndon. Their relationship went all the way back to Lyndon's first election to the U.S. Senate in 1948.1t was Cofer who represented Lyndon on the notorious "Box 13" voter fraud case and Malcolm "Mac" Wallace at his celebrated murder trial in 1952.

Some three weeks before his first trial, Billie Sol, impetuous, emotional and still the born promoter, told me that he had conceived the idea that he could absolve himself by going on the stand and telling the whole truth about everything and everybody. But Cofer vehemently disagreed. Billie Sol then decided to fire Cofer and hire an other attorney, the liberal lawyer Warren Burnett of Odessa, for a fee of $30,000. However, Cofer refused to be fired. He had already been paid $85,000 by "someone else" and he was adamant against spreading the web of truth through confession.

Billie Sol was confused about the tactics that Cofer used during both the El Paso and Tyler trials. No witnesses took the stand. He was reminded that this was Cofer's trial strategy and this was how he obtained Mac Wallace's suspended sentence. However, Billie Sol felt that this was done to make sure there was no opportunity of implicating Lyndon during any testimony or cross-examination. I do not believe that Lyndon wanted Billie Sol convicted, but it was Lyndon's only way out.

Again, in a case connected with Billie Sol, carbon monoxide was held to be the legally blameless killer of Harold Eugene Orr, the late president of the Superior Manufacturing Company of Amarillo. Orr and the company had played a key role in Billie Sol's finance frauds, and Orr was arrested with Billie Sol and given a ten-year federal prison sentence, some two months after Lyndon became President.

February 28, 1964, just before he was to begin serving his term, Harold Orr went out to his garage, ostensibly to change the exhaust pipe on this car. There a few hours later, with tools scattered about-again by report, tools unsuited for this purpose-Orr was found dead. Another murder occurred involving Howard Pratt, a Chicago office manager of Commercial Solvents, Billie Sol's fertilizer supplier, who was found in his car, also dead of carbon monoxide.

In a federal court on August 10, 1964, I was saddened as Billie Sol was convicted of conspiracy and mail fraud charges for mortgaging nonexistent fertilizer tanks. His beautiful family was devastated. Patsy, his wife, collapsed as the verdict was rendered. There was disbelief in the courtroom. He would eventually be incarcerated for over half a decade.

Billie Sol remained loyal to Lyndon even though Attorney General Robert Kennedy visited him in prison to persuade Billie Sol to testify against the man who followed his brother to the White House. RFK was determined to put Lyndon behind bars. He also questioned Billie Sol about J. Edgar Hoover's association with Clint Murchison. Jesse informed me that Lyndon believed his image had been damaged through guilt by association. T he Kennedys were exploiting all publicity surrounding Billie Sol's indictments to try to hang Lyndon. Perhaps they would have succeeded, but the assassination of President Kennedy "hushed" most of the political arena.

Now still alive and hearty, Billie Sol is home with his loving family in West Texas, slowly healing from the scars that prison has seared into his soul. Sometimes, country and western star Willie Nelson drops by to lift his spirits.

I am sure Billie Sol still holds political secrets and historical facts that could expose the murky inner workings of our government by the high rollers in public office. The IRS, which claimed Billie Sol owed over fifty-two million dollars in back taxes, finally dropped its charges. One day, perhaps, he will end the chain of silence and speak out fully, when the fear of reprisal no longer exists.

Former U.S. Marshal Clint Peoples of Waco, Texas, who figured so prominently in the Billie Sol Estes case, was killed in an auto mobile accident on June 23, 1992. Despite his advanced age, some of Peoples' close friends suspect foul play. Like Billie Sol, Peoples' knowledge of Texas irregularities in politics was also deep and rich.

26

Lyndon's Big Texas Morning

It was half-past 2:00P.M. when Larry Buchanan, creative director of our agency, buzzed me on the intercom, "Come on and go with me to Ruby's – we need to have a brain session for Southland Life Insurance (one of the agency's political accounts). Joe Josephson just called and said they are releasing some big bucks for their new ad campaign, 'Hearts of Gold.' Who knows? We may pick up some underground news. Jack can inform us who has paid their dues so we'll know where we can safely gamble."

It was common knowledge that Jack Ruby knew every "goin' ons" in "Big D." Even more so. Jack was a gracious host and a barrel of fun to be around. Although the club was closed to the public until 7:30p.m., he would greet us with his warm smile. "Come on in, you classy guys!"

In front of the well known newspaper and magazine store, known as "Commerce Street," we ran into Dallas Police Captain Charles Batchelor, Mayor Earle Cabell, and H.L. Hunt, the big daddy of Dallas and the rich 8F group. After exchanging greetings, H.L. extended an invitation to the upcoming John Birch Society meeting he was about to host at his lovely Mt. Vernon home, the "White House of Texas," overlooking scenic White Rock Lake. "You'll miss out on some important messages if you don't come!" We assured him we would be there and continued on a block and a half to Jack Ruby's Carousel Club.

Larry chuckled and said, "You know what those messages will be about?"

"Yeah," I replied. "President Kennedy and the miserable mis takes H.L. thinks he has made ... and of course, the oil depletion crisis. That's all you hear when you're around H.L. and Clint."

Larry continued talking about the 1963 World Petroleum Congress meeting and Austin lawyer, Charles Herring, Lyndon's long time friend and business associate. (Herring, in earlier years, had represented Jack Halfen, a Houston mafia man and also a friend of Lyndon's, over IRS difficulties. Carlos Marcello, the kingfish of the New Or leans mafia, was an ally of Halfen's and coordinated the organized crime syndicate in Texas.

Sure enough, Jack Ruby met us with, "You classy guys, come on in-it's colder than a well digger's ass in Alaska."

My teeth were still chattering when Jack handed me an ol' Southern peach brandy hot toddy, the kind that if it doesn't make you warm up-will make you feel good.

Andrew, the porter, was busy cleaning up the club, making it ready for the Wally Weston and Chari Angel (Bobby Lou) Show, that was sweeping Dallas. It was always a contest between Jack and Abe Weinstein, the owner of next door's Colony Club, as to who could provide the best entertainment. Abe had recently employed a beautiful young girl named Beverly Oliver, and she was generating lots of applause.

It was during this time that we saw a man later identified as Lee Harvey Oswald in deep conversation with Jack Ruby. All the so called "insiders" knew about Ruby's involvement with Dallas' organized crime, which had been in operation since the early 40s. Jack's main activity was a gun-running operation to Cuba.

Often we told Jack that he was going to get "wasted" for doing such things, particularly playing with bad boys. His reply would be, "You goin' to catch me?" We knew enough not to carry the conversation any further. Actually, since Dallas operated so wide open, Ruby's activities probably would have been overlooked, had he not become a key figure in history.

We had been at the club an hour or so when Jack came over to our table waving a map of President Kennedy's motorcade route for his planned parade through Dallas. In fact Ruby had specific knowledge of the President's entire Texas trip. It was a tight schedule, covering San Antonio, Houston, Fort Worth, Dallas, and Austin.

"You know what this is?" Jack was waving the map in our faces.

I was a little shocked and stunned that Jack would have this type of secret information, but again we always called him P.C. (Privileged Character). Lightly brushing the incident off-we smiled and said-"No question about it Jack, you do hob-nob with the people in the 'Know.'"

Jack began angrily, "By damn, some of our Democrats here are telling Kennedy, 'Don't come to Dallas.' 01' Barefoot Sanders has told him to scrub the Dallas visit-the climate ain't good here. Even that Mexican guy in San Antonio-! forget his name-said, 'Don't come to Texas.'"

We refreshed Jack's memory and told him it was Henry Gonzales. Henry spent the next thirty years or more in Congress, becoming head of the Banking Committee, and briefly the Chairman of the House Select Committee on Assassinations, in 1977, which investigated the assassinations of Martin Luther King and President John F. Kennedy.

Jack continued, "Hell I'm not one of them smart 'Big Guys,' but I do know two and two makes four. Some of these 'Biggies' will have Kennedy's head blown off. 'Cheeze,' these jocks will shoot you, then ask questions later. Can't Kennedy figure that out?"

Larry and I didn't say a word.

Later that night, while I was dining with my two handsome sons, Jimmy and Steven, at the beautiful private club, "Top of the Cliff," I told them about Jack Ruby having this information. We often discussed my daily work because they were well acquainted with all my business contacts.

Steven, approaching his 13th birthday, exclaimed loudly, "Have you been watching the news on Channel4-Dallas is a 'Hot Bed' now-maybe the President doesn't need to come to Dallas."

I was pleased at Steven's interest in current events. However, since we were hunting buddies with the anchorman, Warren Fulks and Dick Wheeler, both Weimaraner fanciers, I believed Steven's interest was primarily based upon his friendship with Warren and Dick.

Still, I felt unnerved by strange incidents plaguing Dallas as well as the intensity of what I called an atmosphere of "hate" boiling in the city.

Many years prior to Dallas Police Chief Jesse Curry's taking office, Dallas had captured the dubious title of being the "murder" capital of the world.

Curry was 46 years old when he was sworn into office. I often wondered if it was a surprise to him that our city was controlled by a powerful oligarchy-Clint Murchison, H.L. Hunt, banker R.L. Thornton, Mayor Earle Cabell, and perhaps a hundred other influential people off limits to the Dallas Police. I had always known Dallas operated with organized crime, including Jack Ruby's people.

It was public knowledge Dallas' very beginnings in 1841 was land stolen from the Indians. John Neely Bryan, a native of Tennessee, had cleared timber along the sluggish Trinity River, and constructed the first log cabin in what was to become Dallas.

I often entertained Jimmy and Steven with the stories about how our government betrayed the Indians. President Sam Houston of the Texas Independent Republic of 1836 signed a treaty giving them title to their own land. Our first congress, however, soundly rejected the treaty, leaving them homeless in their own country. They became hostile, and joined with the tribes of North Texas. Fierce bloody battles took place. Men, women, and children died attempting to protect their rightful ownership of Dallas County land. By the tum of the century, there were still a few Indian problems.

However, massive numbers of settlers overlooked these dangerous obstacles and hardships. They continued to arrive daily in ox and horse drawn wagons. Joining John Neely Bryan, they constructed a general store, saloon, dance hall, church, and log cabin homes. Neely named the small community Dallas. Many believed it was in honor of George M. Dallas, at that time Vice President of the United States.

The Civil War left many Southerners bitter and overcome with hate. KKK (Ku Klux Klan) membership began to mushroom. They would dress in full regalia, and charge down the muddy Dallas streets while committing dastardly crimes against Blacks, Catholics, and Jews. Outnumbered law officers either joined the group or turned their head while the crimes took place.

The great Dallas fire of July 1860 brought more bloodshed. Eighty percent of the town was destroyed by fire, including the new courthouse. In panic, a gathering of white racist men attributed the fire to northern abolitionists and slaves. One of the first settlers, Wm. Brown Miller, a rich man from Missouri, who had settled in the Oak Cliff area, had to forfeit one of his best slaves. They hung the slave, along with two others, in downtown Dallas. Other slaves were ordered beaten and whipped. Grandfather Lee's tales about those turbulent times always amazed me. When I passed them on to Steven, he was equally fascinated, and as repelled as I had been about the treatment of blacks.

Granddaddy Lee often declared that I was a historical child because I was born on July 5, 1925, the same month the Houston and Texas railroad brought rails to Dallas (in July 1872). "You know," he would say proudly, "It only took that wood-burning locomotive fifteen hours to make the 250-mile trip!" Central Expressway was the southern exit and Preston Road was the North exit. The new safer mode of transportation replaced stagecoach lines. Thus, the population began to snowball, making Dallas as fast-growing as a mining boom town.

Crimes continued to increase rapidly. Belle Starr, the bandit queen, lost her life violently in Indian Territory. Other notorious criminals took their places in Dallas history-Cole and John Younger, Sam Barr, Frank and Jesse James, Frank Dalton, Doc (John) B. Holliday, Bonnie and Clyde. The list goes on and on. Another racketeer with the unlikely name of Lois

Green was gunned down at the age of thirty, because he was a threat to new racketeers moving into Dallas.

Big time syndicate gambler Benny Binion, owner of the University Club located across the street from Jack Ruby's Carousel Club, as well as the Golden Horseshoe in Las Vegas, lived in Oak Cliff. The silver-haired Herbert Nobles, known as "the Cat," survived 15 bloody attempts on his life. Eventually both he and his wife lost their lives violently.

Dallas continued to make headlines in the mid 1950s. The beautiful stripper and mistress of mafia boss Mickey Cohen, Candy Barr, lived a lifestyle considered blasphemous by Baptist Bible Belt citizens. Candy appeared in black-and-white pornographic movies. She even shot one of her husbands. Once, she was wrongfully "set up" by one of many questionable Dallas Policemen on a narcotics charge, and sentenced to a 15 year prison term. Her trial was a dis grace to our judicial system! Judge Joe B. Brown, known to have roving eyes for pretty ladies, took photographs of lovely Candy from the bench. He always ran an entertaining carnival in court, and spectators jammed his courtroom. More than a decade later, he read comic books as he presided over Jack Ruby's trial for killing Lee Harvey Oswald. Ironically, his son, Oak Cliffite Joe B. Brown, Jr. (now a district judge), ordered the autopsy of Dallas Police Office J.D. Tippit, who was killed the same day as President Kennedy.

And there was always the ever present racism-"leftovers" from the Civil War days. The KKK was very strong. Dr. Martin Luther King was not even permitted to speak at Southern Methodist University.

A small wealthy group of Dallas leaders made all the decisions, and elections were reduced to rubber stamps. All the nasty components were "ready made" to assassinate President Kennedy, or anyone else who got in their way. The conspiracy and cover-up was easy, because of the longtime powerful fraternity of the Texas 8F group, and their pocketbooks.

Lyndon had been Texas' "favorite son" because of his total loyalty to the Democratic Party. He was a compromiser and a maneuverer.He would say, "Madeleine, while people stand around picking their nose and scratching their ass, I get something done .. . and that is the way our system works."

During lunch hours, we saw our manipulative Great White Fathers heading for Louie's Oyster Bar on Ervay Street or Billy Hodges' Gun Shop, where discussions effecting our beautiful city were made.

For many years, dating to the days of President Roosevelt, Texas had gained a powerful foundation in our federal government operations, because of its rich black gold.

Before 1960, Clint Murchison and H.L. Hunt were convinced the leading Democratic contender for the presidency was none other than Lyndon Johnson. Somehow, the oil giants overlooked the mighty Joseph Kennedy's Irish mafia clan.

The 8F group had been gratified with Lyndon's performance in the Senate, particularly his stand on importation of foreign oil and the oil import bill that President Eisenhower had signed. Clint and Sid told Lyndon if he could get the support of Knowland of California, Nixon and J. Edgar Hoover, he could control the United States.

On one occasion. Lyndon was talking about his faithful friend, Clint, telling me he had received a letter from Clint and, to substantiate how much power Texas oil people wield:

> January 20, 1958
>
> The Honorable Lyndon B. Johnson The United States Senate Washington, D.C.
>
> Dear Lyndon:
> I have been doing quite a bit of thinking about the Near Eastern oil intrusion into the United States which is vitally affecting our markets for producers, refineries, and distributors all over the United States.
>
> It occurred to me two years ago to try to control this enormous influx of oil to the extent that it would prove beneficial to all parties concerned. I consulted with Secretary Humphrey about it at length, and his only question was where he would get the money.
>
> My thinking is that you could shut in the East Texas field and the Conroe field and provide storage facilities in those two fields to the extent of approximately three to five billion barrels of oil. In shutting in these fields it would also take away approximately 20,000 barrels per day in the East Texas field, which actually would create a local shortage for oil. (These figures are based on twelve producing days per month and would vary according to the number of pro-rated days set out by the Railroad Commission.
>
> It is needless to tell you that in case of an all-out war the first thing which would happen to the United States would be an oil shortage. By putting 500,000 barrels per day in these storage areas, if the war could be held off long enough, it would suffice to build up our production in the most economical manner.

> I am sure a deal could be worked out with the major companies whereby they could take scrip for both their oil and their transportation at a lower price than is now being received in the open market. It goes with out saying that if you give some income tax features to this idea all the major companies will get behind it very solidly, in my opinion.
>
> If this merits any consideration in your thinking, I believe we could get the full collaboration of Bob Anderson in a project of this kind.
>
> My sincerest personal regards to Lady Bird.
>
> Clint

During the Bay of Pigs, Kennedy incurred the wrath and hostility of both the Pentagon and the CIA, which emerged from the fiasco appearing incompetent, deceitful, and untrustworthy. President John Kennedy initiated a thorough house cleaning of the Agency, demanding the resignation of its Director (Allen Dulles, later a member of the Warren Commission) and Deputy Director General Charles Cabell, whose brother was mayor of Dallas at the time of the assassination. Kennedy had gone on record "to splinter the CIA into 1,000 pieces and scatter it to the winds." He was determined to curb the Agency's power and independence, and discussed plans to place it under the authority of Attorney General Robert F. Kennedy.

Political advisers knew President Kennedy and his administration were in big trouble in Texas in particular and the South in general. Kennedy had angered some of the giant independent oilmen. Many Texas Democrats were disgruntled over the continued rumors suggesting that Lyndon might be dropped from the 1964 ticket be cause of the Billie Sol and Bobby Baker scandals.

President Kennedy had begun, in 1962, making what the oil industry, especially major companies, must have viewed as ominous signs of reform. On July 12, 1962, a Treasury Department official acknowledged that "It is no secret that we are collecting financial data on percentage depletion in the oil and gas industry, and that we are considering this issue in connection with tax reform." This meant the 27.5 percent oil depletion allowance, the industry's most treasured piece of government favoritism, might be reduced or abolished altogether. By May of 1963, Attorney General Robert Kennedy was talking openly of "an apparent tendency toward concentration in this industry" and the need for an anti-trust probe. A cabinet-level Petroleum Study Committee suggested radical changes, which many industry observers believed would certainly be put into operation by January 1, 1964, when a new import quota period was scheduled to begin.

Meanwhile, in Texas, minor politicians representing the smaller oil operators, who were in dire straits, prepared a last-ditch effort to get fast action out of Kennedy. Lyndon's long time friend and aide,

Austin lawyer and State Senator Charles Herring, who, years earlier, had represented mobster Jack Halfen, was one of three Texas senators who had attended the 1963 World Petroleum Congress. Upon his return, he authored a furious report setting forth the Texas independent oil man's troubles in competing with import programs dominated by the international giants. It was a thirty-six-page report telling how the program came into existence, who was profiting, and who was being put out of business. Herring and other representatives of the independents obtained a firm commitment that, when Kennedy reached Austin on November 22, the report would be put in his hands along with a confidential letter from Herring. This letter addressed the import programs' "potential for scandal ...perhaps dwarfing the Teapot Dome scandal of yesteryear." The report and the letter were never seen by Kennedy.

It is unlikely that Kennedy, who was not a talented manipulator of Congress, could have taken away the oil depletion allowance. But this form of favoritism was not at all popular with many Congressmen, and it is not unthinkable that he might have trimmed the allowance, perhaps to 25 percent. Once reduced, the allowance would never again be secure, as it has been for over a generation. One must consider what even a 2.5 percent reduction in the present allowance would have meant to the Treasury.

Suppose further that Kennedy might have been able to wangle some adjustments, even a minor one, in the depletion allowances under which favored oil companies based in this country operate abroad allowances which now permit some of these billion-dollar companies to escape any U.S. taxation whatsoever. Suppose also – the most likely possibility of all-that he had decided to adopt the quota-auction system, with the proceeds going to the U.S. Treasury. This proposal was actually under consideration at the time of Kennedy's death. Put all of the possibilities together and it adds up to several billions of dollars that the government is now missing.

H.L. Hunt's criticisms of Kennedy were constant throughout the President's term of office. Hunt was very vocal and almost paranoid. "John Kennedy is a political phenomenon-a product of his old man, Joe ...but he won't take any advice. Mr. Sam could handle him some, but Rayburn is no longer around. Joe Kennedy is no longer a political factor. This is America and we need to stop him before it's too late. He's wearing the shoes, taking over the nation's biggest job without any experience in business or in public administration.

"Just look at the mistakes he's made. None of us appreciate the treatment he's dishing out to Lyndon or Edgar."

H.L. could run through multiple issues all in virtually one breath-"Laos, Vietnam, the Bay of Pigs, look what he did to Charles Cabell and Allen Dulles, civil rights, the Berlin Wall, Cuban missiles, home front, wheat deal, Alliance for Progress, NATO, the coming missile gap, Indonesia ...and 'lord,' the oil depletion-he's wanting to cut our pocketbooks by a fourth!

"How long are we going to let this go on? Are we goin' to have to shoot those mafia bastards to get them out of office?"

Some of us would offer him bad advice-"Smoke his cigars calm down-better still, go on down to the Lamar and get into a good game."

Sadly, H.L. would say, "Well, ol' Sid's gone; Clint has given up gambling since he married that pretty lady, Ginny; Hofheinz is still chasing girls; Jesse Jones is in retirement, and Edgar doesn't get down here much."

Grinning H.L. said, "Who do you want me to play with myself?"

If any relief was felt within the oil industry at Kennedy's assassination, it was not felt in vain. Five days after the assassination, Senator Herring wrote Walter Jenkins at the White House, "Powerful forces doubtless are seeking to utilize the present period of transition to delay further the overdue shake-up in the oil import control system."

However, the oil giants knew they had Lyndon in their pockets after Kennedy's death. They were confident there would be no further problems-and they were right.

W hen Lyndon lost the presidential nomination, but secured the vice presidential spot, H.L. proclaimed like a prophet."We may have lost a battle, but we will win the war."

H.L. often praised Lyndon-"After all, he ruled the Senate for years. He is a product of the great Speaker of the House, Sam Rayburn. He cut his teeth under his father, Sam, who served in the Texas legislature. Lyndon may not be a Harvard graduate, but he knows his way around.

"Lyndon knows how to communicate with people. He is our backer when it comes to problems facing oil folks. In any kind of business deal, and I don't give a damn what it is, he knows how to work it out, and with speed, particularly if you grease his palm. Lyndon is our man every hour of every day. Ike and Nixon found that out. J. Edgar believes him to be infallible."

I lost a great friend in H.L. Hunt when he passed away in October, 1971. He was given elaborate services at the downtown First Baptist Church, which has continued to pay great tribute to him and his devoted family.

The ugly atmosphere generated by the wealthy ultra-right wingers-the independent oilmen, all three warring Texas Democrats (Senator Ralph Yarborough, Governor "Big John " Connally, and Vice President Johnson) who possessed a colorful heritage of back-biting, backstabbing, and bickering-did not dampen President Kennedy's enthusiasm as he departed for Texas, leaving drizzling cold weather behind him in Washington. He had been adamant about coming to Texas, even though concerned Democrats had advised Kennedy openly to drop the visit.

President Kennedy's main concern in Texas was to help unite the Democratic party ...and smooth the hostility of angry oilmen.

T he difference between Yarborough and Connally was largely a matter of political philosophy. The rift between Yarborough and Lyndon had developed from previous campaign wounds and a continuing power struggle between the two for distribution of political patronage. Lyndon told me, "I hate Yarborough!T hat monkey ass is nothing but a yellow scoundrel in politics!"

T he feud reached its climax almost immediately after Kennedy and the Texas politicians arrived in San Antonio. Yarborough refused to ride with Lyndon in the motorcade as had been planned in that city. It was in San Antonio that Lyndon screamed at the crowds,

"I'll put the evil eye upon you," and Kennedy, with his polished manners, tried to calm both Lyndon, and Lady Bird.

I knew Lyndon had arrived back in Texas before the President. He attended the Pepsi-Cola Convention in Dallas where Richard Nixon was guest speaker. Jesse said that Lyndon could squeeze forty-eight hours into eight. He left Dallas to join the First Family in San Antonio, then flew on to Houston. He met with the ultra-rich 8F Group whose home was in the Lamar Hotel. Lyndon was very fond of this hotel and stayed there often. Bells often ring in my ears be cause some of our "hottest rendezvous" were at the Lamar.

When Air Force One arrived in Houston on Nov. 21st, Kennedy was greeted by the Houston Post headline, "JFK's Visit Accents Division in Party."

Yarborough refused to ride with Lyndon because the dignity of the U.S. Senate was at stake. Over radio and TV waves, Yarborough declared that he wouldn't have traveled in the same car with Lyndon, even if it cost him the election. He resented Lyndon as much as Lyndon despised him.

The following day, a story appeared in the Houston Chronicle under the headline: "YARBOROUGH CHOOSEY ABOUT HIS PARTNERS, SKIPS RIDE WITH LBJ."

Adding to Yarborough's pique was his exclusion from the invitation list for a reception honoring Kennedy at the Governor's Mansion. In addition, Yarborough was originally told that he would march into the auditorium for the Austin fund-raiser with state legislators, rather than with Kennedy, Lyndon, and "Big John" Connally, which would further drive a wedge into the Democratic party.

Even as the tables were being set in Austin's Municipal Auditorium, efforts were still in motion to create a public impression that the bickering, warring Texas Democrats had achieved harmony. Albert Thomas, who had been honored on Wednesday night for his role in bringing NASA to Houston, became the mediator, and settled the final arguments. A last-minute compromise was reached which allowed Yarborough to sit at the head table. He would even be permit ted to make brief remarks. Yarborough then agreed to share the car with Lyndon in Fort Worth and Dallas.

On Thursday night, Nov. 21, 1963, the last evening prior to Camelot's demise, I attended a social at Clint Murchison's home. It was my understanding that the event was scheduled as a tribute honoring his long time friend, J. Edgar Hoover, whom Murchison had first met decades earlier through President William Howard Taft, and Hoover's companion and assistant, Clyde Tolson.

The impressive guest list included John McCloy, Richard Nixon, George Brown, R.L. Thornton, H.L. Hunt, and a host of others from the 8F group.

The jovial party was just breaking up when Lyndon made an unscheduled visit. I was most surprised by his appearance, since Jesse had not mentioned anything about Lyndon's coming to Clint's. With Lyndon's hectic schedule, I never dreamed he could attend the big party. After all, he had arrived in Dallas on Tuesday to attend the Pepsi-Cola convention.

Tension filled the room upon his arrival. The group immediately went behind closed doors. A short time later Lyndon, anxious and red-faced, re-appeared.

I knew how secretively Lyndon operated. Therefore, I said nothing ...not even that I was happy to see him. Squeezing my hand so hard it felt crushed from the pressure, he spoke with a grating whisper-a quiet growl into my ear not a love message, but one I'll always remember: "After tomorrow those goddamn Kennedys will never embarrass me again-that's no threat-that's a promise."

I visibly trembled. He said nothing else, but was off in a flash to join a party at Pat Kirkwood's "Cellar Door," an after-hours night club in Fort Worth.

It was at that same club that night where many of President Kennedy's Secret Service detail stayed as late as 4 A.M. No wonder they were so slow to react a few hours later when the shots rang out in Dealey Plaza.

*****

I woke up early on November 22, 1963, excited about the big day crammed full of activities. I had a meeting scheduled for 11:30 A.M. with some of Dallas' influential Democrats to finalize the Austin fund raiser.

As I was packing my automobile,Lyndon surprised me again with a phone call from the lobby of the Texas Hotel. It was evident that the tone of fury in his voice from last night had not dissipated. I had barely eked out the words, "About last night…" when his rage virtually went ballistic. His snarling voice jolted me as never before " That son-of-a-bitch crazy Yarborough and that goddamn fucking Irish mafia bastard, Kennedy, will never embarrass me again!"

I managed to say,"I'm looking forward to tonight," when he blasted out even louder,"I've got about a minute to get to the parking lot to hear that bastard!", and he slammed down the phone. I was startled ...an uneasiness gripped me over Lyndon's actions and temper.

As I was preparing to leave,Jesse called to confirm my schedule.He warned,"You know,you probably won't be able to see Lyndon for more than fifteen minutes. "

Flashes of wild lovemaking danced in my head. Five minutes with Lyndon could capture my body and soul for days … an additional ten minutes sounded just heavenly.

"Jesse,for any time I have with Lyndon,I'm grateful."

Jesse added,"Lyndon is in a terrible mood,screaming about the Kennedys. All he can say is,'Those goddamn Kennedys will never embarrass me again after today.' "

"Yes,I know," I said,"But after my fifteen minutes with him, he'll love the world!" We both broke into laughter,feeling that the two of us really knew and understood the mighty LBJ ... at least thought we did.

Jesse then gave me a run-down of the scheduled Dallas visit and said the motorcade would be winding its way down Main Street around 12:30 p.m., en route to the Trade Mart's luncheon. Then, at approximately two p.m., everyone would be on their way to Austin for the grand finale, the giant fund-raiser.

"Jesse," I interrupted, "the Democrats are in a turmoil. There is a very hostile, sarcastic, 'Welcome, Mr. President,' full page ad by some ultra right-wingers in today's paper, and a circular with mug shots of Kennedy is being handed out saying, *'Kennedy-Wanted for Treason.'*

"H.L. gave me one several days ago. I told him he was going to get into big trouble and he said, 'The hell I will. I'm the richest man in the world and I'll do as I damn please!' I mentioned to you several weeks ago about Jack Ruby who was flashing a copy of the motorcade map. Jack is really 'in' with the great white fathers."

"Too bad," Jesse replied, "something should have been done about those guys a long time ago."

A chill went down my spine, for I had known from the beginning Jesse Kellam was Lyndon's hatchet man, and politics was hardball.

"See you tonight, Madeleine."

I sat for some time, remembering various incidents. Dallas had given Richard Nixon the largest margin of votes over John Kennedy of any city in the country. In elections during the next three years, eight of Dallas County's nine state legislative seats went Republican. Peter O'Donnell, John Tower, Bruce Alger, Frank Crowley, and Duke Burgess (the first self-avowed Republicans in Dallas) worked night and day to help achieve this goal.

But, while mainstream conservatives dominated the parties, extremist conservatives dominated the political image of Dallas, considered a major center for a fiery far-right movement that was sweeping the country, the John Birch Society.

I had witnessed a disturbing incident that occurred in November 1960 (see Chapter 21), four days before the Kennedy-Nixon presidential election. Lyndon and Lady Bird had encountered a throng of Nixon supporters at the Adolphus Hotel. This scene was terrible, with the crowd jeering and shouting, "Carpetbagger, go back north!" It took Lyndon and Lady

Bird over thirty minutes to cross Commerce Street from the Baker Hotel to the Adolphus.

Later, at the first National Indignation Convention in Dallas, November 1961, we heard a phone message from Eastern Airlines chairman, Eddie Rickenbacker, praising the late Senator Joseph McCarthy, and a recorded message from film star Ronald Reagan denouncing income tax as "spawned by Karl Marx a hundred years ago. " (Ronald Reagan was the talent I used for a Dallas Power and Light commercial. However, we could not run the commercial in Dallas due to Reagan's controversial statements in California.)

All of the "coffee cronies" at Vick's began kidding our good friend and soft-spoken billionaire, H.L. Hunt. He had become an over night celebrity when magazines started featuring his great wealth and ultra-conservative political viewpoint. He worked diligently in spreading his message throughout the nation, utilizing his Facts Forum and *Life Line* radio programs. Many thought H.L. passed money under the table to have his program granted tax free status. That's rather doubtful, because his political conservatism was matched by his refusal to spend money. He never wanted to pay for anything.

H.L. would raise his voice stating: "This is America and some one has to stand up and speak. I' m not afraid of anything! I'll continue to speak as long as there is breath in my body." He held true to these words until his death.

Dallas was also known as the home of retired Major General Edwin A. Walker, also a good friend of H.L.'s. Walker had become the hero of the far right when he was cashiered from the U.S. Army in 1961 following a controversy over his use of John Birch Society material in training troops. H.L. often expressed his admiration for General Walker and candy manufacturer Robert Welch, the founder of the John Birch Society.

In April, 1963, Edwin Walker and Dallas again appeared in the national news when a single shot was fired at Walker while he sat in his home going over his income taxes. The bullet narrowly missed his head. Walker resided in North Dallas' affluent Turtle Creek. Jack Ruby told me that Lee Harvey Oswald, visiting his Carousel Club, acknowledged he was the one who fired the shot.

"Ah come on, Jack," I said, "No one admits trying to kill some-one."

Grinning with his beautiful brown eyes glistening like a pair of rare diamonds. Jack said, "Wake up-this is Dallas!"

I always believed it was South Texan Mac Wallace who fired the gun narrowly missing Walker. It was Mac Wallace's style. I saw him often at the Dallas Gun Club practicing with a .22 single shot pistol.

There were other disturbing incidents involving Dallas down town store fronts owned by Jewish merchants, and three months prior to the fatal day of November 22nd, windows were knocked out of the Dallas County Democratic headquarters twice within a 24 hour period.

Looking back, I believe that there truly existed a powerful spirit of hate in Dallas at that time.

The editorial page of the Dallas Morning News had gained a national reputation among journalists and politicians for its unswervingly conservative and often acerbic viewpoints. An editorial columnist referred to the New Deal as the "Queer Deal." The American Civil Liberties Union was characterized as the "American Swivel Liberties Union." The U.S. Supreme Court was renamed the "Judicial Kremlin."

Even at the height of their activity in Dallas, the wealthy and powerful right-wing extremists were a small group, but they man aged to attract a great deal of attention to the city.

In that climate, there was a palpable undercurrent of violence. Dallas was a Petri dish-a spawning place for the bacteria of seething anger ready to multiply in leaps and bounds.

Only one month before the assassination, October 24, 1963, Dallas had greeted Ambassador Adlai Stevenson with outdoor bulletins and bumper stickers featuring the extremists' motto:

GET THE U.S. OUT OF THE U.N. AND THE U.N. OUT OF THE U.S.

The Ambassador addressed a U.N. group of approximately two thou sand people at Dallas Memorial Auditorium which turned into "Dal las' Disgrace." A group of one hundred extremist right-wingers showed their disdain for the United Nations. Protesters, using bar room tactics, walked the aisles with flags upside-down. Frank McGehee, a radical Dallasite and leader of the Indignation Commit tee, was escorted from the auditorium by Dallas police when he stood up, jeering and shouting protests. The Ambassador, on the other hand, gracefully brushed off the incident and continued his speech.

The embarrassed audience gave Stevenson a prolonged ovation to show their disapproval of radicals.

Stanley Marcus, of Neiman-Marcus fame and a longtime friend of Lyndon's, escorted the Ambassador to a waiting limousine. Eager reporters crowded around, note pads in use. All sorts of cameras were recording the historic event when an Oak Cliff housewife, tongue stuck out, struck Ambassador Stevenson with her U.N. placard. (She later said someone had pushed her.) At the same time, an Irving college student spat on him. Marcus shoved the Ambassador into the limousine and the protesters, chanting insults, rocked the car. The driver was guilty of extremely hazardous driving in making his es cape. I was totally horrified at the mob scene being acted out before me.

The incident made national news. Film was shown on CBS in excruciatingly slow motion by Walter Cronkite the following evening. Newspapers published revealing photos on front pages. It was a dis grace to Dallas, which prides itself for being a cultural mecca and art center of the world.

In the wake of the Stevenson incident, Dallas leaders reacted strongly to the outrageous behavior of the out-of-control ultra-conservatives.

Dallas Mayor Earle Cabell, supported by other leaders, angrily stated: "They are not conservatives-they are radicals." In a statement issued two days after the October, 1963, incident, Mayor Cabell declared that civic leaders must accept some responsibility for the problems in Dallas. "The constructive thinker and civic builder, although in the majority, had become engrossed in his own affairs and had permitted a small but highly vocal minority to project the image of our city to the world at large. One can do that with money and media."

But Mayor Cabell, who did not particularly like Kennedy, said he wanted to improve the city's image. "We have an opportunity to redeem ourselves," he said, "when President Kennedy pays us a visit next month."

Dallas was embarrassed and repentant over humiliating Stevenson. The Dallas Morning News, on October 25, published an editorial extending a "community apology" to Stevenson, assuring him that "the actions of a few do not represent the demeanor of the rest." The editorial, denouncing "the shameful treatment" of Stevenson, noted that the News did not support his candidacy for president, and it had disagreed with many of his stands on public issues, "But this newspaper defends his right to say what he thinks, and will defend it anywhere,anytime."

Also in reaction to the Stevenson incident, and on the same day, the Dallas Times Herald published a front page editorial under the heading, "Dallas Disgrace."

Telegrams signed by 100 civic leaders, the people off limits to Dallas Police, were sent to President Kennedy and Ambassador Stevenson saying that Dallasites were "outraged and abjectly ashamed" of the incident.

The City Council quickly passed an anti-harassment ordinance-too little, too late.

The rhetoric of the right was powerful. And sometimes reactionaries advocated violence, such as the hanging in effigy of United States Chief Justice Earl Warren.

Most Texas politicians agreed President Kennedy wanted to come to Texas to shore up his support for the upcoming 1964 presidential election, and to mend political fences in the Party with some of the independent oil and gas giants. In addition to the liberal labor coalition's disagreements with conservatives, the infighting was made even more intense by the powerful and ambitious personalities of the leading characters in the Democratic drama.

According to Lyndon, Kennedy believed his trip would help heal the personal and philosophical rift existing between Connally, Yarborough, and himself. He was still painfully trying to accept being "number two" as Vice President. However, Lyndon's real power of access was being head of the strong Invisible Government, unknown to most Americans. Lyndon told me, "Congress didn't know how the Agency (the CIA) spent their $4,000,000,000 budget. The CIA, FBI, and military are intertwined."

I asked, "What do our representatives and senators think about this? W hat is the Invisible Government?"

Lyndon said, "The Agency controls private companies, radio stations, a steamship company, and a publishing house. It is dangerous, and has overthrown some foreign powers. Some of the operations played a crucial role in the Kennedy-Nixon campaign. And the average person doesn't know a damn thing about it." I was stunned, because my own advertising agency handled the account of one of the world's largest steamship companies.

Lyndon explained, "Harry S. Truman established the CIA after World War II and Allen Dulles, John Foster Dulles' brother, was the Medusa head of the organization." He then scornfully added, "Haven't I told you repeatedly, you don't hear, see, or repeat any thing?!"

My mind and my mouth were sealed.

Governor Connally had risen from the level of a "poor dirt farmer" to achieve wealth and power. He had gained much of his political acumen from Lyndon-with strong assistance from rich oil man Sid Richardson. Newspapers in 1959 reported Connally had earned a cool two million dollars as executor of Sid's estate. Big John was rapidly becoming a favorite of the state's business and legal community with his own desires and ambition of becoming U.S. President. Lyndon often seemed jealous when Connally's name was mentioned.

Liberal Senator Ralph Yarborough, the East Texas populist lawyer, had angered Lyndon when he supported Kennedy. He strongly suspected that Lyndon and Connally were searching for a candidate to unseat him. Jesse told me that was, indeed, Lyndon's intent-to dump Yarborough. Lyndon's anger was like a volcano when it erupted. Anyone who got in his way would get suffocated by problems, many provided in the form of painful IRS investigations.

In spite of all the bickering between the "Three Great Giants," a Houston Chronicle survey indicated that Yarborough would be hard to beat in the primary. It showed Governor Connally winning re-election almost without effort. The disaffection for Lyndon had increased in Texas, primarily because of his identification with Billie Sol Estes and Bobby Baker. The stigma of the collapsed New Deal of Roosevelt was another negative factor against him.

Surveys also showed that, if the election had been held that day, conservative Republican Barry Goldwater would have carried Texas against Kennedy. Three years earlier, Kennedy had beaten Richard Nixon, champion of conservatives, in Texas by a mere 46,222 votes, an infinitesimal number out of 2.3 million cast. Many analysts attributed Kennedy's Texas victory to Lyndon and the strong participation of the Invisible Government.

Upon hearing my antique grandfather clock chiming 11:00 A.M., I realized I would have to rush to meet my friends and political associates. . .

*****

A large cheering crowd had gathered in the parking lot to hear John Kennedy's last speech in Fort Worth. Kennedy thought he had made some headway with the feuding Democrats-Lyndon and Yarborough-since they had agreed to sit together in the Dallas motorcade.

Thirty-five minutes later Lyndon arrived at Dallas' Love Field only three minutes before the President. He had already turned on his charming dual personality. He was supporting a broad smile as he joined Mayor Earle Cabell and his wife, Dearie, who graciously presented Jackie, glowing in her hot pink suit, an armful of American Beauty roses. After a short greeting and handshakes with the crowd, which was shouting warm welcomes, the party boarded the motorcade.

Sheriff Bill Decker and Dallas Police Chief Jesse Curry took their places in the lead car. Others in the motorcade were my love, Vice President

Johnson and Lady Bird; Mayor Earle Cabell and his wife, Dearie; Lady Bird's press-secretary, Liz Carpenter; Houston's P.R man, Jack Valenti; East Texas Lawyer, Ralph Yarborough, who only moments before had settled the Democratic feud. He had agreed that Governor Connally-known for his excellent extemporaneous speaking-would announce the "historic event" at the fund-raiser.

The press bus, which usually was positioned near the President, was located near the end of the Dallas motorcade. There were other impressive dignitaries and Secret Servicemen. The motorcade route, according to Jesse, had been unofficially changed by Dallas Police Captain Charles Batchelor, routing it through the "Birch Alley" on Turtle Creek. Batchelor was in charge of security precautions for both Kennedy's motorcade and the transfer of Oswald to the county jail. He lost both his charges and was promoted to Chief of Police later on. That's how things worked, there.

As the motorcade turned onto Main Street, the ugly gray clouds briefly opened to a beautiful bright sun and vivid blue skies. The normal Texas cold, blustering winds (separated from the North Pole by nothing more than a piece of barbed wire) had disappeared and the day had blossomed into Indian Summer for the First Family. Cheering multitudes of people, waving American and Texas flags resembling demented windmills, lined the streets. All the open hostility had vanished.

Meanwhile, according to John Curington, he, H.L. Hunt and

Jerome Ragsdale, watched the motorcade pass their windows at the Mercantile Bank Building. John Kennedy gave them a big smile. Lyndon also smiled and waved a big "V" with his arms. Hunt sighed, "That son-of-a-bitch's days are numbered," he said, referring to the President. Then the motorcade turned right onto Houston Street at Dealey Plaza, and then left onto Elm Street, the perfect "set-up" for an ambush!

My long time friend, Doris Clyce, standing on the comer of Main and Houston Streets, heard the first two shots that sounded like firecrackers, but other shots reverberated across Dealey Plaza, killing America's youngest elected President. Kennedy fell slightly forward, then violently backwards, as Jackie cried out, "They've killed my husband" while climbing across the back of the limo apparently to salvage pieces of the President's skull and brains. An assassin's bullet also struck John Connally, and he exclaimed, "My God, they are going to kill us all."

Panic, hysteria, and pandemonium prevailed in Dealey Plaza as William Greer, the driver of the Presidential limo, began accelerating at a high rate of speed, upon receiving instructions to proceed to Parkland Hospital. Screams from spectators echoed through the area, "President Kennedy has been shot! President Kennedy has been shot!"

The racing motorcade passed Trammell Crow's Apparel Mart where 2500 people had gathered to hear President Kennedy speak on the John Birch Society. When the motorcade arrived at Parkland, a team of doctors frantically worked on President Kennedy and Governor Connally. The medical staff realized Kennedy's wounds were fatal. Father Oscar Huber, a Catholic priest at Holy Trinity on Oak Lawn near Parkland, was summoned to administer last rites. The priest anointed President Kennedy's five senses with holy oil. Shocked and stunned, the heartbroken First Lady placed her wedding ring on his finger. A sheet was pulled over his head by nurse Doris Nelson. A few minutes later, after one o'clock, there was a public announcement that President Kennedy was dead. Gov. John Connally's condition was described as critical, but he was expected to survive.

Meanwhile, I had been at the old Red Courthouse listening to a group of angry Democrats still upset over Kennedy's coming to Dallas. I bade them farewell with hopes they would be in a better mood by the time we arrived in Austin.

Unaware of the tragic events which had transpired, I gleefully drove the five minutes to Oak Cliff near the connecting highway to Austin. Faintly, I could hear the beautiful chimes from Christ Episcopal Church. On an impulse, I decided to stop at Titches in Wynnewood to have my hair redone and was greeted by the news that the President had been shot. I felt as if someone had struck me with a sledge hammer.

With shaking hands I called my friend, County Judge Lew Sterrett (known as "The Fixer" in the Dallas County Courthouse). Lew said both Lyndon and Kennedy had been shot, "Maybe every one." Stunned and almost hysterical, I raced frantically home and called Jesse who reiterated what Judge Sterrett had told me.

The first fragmentary reports indicated that Lyndon, rather than the Governor, was the second victim. In those hectic and con fused moments, Secret Service agent Rufus Youngblood said that upon hearing the gun shot, he had pounced on Lyndon in his seat and slammed him to the floor to protect him. The jolt had apparently injured Lyndon, and he was still in pain when he arrived at Parkland Hospital. Seeing him bent forward and holding his chest, some re porters naturally assumed he had also been shot.

Jesse always had a calming effect on me. He said he would be calling with further information. I then turned on the radio and TV, shamefully relieved but still stunned by the horrible news. More de tailed reports indicated that it was Big John Connally, and not Lyndon, who had been wounded.

At Parkland Hospital, the President was pronounced dead. Lyndon, waiting for information, stood in a small anteroom known as Cubicle 13, dramatically muttering over and over, "The International Communists did it ... the International Communists did it."

The V ice President was notified at 1: 13 P.M. that President Kennedy had died. Thirteen minutes later, Lyndon was hustled into an unmarked police car to be driven at considerable speed to Love Field Airport, where Air Force One, the Presidential Jet, was waiting. Apparently fearing conspirators in his midst, Lyndon made the trip crouched on the floor of the police car. Had number 13 come back to haunt Lyndon?The box 13 scandal, cubicle 13, the news of Kennedy's death reaching him at 1: 13 P.M.-or was it a strange sort of political karma? Even after Lyndon's death the number "13" surfaced again when his own son passed away on Friday, September 28, 1990 at exactly 1: 13 P.M.

At home, I continued to watch post-assassination events through glazed eyes. A somber-faced Lyndon took the oath of office in the cramped executive suite of Air Force One. At his right stood Lady Bird; to his left the numbed Jacqueline Kennedy. Federal Judge Sarah T. Hughes, an old and dear friend of mine, and of Lyndon's, administered the oath. She used a Roman Catholic prayer book rather than a Bible. Judge Hughes, in her usual polka-dotted dress, remained very calm and collected during the ceremony. She showed no signs of emotion-and certainly no traces of hysteria.

As she left Air Force One, Judge Hughes said to the new President, "We'll back you, Lyndon." Everyone was shocked that Lyndon had chosen Sarah because she was not a favorite of Dallas court lawyers. She was high-tempered and often would threaten the lawyers with what she called "contempt," and order them to jail. When she would cool off, she would have the bailiff return them to the court room. Lyndon had surmounted many difficulties in obtaining her appointment as a federal judge.

Sometimes pictures speak louder than words. I was dismayed no end when Albert Thomas winked at Lyndon while Lady Bird smiled-and Jackie was in deep shock.

I was also overwhelmed with sadness. I could hardly cope with my emotions. I wept for the fallen President's family-but not just for them. I was sorry for Lyndon, who had just been catapulted into what, at the moment, appeared to be the most dangerous job in the world. I was even more sorry for myself. I knew Lyndon would be so busy I probably would not get to see him – even for a rare and precious fifteen minute interval. Eventually these morbid fears gave way to the more depressing consideration of the Presidency itself.

Dallas was in a total state of disgrace, disbelief, and despair as the world was repeatedly exposed to the horrible scenes of the assassination. How did this happen? Had one unstable individual followed an irrational impulse? Had the powerful 8F rich ultra-conservatives finally succumbed to violence?Was it the act of the Invisible Government (FBI, CIA, or Military)? It could have been a combination of more than one of these elements.

In the anguish of that Friday afternoon, little work was done in the city! Many places of business closed in the shock and confusion.

Tear-stained, frightened parents, fearing further violence, rushed to schools to get their children. Mr. Ragsdale went to St. George's Episcopal School to pick up Jimmy and Steven.

Great numbers of the normally busy population filled the churches and synagogues. Across the breadth of the city, people knelt at altars or sat solemnly in pews. The silence of prayers and meditation were broken only by occasional heart-rending sobs.

The spontaneous expressions of sorrow extended into the night. Downtown, in the chapel of the First United Methodist Church, mourners remained a full forty hours after the assassination. At Temple Emanuel, mourners overflowed the High Sanctuary.

Almost all city services closed in response to the tragic event.

Only emergency crews remained active.

Mayor Earle Cabell, despite his negative view of Kennedy, immediately called for a day of prayer on Saturday. He requested that churches and synagogues remain open from midnight to midnight. Ministers estimated that more than half a million people filled Dallas places of worship in search of solace.

Air Force One arrived at Andrews Air Force Base. A navy ambulance was waiting to take Kennedy's coffin to Bethesda Naval Hospital for an autopsy.

Lyndon delivered a brief statement to the nation hurriedly writ ten by Liz Carpenter only minutes before landing, "This is a sad time for all people. We have suffered a loss that cannot be weighed. For me it is a day of deep personal tragedy. I know the world shares sorrow with Mrs. Kennedy and her family. I will do my best. That is all I can do. I ask for your help and God's." He quickly departed to the White House to begin work.

Back in the capitol, the marquee outside Austin's Municipal Auditorium still carried its greetings to the Kennedys.

The sixteen-ounce steaks had been prepared, $300,000 worth of tickets had been sold and 3,00 souvenir programs had been printed with the ironically prophetic message from Gov. Connally. "A Day Long to be Remembered." Another item awaited, the unopened letter from Senator Herring concerning the oil depletion allowance.

Confusion and hysteria prevailed. There were newspaper extras as the assassination story dominated the media. Shortly after the assassination, a Dallas policeman, J.D. Tippit, was killed halfway be tween Lee Harvey Oswald's and Jack Ruby's apartments.

Oswald was apprehended in Oak Cliff at the neighborhood Texas Theatre. He was arrested by Officer Nick McDonald after a struggle, and taken to the Dallas City Jail. During the interrogation, young Lee Harvey Oswald denied firing the fatal shots at President Kennedy. He also denied killing police officer J.D. Tippit. He insisted that he was a patsy. Today many researchers believe Oswald never fired a shot.

Jimmy, Steven, and I remained at home. I was hoping to hear from Jesse. The silence was agonizing! How I wished I could talk to Lyndon.

Sunday, the boys and I attended a special high Mass at St. George's Episcopal Church celebrated by the Reverend Father Frank Jarrett in tribute to the Kennedys and the new Commander-in-Chief, President Johnson, and his family. People were still weeping over the tragedy.

As we arrived at my mother's, Miss Laurie, my grandmother, met us at the door with the news that crazy Jack Ruby had just shot Oswald under the watchful eyes of Dallas police officers in the basement of City Hall! She was almost hysterical, crying, "This city is going loco. It's like a lunatic asylum." She finally calmed down enough to tell me I had an urgent message from Mr. Ragsdale.

Ragsdale was blunt and curt, "Madeleine, you and the boys may be in big danger. You need to get the hell out of Dallas as soon as possible."

I didn't understand why we were in danger!

Ragsdale explained, "You are too close to Lyndon-you and Jack Ruby have been seen together, along with me, H.L. Hunt, and Jesse Kellam. You've been at socials where Hoover and Tolson have been, and God knows where else. I know you have been to the Campisis' 'hot spot' Egyptian Lounge on Mockingbird. The FBI has continuously photographed people who dine there. You just need to exercise extreme caution. Don't call me or Jesse Kellam. I'll contact you as soon as I can."

I took a deep breath, hastily regained my composure, turned and said, "Miss Laurie, let's go to the farm in Josephine for a few days. Let Dallas go loco without us."

As we hurriedly packed, Jimmy, Steven, and our gorgeous Weimaraner hunting dogs (Karla Frau, Hienie Achtung, and field trial champion Schnapps Achtung) took their places in the station wagon. We were desperate for peace and quiet.

*****

It was quickly apparent from the frenzied reports of TV comment after that Lyndon's newly gained power caused people to hate and resent him. Some people were asking who had the most to gain from Kennedy's death? After all, Lyndon was being investigated over the Bobby Baker scandal. Other names mentioned included Billie Sol Estes and Walter Jenkins.

It was extremely painful for me to hear anything negative about Lyndon. My mouth continued to be sealed. Jesse Kellam and Mr. Ragsdale were being very, very quiet.

I wish I could have been by Lyndon's side, when, under the gravest of circumstances, he took the reins as President of the United States. He said in his initial address to congress, "Let us continue." It was apparent that he meant to oversee the passage of Kennedy's en tire legislative program, including Civil Rights laws and an unorthodox tax reduction to stimulate the economy, Kennedy had been pulling out of Vietnam, but Lyndon rescinded that order.

The Vietnam War was heating up, racial conflicts were tearing apart our cities, our educational institutions were in an explosive state, and millions of impoverished Americans were still waiting for the promised benefits of the Kennedy programs. Lyndon was not an elected President, and therefore had no way of knowing how much public support he could anticipate. I heartily supported him. I prayed for him, but I was heartsick over his Vietnam policy!

Lyndon, who was only fifty-five-years-old when he became President, was subject to public abuse. During every day and every working hour he would have to make decisions affecting millions of people in America and throughout the world.

I heard Lyndon in his rich southern drawl telling Congress, "We have talked long enough in this country about equal rights. We have talked for a hundred years or more. It is time to write in the book of law." I don't think there was ever a time when I was prouder of him, for I knew that Nobel Prize winner Dr. Martin Luther King's "Dream" was about to come true.

Lovely, beautiful Mildred Teel and others like her would never have to shed tears over their skin color.

Signs saying "White Only" would be removed forever. I knew from "the other side"-the ones who had fought for civil rights-my Grandfather Lee, John F. Kennedy, Mr. Sam Rayburn, and a host of others, would sing "Hallelujah!"

We stayed at the cotton farm for two weeks before Ragsdale called to say it was safe to return home. Rumors at Vick's were that our friend H.L. Hunt was on sabbatical at the Atilano De La Garza Ranch in remote northern Mexico, but according to John Curington,

H.L. spent only a few days at the ranch because Lyndon called him to Washington to resolve the oil depletion crisis.

*****

We were also stunned about Jack Ruby killing Lee Harvey Oswald. Ruby had often bragged about personally knowing all of "Big D's" policemen, as well as city and county officials. His Carousel Club was located at 1213 1/2 Commerce Street across from the Adolphus Ho tel. He also had a western club, the Bridgeport, on Lamar Street Strip, and still another club on Oak Lawn. I knew most of his beautiful girls who worked there. Through the years, the city's great white fathers, both city and county, were often seen in the company of Jack Ruby. He was a good friend to everyone, always helping people! He was especially good to his girls.

He was also a great dog lover and to us a lover of dogs and animals was "good people." He bragged about his dogs and we kidded him about Sheba's "waistline" after hearing he fed her round steak. Jack Ruby was fun, but rather mysterious! We all knew he had worked for AI Capone before coming to Dallas, but we accepted Jack for what he was. I was introduced to him in the early 1950's when he was manager of the famous Longhorn Ballroom. However, he did not remember meeting me then. During his confinement in the county jail, we wanted to visit him, and later in Parkland, but Ragsdale advised, "Stay away."

We did meet his famous, flamboyant attorney, Melvin Belli, of San Francisco. Everyone was so impressed with Mel. We passed the hat at our coffee bar to help pay Jack's attorney fees. Jack would have been freed had

Melvin Belli tried his second case. It didn't take Mel long to learn the inner workings of our local judicial system.

Dr. Jack Barnett did not believe Ruby's contention that he had been infected or sprayed with poisonous gas. He felt that Sheriff Decker would never have allowed this to happen. Dr. Barnett, who cared for jail personnel while in medical school, knew Sheriff Decker very well. He said Jack Ruby was "far too gone" to be helped by medical science by the time they had received him at Parkland Hospital. Ruby, like John Kennedy and Lee Harvey Oswald before him, died at Parkland on Jan. 2, 1967.

Dr. Barnett and I have been long time friends-hunting and field trailing together. He is a wonderful sportsman. We've talked a lot about Jack Ruby. He said he had received thousands of letters from all over the world advising how to treat Ruby. Later all the letters mysteriously disappeared from his office.

I would like to pay a special tribute to Dr. Barnett. He has always been a gentleman and contributed much to the medical field. His warm friendship helped sustain me during Steven's long illness.

Often he would quietly open the door to my son's hospital room to either offer assistance or give reassurance that I was not alone.

November 22, 1963 spelled the end of Camelot, but it was also the biggest "Texas in the morning" for Steven Mark's father, Lyndon Baines Johnson. For Lyndon's mother, Rebekah, and father, Sam, it was a lifetime dream come true. While the timing and circumstances of his achievement were tragic and unfortunate, I sensed some ambivalent feeling of joy for him because I could still remember his disappointment at failing to receive the 1960 Democratic Presidential nomination.

27

My Sandow, The President

The shock and horror of the assassination had paralyzed Dallas, yet the joy and hope of Christmas with its message of renewal permeated the air. Beautifully wrapped Christmas packages had been arriving at the advertising agency ("payola" we called them).Mayor Cabell had requested that all social functions be canceled. Many elegant social parties were victims of the thirty-day mourning period.

Turmoil on a world-wide scale was caused by the assassination and the activities of the CIA. Former President Harry Truman made a formal statement on December 21, 1963, stating, "For some time I have been disturbed by the way the CIA has been diverted from its original assignment. It has become an operational and at times a policy-making arm of government ...

"I never had any thought that when I set up the CIA it would be injected into peacetime cloak-and-dagger operations. Some of the complications and embarrassment that I think we have experienced are in part attributable to the fact that this quiet intelligence arm of the President's has been so removed from its intended role that it is being interpreted as a symbol of sinister and mysterious foreign intrigue-and a subject for cold-war enemy propaganda."

One of Lyndon's first duties after taking over the reins as President was the appointment of the Warren Commission, composed of eight prominent Americans: Representative Gerald R. Ford (The Fords were close friends of the Johnsons while in Washington); Representative Hale Boggs; Senator Richard B. Russell (bachelor and good drinking buddy of Lyndon's brother, Sam); Chief Justice Earl Warren; Sena tor John Sherman Cooper; John J. McCloy (a financial ally to the oil tycoons, H.L. Hunt, Clint Murchison, and Sid Richardson, and a long time chairman of the Chase Manhattan Bank); and former (JFK fired him!) CIA Director Allen W. Dulles. J. Lee Rankin was the General Counsel of the Warren Commission, organized their work, and did more of it than anyone else-commissioners or staff.

Long before their report was released, a group of "gun lovers," headed by C.G. West, took the same kind of 6.5 mm rifle Oswald was supposed to have used and set up a similar scene to the one at Kennedy's assassination. After test-firing the gun, each expert said it was impossible to fire this gun as reported. They stated there had to be three or more people firing rifles. It was the consensus of the Winchester Elm Fork Gun Group that the first shot came from the top of the Records Building, the second came from the railroad trestle running over the triple underpass, the third from the grassy knoll near the railroad trestle and the fourth shot came from the roof of the Texas School Book Depository. Even though these gentlemen tried desperately to get in touch with the Warren Commission, no one in power would give them the opportunity to present their theory. Later events showed this to be a dangerous endeavor because so many of the witnesses interviewed by the Warren Commission have died violent deaths. Today, when these old time gun enthusiasts discuss the assassination, many agree those original findings were roughly correct, and that the Warren Commission ought to have listened.

Former Speaker of the House, Thomas P. ("Tip") O'Neill, Jr., in a public forum, discredited the Warren Report completely. Lyndon had the records sealed until the year 2029. I asked him "Why?" He smiled his little boy smile and said humorously, "Remember Box 13?" Jesse's expected call finally came late on December 24th. "Rejoice, Madeleine, this will be the best Christmas of your life. You have an invitation from the Honorable Mr. President to be at the Driskill on December 31, 1963."

I think my heart stopped beating for a few seconds as he read me the agenda.

Air Force One would be bringing Lyndon to his beloved Hill Country on Christmas Eve. He would check in the Governor's Mansion on "Big John" Connally, who was rapidly recovering from wounds received while riding in the Kennedy motorcade.

There would be a big family Christmas, with uncles, aunts, cousins, and much food. Lyndon loved Christmas, so this was a very extravagant occasion.

I interrupted Jesse, "What Lyndon would miss is a rite of pas sage for our son, Steven, who is about to become a teenager."

Jesse's tenderness showed for a few seconds. Then he paused and said, "Everything will be all right. "

He continued with Lyndon's itinerary: "You know German Chancellor Ludwig Erhard will be at the ranch. Do you remember when he asked

Lyndon if he had been born in a log cabin and Lyndon told him. 'Hell, no. I was born in a manger."' We both had a good laugh.

"Lyndon and Jake Pickle will get in a few hours of deer hunting," I said. (The ranch had elaborate deer stands, equipped with elevators. Pickle was a long-time Democrat and a good friend of Lyndon's.)

Jesse said, "Yes, then it will be your time, Madeleine."

The "zillion butterflies" hit my stomach and head. Oh happy day!!!

Time was an eternity. When I arrived, I almost felt like a stranger at the Driskill. The Secret Service, aided by Texas Highway Patrolmen, had blanketed the hotel. Much had changed on the floor of the suite. The madness of this! It would take some time to get used to, but I would endure almost anything to see Lyndon.

There was a quiet little man sitting outside the door of the suite. He held a black briefcase. I was frightened, but Lyndon later told me the briefcase contained top-secret information, a secret code with which he could order the launching of nuclear weapons against an enemy. By law, the bearer must accompany the President every time he leaves the White House, always staying within easy reach. Over the course of the next few years, several different, deliberately bland and colorless men carried that secret code. I was never introduced to any of them, nor did I ever learn their names.

As I opened the door to Lyndon's suite, I discovered he was totally naked with an erection (that was Lyndon; he never wasted valuable time). He smiled his little boy smile, oddly innocent. Then we melted together. I was muttering, "Mr. President, my Sandow, I love you so!"

Finally, we separated and he handed me a crystal thin glass of bubbly champagne. Toasting with our glasses, we agreed to the toast. "Here's to a hell of a better year than '63!"

I lifted the rim of the glass and took a sip.

"Dom Perignon, of course," he said before taking my other hand, he led me to the bedroom.

If I thought he would change his manner because he was President, I was wrong. Lyndon was wild with passion as he stripped my clothes off and threw me on the feather bed.

"Hey, don't eat me up! I want more of you. Goddamn, you feel good," he breathed passionately, gently, while firmly pulling my nipples.

"Jesus Christ!" Lyndon was bellowing like the bull he had always been. As he climaxed, I felt myself whirling in ecstasy. After playing and experimenting with each other, discovering each other for the first time or perhaps the hundredth, we fell asleep in each other's arms, our legs intertwined.

Two hours later, the rising orb of the sun broke through the draperies and Lyndon sprang up in bed.

With his famous bellowing bull sound, he roared, "Goddamn, Madeleine, there ain't nothing better than Texas in the morning!!"

As he leaned back in my arms, I noted for the first time how he looked. As Texas cattlemen would say, he looked "drawn."

"Are you really doing all right, my love?" 1 asked him as I gently ran my fingers through his hair.

"I'm just tired and run-down, that's all. I don't have anyone that I can tum to like I used to with Mr. Sam." Swallowing hard, he added, "I wish he was here. I need him. I have to put my mind at ease. "

"Lyndon, you know that a lot of people believe you had something to do with President Kennedy's assassination."

He shot up out of the bed and began pacing and waving his arms screaming like a madman. I was scared!

"That's bullshit, Madeleine Brown!" he yelled. "Don't tell me you believe that crap!"

"Of course not." I answered meekly, trying to cool his temper.

"It was Texas oil and those fucking renegade intelligence bastards in Washington."

"What are you talking about?" I asked, my eyes bulging. "Hell, that son-of-a-bitch Irish mafia Kennedy-with advice from the Invisible Government-came out for suicidal cuts in the oil depletion allowance. More than two hundred eighty million dollars per year! He stopped half a dozen mergers under the anti-trust act. In '62s sag, the market dropped one hundred and thirty-seven billion fucking dollars. Steel fell fifty percent, and he had the impertinence to talk about 'rollback' of prices, or worse a freeze. This was war, Madeleine, to some rich, fat cats in Texas you and I both know. He campaigned on an increased defense budget. Then he made plans to close fifty-two military bases in twenty-five states, plus twenty-five overseas bases, and he was getting ready to quit in Southeast Asia. And for the first time in history, he had sent in one intelligence agency, the FBI, to dismember another agency, the CIA. America simply could not have this!

"Goddamn it, Madeleine, in the last fifteen years we've lost eight hundred million people to the Communist conspiracy-and price less resources and markets-and not a single Russian soldier has been killed. We're being nibbled to death in Vietnam, and now in our own hemisphere, our oil boys and the intelligence boys didn't like Kennedy's talk about 'disarmament' or the 'Peace Corps.' They believed that the only thing the goddamned Communists understand is power!

"And, my God, they couldn't tolerate the Negroes. These boys thought Kennedy was going to lead the Negro revolution instead of fighting it. They got real uncomfortable when they saw 250,000 American Negroes and their supporters march in Washington in the Fall of '63."

"Who were the Texas oil men, Lyndon? Who are we talking about?" I asked boldly.

He turned and stared me straight in the eyes with a cold glare, saying, "Behind every success there is a crime," and "Do you remember what I told you years ago, Madeleine?You see nothing, you hear nothing, you say nothing." As he stormed off to the bathroom, he added, "I can see that I have already told you too much. I should have listened to my own advice."

I began to hyperventilate. I shivered like an earthquake registering number ten on the Richter scale. I do not claim to be a Kennedy assassination researcher. I have not meticulously studied the history of November 22, 1963, but I saw and heard and knew enough to unnerve my senses. My views, like a jigsaw puzzle, include pieces of circumstantial evidence and odd associations and persistent stories too sinister to dismiss as pure coincidence:

> 1ack Ruby did have possession of the motorcade map and Ruby "knew" the Dallas Police Department.
>
> • Lee Harvey Oswald and Ruby together at the Carousel Club.
>
> • Ruby's friendship with Jerome Ragsdale.
>
> • Rumors of high level authorities changing the motorcade route and the lack of security and press in Dealey Plaza at the crucial moment.
>
> • Witnesses who claimed the motorcade slowed down or virtually "stopped" during the shooting.
>
> • Lyndon's close relationship with Murchison and Hoover since the Box 13 scandal.
>
> • The Texas 8F meeting at Murchison's home on Nov. 21, 1963.
>
> • -H.L. Hunt's confidence in being the richest man in the world, that he would never get in trouble, and his complete disdain for JFK.

- -Lyndon's intention of visiting Pat Kirkwood's nightclub after leaving Murchison's home. Nine of Kennedy's Secret Servicemen were later criticized for visiting Kirkwood's club 'til the early-morning hours in clear violation of curfew regulations. Years later Kirkwood admitted that some of Ruby's strippers had kept the security men entertained during the night.
- -Lyndon's prophecy of never being embarrassed by the Kennedy's again.
- -The swirl of witnesses and evidence seriously supporting the theory of multiple shooters and questioning Oswald's guilt.

The list goes on and on-I was frozen with shock. As I dressed to return to Dallas, Lyndon remained in the bathroom. All the old plus some new fears, concerns, emotions, doubts, plagued me.

How could I be so desperately in love with someone who had openly implicated himself in cloak-and-dagger tactics?

After all these many years, I still cannot honestly answer this question, even to myself.

I have no doubt that Lyndon told me the truth about the assassination. I believe Lyndon and the 8F people did what they felt they had to do to protect their own interests.

28

Embarrassing Moments

In July 1964, Lyndon proudly signed into law the most sweeping civil rights bill since Reconstruction days.

The bill, which had been submitted in June 1963 by Kennedy, passed the Senate after a fifteen-week Southern filibuster. It outlawed discrimination in places of public accommodation, publicly owned facilities, employment, and union membership, as well as federally aided programs. A major feature of the legislation was the new power it gave the attorney general to speed school desegregation, and to enforce the Negro's right to vote. It was designed to end all racism.

To get the legislation he wanted, Lyndon had used with great success what many of us in Texas had known for years as the "Johnson treatment." This consisted of a combination of empty flattery, insistent coaxing, arm-twisting, threats and solicitous wooing, all placed in motion by Lyndon with an endless succession of telephone calls, booze-saturated lunches, vulgar and shocking barnyard jokes, physical contact, compassionate arm-around-the-shoulder comraderie, and the cold stare when crossed. The technique was very good at exposing the most sensitive nerve in Lyndon's target, and, he said, "Most often, that was the target's self-interest."

Lyndon's record in the months after Kennedy's assassination, in addition to his previously unconcealed presidential ambitions, left no doubts in the minds of Democrats and Republicans alike that he would be his party's favorite in the 1964 election.

However, when we met in Austin during the long Fourth of July holiday, celebrating the passage of the Civil Rights Bill and my birthday, Lyndon told me he wanted to get out of the White House, but there was no way out now.

"Lyndon," I urged him at our suite at the Driskill, "I hope you will run. I want you to do whatever is best for democracy and the American way. I know that you can do it, even though it will take you away from me and cause my heart to break. Then when you are re elected president, announce to the world that you are going to do what is best, for blacks and whites, Democrats and Republicans, Protestants, Jews and atheists without paying homage to the monied class," meaning the 8F group ...

As we dallied in bed, we discussed who would be his running mate. Up to this point, Lyndon had achieved-with suspense, titillation, and manipulation of the press-a hodgepodge of names and no one except me, knew who the main contender would be. Of course, it was Hubert H. Humphrey of Minnesota. I think he chose Hubert as a foil to his Republican opponent, Barry Goldwater, Arizona's conservative knight. Goldwater's itchy fingers, if elected, might press the button that would unleash nuclear holocaust.

On both sides, the campaign was a relatively clean one. Lyndon's supporters had only two episodes verging on the scandalous that had to be explained to the voters.

One involved Bobby Baker, a good and loyal friend of Lyndon's, who had served as secretary to the Senate Democratic majority at the time Lyndon was the majority leader. Just before the assassination of Kennedy, it was disclosed that Bobby Baker had used official influence to amass a sizable fortune.

A Senate subcommittee investigation disclosed that Baker had arranged a deal between an insurance man and the LBJ Company, the Johnson family's communications empire in Austin.

The Baker investigation never officially linked Lyndon to Baker's alleged unethical practices, but the whole affair remained a source of embarrassment for Lyndon.

The second embarrassing incident indicated that Lyndon, who was noted for being intensely loyal to his friends and aides, could also be ignorant of some of their weaknesses. He failed to note a flaw in the personality of Walter Jenkins, the chief assistant and coordinator of Lyndon's White House staff.

Shortly before the election, Jenkins was arrested on a morals charge in the men's room of the downtown YMCA in Washington. It turned out that he had a record of a previous arrest in the same place, a notorious gay hangout. J. Edgar Hoover, a suspected closet homo sexual, had failed to notify Lyndon, and considering how efficient Hoover was, it seems very strange that the deviant behavior had not been reported. I knew Walter personally, and have always felt he was framed. (Oddly, Jenkins' brother was an FBI agent in Lubbock, Texas.)

The Bobby Baker investigation was proceeding and Lyndon was concerned about Walter's testimony. Walter represented the American Dream

Family turned into a nightmare (he had five children), and I felt sorry for the entire Jenkins family as they returned to Texas as outcasts, the sad flotsam of Washington. D.C.

On November 3, 1964, Election Day, Lyndon was at his ranch, the new unofficial White House during Lyndon's administration. Lyndon voted, then spent the day driving his Lincoln Continental around his lavish spread.

That night, as the votes were counted across the nation in the dark hours, it quickly became apparent that tens of thousands of Re publicans had deserted their party to vote for Lyndon. The people rewarded his good work and powerful campaign with a record-breaking majority of sixty-one percent of the popular vote. Lyndon called this result a "mandate for unity."

I met Lyndon two more times during his prolonged stay in Texas after the election. Like many friends and influential people, I received the well publicized "Ya'll Come" in a gold-engraved invitation to his inauguration.

I flew to Washington with several Dallas political dignitaries aboard Earle Cabell's personal DC-3, where a festive atmosphere abounded. From all the advance publicity, many on board had visions of an exciting luxurious Roman holiday. They hoped for the opportunity to rub elbows with the great and near-great and perhaps engage in a private chat with Lyndon. (Jesse had already informed me that there would be no time for Lyndon and me to have a Washington rendezvous.)

The beautiful ball gown I was wearing had been designed by the internationally renowned de Rauch Madeleine, and I'm sure it had cost Lyndon thousands of dollars. He said that he didn't want me to look like the women in John Steinbeck's Grapes of Wrath!

Although Lyndon had publicly announced he would not wear a top hat or formal attire for the swearing-in ceremony, most of the men wore tails or tuxedos for the various parties and the final gala ball.

Several inaugural balls took place on the night before the swearing-in. Each was like an indoor Disneyland, with thousands of fancily dressed Democrats having a great time.

Besides the number one ball held at the Mayflower Hotel, I attended the big fund-raising gala which featured a lot of entertainers from Broadway and Hollywood. Johnny Carson was the master-of ceremonies.

Considering how exhausted I was after attending the inaugural festivities, I could only imagine how poor Lyndon must have felt, particularly since he was forced to attend all the functions and keep smiling throughout.

Lyndon's 1,500-word inaugural address on January 20, 1965, was one of the shortest in history. In it he said: "In a land of great wealth, families must not live in hopeless poverty. In a land rich in harvest, children must not go hungry. In a land of healing miracles, neighbors must not suffer and die unattended. In a great land of leaming and scholars, young people must be taught to read and write."

To the world Lyndon said, "We aspire to nothing that belongs to others. We seek no dominion over our fellow man, but man's do minion over tyranny and misery." As Lady Bird stood next to her husband on the inaugural platform, for the first time I really under stood that I cherished vague hopes for the future, but I shrugged off the feelings of certain disappointment by whispering Lyndon's favorite line: "Today is today. Tomorrow is tomorrow."

29

Shadows

With the inauguration out of the way,Lyndon suffered a dreadful case of influenza. His diseased heart was bothering him. He was cross and ill-tempered,and made a costly foreign relations mistake when he refused to let Vice President Hubert Humphrey attend Winston Churchill's funeral as the U.S. representative. Churchill's demise ended the colonial grandeur of Britain. He was Britain's savior from the Nazi horror. Hubert Humphrey was deeply hurt when he had not been allowed to honor him, and it created more tension within the executive branch.

Lyndon believed many of his dreams for a better America could become reality. The landslide victory which put him into office had also given him a Democrat victory in the House as well as the Senate, and both were ready to follow Lyndon's lead with little opposition. The fabulous 89th session soon began rubber-stamping his "Great Society " program-passing legislation that had been squashed for 30 years. The Republicans bitterly claimed it was unwise to pass such sweeping legislation.

Early in his Administration, Lyndon declared "war on poverty." He made two trips to the distressed Appalachia area to dramatize the need for an anti-poverty drive. Now he asked Congress to appropriate $1 billion for this cause.

"I asked you to march with me along the road to the future," he said,"the road that leads to the great society,where no child will go unschooled ...where every human being has dignity and every worker has a job, where education is blind to color and employment is unaware of race, where decency prevails and courage abounds..."

Among the measures that would have the most far-reaching effect on the quality of American life in the future was the bill to provide virtually free medical and hospital care for the aged under Social Security, known as the Medicare Bill. (Little did Lyndon know that his health care program would be smashed by the iron hand of inflation.) He signed it into law on July 30, 1965. Lyndon flew to Missouri, and gave former President Harry Truman Medicare Card No. 1; Bess received Card No. 2.

In the first euphoric months, Lyndon's love for education ex pressed itself with massive federal dollars earmarked for primary and secondary schools as well as to colleges and college students; new safeguards for black voting rights; reform of the immigration laws; grants for the "model cities" development program and a program for rent subsidies for poor tenants; a higher minimum wage; increased funds for the anti-poverty program; a series of measures to protect the consumer from fraudulent packaging and advertising; and a substantial start on efforts to rid the air and streams of pollution, which was so close to our own son's heart.

All these and tax cuts, too, were realized by Lyndon, with the help of the 89th Congress, which expanded certain areas of government and allowed others to wither and die on the vine.

Robert C. Weaver was the first black American named to hold cabinet rank. Lyndon also appointed the first black ever to sit on the Supreme Court, Thurgood Marshall, who had won fame as a brilliant trial lawyer for civil rights before Lyndon appointed him Solicitor General of the United States.

In fact, he appointed many blacks to high office, which I believe, in the depths of my soul, paved the way for Jesse Jackson to run for the presidency and gave such a role model to the young blacks claiming their place in society. (Many believe that Dr. Martin Luther King's strong leadership and Lyndon Johnson's love for democracy are the driving forces today in giving Jesse Jackson the potential to become America's first black president.) "Now, maybe, every Negro kid in the United States could think, 'Goddamn it, maybe I can be a judge some day – or president.' I want to put some incentive in them," Lyndon said.

On many occasions, Lyndon lent his prestigious Southern ac cent to the voices heard during the nonviolent black demonstrations. Dr. Martin Luther King urged his followers, saying, "We shall over come," and on occasion Lyndon used that phrase-the anthem of the civil rights movement-while urging Congress to enact strong voting rights legislation.

"It is not just Negroes, really, it is all of us," he said, "who must overcome the crippling legacy of bigotry and injustice. And we shall overcome." ... And today, in many ways, we have, even though we still have far to go.

Lyndon was born to be a child of Congress. The passing and shaping of legislation and federal programs was to him the prime function of government.

He was, at heart, an isolationist, and if Lyndon could have, he would have built a wall around America so she could put her house in order and help all Americans up the ladder to success without foreign distractions.

But events were not to allow him to take that course. Through out his administration, a great shadow was cast over all his efforts. It was the shadow of war, of the tragic, ugly, bloody, seemingly endless war in Vietnam.

Even Lyndon's most severe critics would agree that in substantial measure this president inherited the problem of Vietnam.

South Vietnam had plagued both Eisenhower and Kennedy. They sent military advisors to the South Vietnamese army to help them combat the guerrilla tactics of the Viet Cong, who were aided by North Vietnam. Although Kennedy was apparently in the process of withdrawing from Vietnam, it was Lyndon's fate to commit American troops to a long and costly land war in the region.

Many questions arise. Two that bothered me the most were: "Was it Lyndon's desire to feather Brown and Root's pocketbook?" and "Was the Brown and Root Company a secret government agency?"

Don't laugh. Many companies were government operations in deep cover.[3]

The stage for escalation of the war was actually set in August 1964, after Communist boats attacked United States destroyers in the Gulf of Tonkin. Lyndon obtained congressional approval of a resolution granting him full authority for "all necessary action to protect our armed forces."

The alternative for Lyndon was either a powerful assertion of American military power, or humiliating defeat as the Communists took over. He was committed to victory in all areas, he told me, be cause he did not want to start his full term in office with an international defeat, he also knew the dangers of committing American troops. His best information at the time was from Kennedy's military advisors who assured him that just a few months of direct American military intervention would eradicate the Communist problem in Vietnam.

Lyndon took this bad advice and authorized bombardment of North Vietnam, attempting to cut the military supply lines to the Viet Cong in the South. By July 1965, Lyndon had sent 75,000American troops into the war zone and was planning to increase the number to 125,000. By November there were 100,000 American troops there.

In February 1966, there were about 200,000 American servicemen in South Vietnam and, at that time, the U.S. was functioning in the limited capacity of advising and giving logistic support to the weakening native forces. Lyndon received the grim alarm that the Saigon government was

3 Victor Marchetti and John D. Marks, *The CIA and the Cult of Intelligence* (Alfred E. Knopf, 1974) exposed in detail many of these front companies.

in danger of collapse. The Viet Cong insurgents and North Vietnam army units had begun a final drive for Communist victory.

Often, as criticism of his war policies grew both at home and abroad, Lyndon pleaded for understanding. "We will never be second in search for . . . a peaceful settlement in Vietnam," he said. "We remain ready for unconditional discussions."

From time to time he would tell me of his difficulty in sleeping because he was so troubled over the Vietnam War, and thinking about young men like Steven and Jimmy. He was terribly concerned about the loss of many young people on both sides. "War and politics is an ugly hellhole sucking the vitality of so many innocent people. I know one goddamn thing, I'll never allow my son, Steven, to go to war. I promise you that Madeleine, nor Jimmy."

Lyndon tried to become a peacemaker and end the vicious, bloody war by negotiation. However, Hanoi, Beijing and Moscow denounced this as a smoke-screen for further escalation.

The Viet Cong claimed to be the only legitimate governing force in South Vietnam. The United States-backed Saigon government, controlled largely by leaders of the corrupt South Vietnam armed forces, made the same claim.

Lyndon was disappointed, and steadfastly refused to pursue a settlement that would give the Viet Cong too great a share of political power in Saigon. He feared that total power was the enemy's long range aim. The other side refused to settle for anything less.

On all except this central issue, Lyndon tried to be conciliatory, even generous. He refused to whip up hate for the enemy and he offered to spend, after the war, billions of American tax dollars on the rebuilding of Vietnam and help develop the economies of both the North and the South.

But beyond charity, Lyndon believed the dominant issue was whether the United States would keep its word and prevent the forcible overthrow or conquest of a country it had promised to defend. The violation of such a promise, he insisted, would imperil dozens of other nations and hence the peace of the world.

Many Americans agreed, and went along with Lyndon's contention that promises and commitments, once made, could be violated only at the nation's peril.

Lyndon became hated because of his pursuit of the Vietnam War. The passion of the American people ran so high-for or against it-that it polarized our country into hawks and doves. It stood to reason, considering the violent mood across the country, that another assassination might be triggered against Lyndon.

First of all, he was a Texan-that alone was enough to curse him in the eyes of a great number of reporters throughout the country. His accent, his manner, his country-boy candor (and earthy language) all worked against him. Whenever possible, some press members deliberately pictured Lyndon as an uncouth bumpkin with no dignity or social graces. Lyndon brought criticism upon himself be cause of some relatively minor incidents that were gleefully reported to the public.

Once he playfully picked up a beagle by his ears and offended millions of over-sensitive dog lovers. There was never a greater lover of animals than Lyndon. He even wrote legislation to protect animals and usually had a dog with him in the White House.

On other occasions he pulled up his shirt and displayed to reporters the big scars from his gallbladder operation, no doubt dis tressing many squeamish people. He went swimming nude in the White House pool, causing great concern among the church groups of the Southern Bible Belt. He loved to make home movies of animals mating, and during their showing would make comments such as "Ain't it great!" to anyone watching.

Lyndon realized, but seemed not to care, that each of these incidents would spark a negative public reaction. Each episode was an act of perverse defiance against the press, which already held critical views of him because of Vietnam. I can't tell you how many times that Lyndon openly wept in my arms as he described the war as his "endless agony." It was destroying the man I loved.

Partly because of displeasure with the war, a critical Congress tore Lyndon's modest foreign aid program to shreds. In a series of damaging public hearings in 1966, conducted by Lyndon's fellow Democrat, Senator J. William Fulbright, the Foreign Relations Committee challenged Lyndon's policies toward Vietnam, toward Communist China, and even toward Western Europe.

It was the beginning of the end. Violence exploded on university campuses and earlier civil rights marches in Washington gave way to equally large anti-war demonstrations. Lyndon's foes could sense that time was on their side-and so it was!

30

Live, Learn, and Hope

My hopes and desires for Steven were being fulfilled in 1967. He had developed into an outstanding student at my own alma mater, W.H. Adamson High School. He was active in theater productions, debating, speech tournaments, and was an officer in Rare. He won trophies and gold medals-and praise from his teachers-with surprising frequency.

He was a total delight to me. He reminded me so much of his father. His height, his weight, his hair-all his physical characteristics-screamed out that he was Lyndon's son.

Of great concern to me was the day when Steven would find out the truth about his heritage. At times he would catch a glimpse of that fear in my facial expressions. Reminiscent of his father's impudence, he would say, "Lighten up, Mother. Don't sweat the small stuff. Today is today and tomorrow is tomorrow," which would often make me laugh-and sometimes make me cry.

Beside his formal studies at Texas A&M, Steven excelled in many endeavors. Sports came easily to him, but because of my maternalistic fears of crippling injuries, I discouraged his participation in contact sports such as football. Every spring his coach strongly encouraged Steven (who was six feet, four inches tall and weighed two hundred pounds) to play. I imagined him confined to a wheel chair for the rest of his life and was unmoved by the coach's entreaties.

As an expert marksman he had recently won the Dallas Open Gun Tournament at Elm Fork Gun Range. He was shooting a 12-gauge Browning Shotgun (a gift from Lyndon) over and under stacked barrels in competitions across the state. He competed in field trials with "Schnapps Achtung," our Weimaraner champ (a "gray ghost," a dog bred for royalty in Germany). He won ribbon after ribbon, trophy after trophy, until the case in our gun room was filled to capacity.

We benefited from his talent in other ways. Each year he filled the family freezer with dove, quail, pheasant, and, occasionally, a fat deer, although he didn't like to kill them. He said they were too beautiful. He would only do so if we used the skin and all the meat, so there would be no waste. He often said, "God gave us stewardship of the earth and I'm sure he gets ticked off when we waste His good works."

I remember when he was nine years old, I took him and his first shotgun, a single-shot .41 0, for practice with clay pigeons. I knew when he was younger he always shot left-handed with his BB gun. No matter how I tried to coach him to be right-handed with a gun, he could not change. So when he loaded his shotgun and threw it up to his left shoulder, he looked awkward.

The skeet trap was set up in front of what we affectionately called the "club house" which was, in reality, a half-finished cabin on the edge of a large water tank at Clopton's Hunting Resort in Rockett, Texas. Steven, with an extended left elbow, long legs and oversized feet, looked like a young crane stalking frogs.

I couldn't help but chuckle, then I would feel my heart sink as I realized that Lyndon would never experience these moments with his son. He was limited to those which I captured on 8 mm film. He often requested I bring photos and films of Steven. These were the quiet times Lyndon and I spent together enjoying our son. Often tears would flow while Lyndon held me tenderly.

My reflections were shattered by the shotgun blast as Steven "killed" his first clay pigeon. I was amazed that someone as young and awkward-looking as Steven could hit such a fast moving target on his very first try. He very precisely ejected his shell, reloaded, and showed his subdued excitement in a high-pitched voice as he yelled, "Pull!"

His bird flew up sharply on a straight burst of hot Texas wind and then exploded into tiny pieces. In disbelief, I watched as he "killed" twenty-four more and I'm sure he would have gone to twenty-five straight if Schnapps Achtung hadn't interfered on his last shot.

How proud Lyndon would be of Steven!

Steven was very popular with girls and was invited to many functions throughout Texas. One of his favorite girls was Beth Horstmann of San Antonio, the daughter of Col. John and Mrs. Alice Horstmann. He was also impressed with Beth's Weimaraner, Bravo, who ran a close second to Schnapps. For his first real date, I drove him to San Antonio for Beth's Christmas party at St. Mary's Hall, the exclusive all-girl's Catholic school. They were a stunning duo and were acclaimed the most outstanding couple at the party. Beth was glowing in her hot pink, silk gown and Steven was immaculate in his tailored blue suit, a perfect counterpoint to Beth.

Distance kept this romance from blossoming. Unfortunately, Beth and her sister, Alex Short, lost their lives in a fiery plane crash in 1976.

There were other girlfriends who held his attention for a while, but his standards were rather high. They were expected to love the outdoors, swimming, and dancing. A knowledge of firearms, current events, and politics was also important.

"Steven," I would ask, "What about homemaking, cooking, and housekeeping?"

His assumption was that any girl with his qualifications would have those skills naturally built in.

31

Surviving the Worst

On July 20, 1967, Steven was ten days away from competing in the World Championship Shoot in Atlanta, Georgia. He often shot skeet with the boys from Lackland Air Force Base in San Antonio. They encouraged me to register him because he could easily shoot 100 straight without practicing.

As Steven and I were driving home from the Dallas Gun Club, we collided with another car that sped through an intersection over

R.L. Thornton Freeway.

I awoke in Methodist Hospital three weeks later, covered with bandages, and found most of my body suspended in traction. I asked a nurse what had happened because the last thing I remembered was being at the gun club. I thought that my new Remington 1100 automatic had exploded. The nurse told me what she knew about the accident.

The doctors informed me that I was lucky to be alive. Steven suffered only multiple bruises, but my neck, arm, and leg had been broken. Our dog, Schnapps, had to be maced by the Dallas Police because he would not allow the paramedics to remove us from the car. He was then kennelled at Clopton's Hunting Resort.

Worst of all, my face had been smashed and badly cut by bro ken glass. W hen the bandages were removed, I was horrified by my badly scarred appearance.

I stayed in the hospital for two months during which time Mr. Randall Brooks, President of Rogers and Smith (the advertising agency at which I was employed) suffered a fatal heart attack. The agency closed and my medical insurance was canceled. Therefore, I was responsible for all my medical expenses. Thoughts rushed through my mind wondering if this was just a coincidental wreck. From the time I met Lyndon I experienced strange events and saw many unexplainable situations occur-murder included. Was this my fate for having an affair with a married man?

I needed Lyndon then more than at any other time in my life, knowing quite well that it could not be. But I feared I would never see him again.

As I began a long course of recovery and plastic surgery.I plunged into a state of depression, wracked by constant pain from internal injuries. I felt damned for life, and lost the will to live.

Mr. Ragsdale would call and ask how I was coming along. KTBC and other Texas media organizations filled my hospital room with flowers. Lyndon would somehow manage to call occasionally. I could, however, have done without his constant bragging about his new grandson, Patrick Nugent, born on June 2, 1967. The last thing I wanted to hear was how his daughter had given him a "boy to carry on the bloodline." He seemed to me to be insensitive and uncaring. I relived past years and remembered holding Steven, watching him grow up ... not only without his father-but with no public acknowledgement of Steven's existence. My agony turned into anger and hate. I became bitter. Was I being punished for my sin?

Steven and Father Jarrett's daily visits didn't help the pain and anger concealed within my heart. Finally, one day Steven said, "Mother, I'm not going to come see you anymore until you straighten out your act." Somehow his frankness had a jolting, healthy effect. I began to deal with my pain and I started to cooperate with the doctors.

32

Defeated and Disgraced

In early 1968, the Vietnam War still continued. The bitter divisions at home intensified and campus violence increased. At the University of Houston, protesters carried coffins while chanting, "Hey, hey, LBJ, how many kids have you killed today?" We were living near the university and my emotions were violently stirred when I heard this, but I must confess I agreed with some of their messages on the Vietnam War issue. Even though Lyndon did not consider Eugene McCarthy and Bobby Kennedy as serious political threats in his bid for re-election, his narrow victory in the New Hampshire primary came as a real shock.

On the evening of March 31, he made a nationwide address on Vietnam. First of all, he set a ceiling of 549,000American troops, clearly stating that the only new men would be support troops previously committed.

Secondly, we would accelerate our training and equipment for South Vietnam's forces so that they could take over major combat responsibilities previously assumed by U.S. troops.

Thirdly, speaking directly to Hanoi, he offered to greatly re strict our bombing of the North as an inducement for an immediate start of peace negotiations. And then he dropped his own bombshell at the end:

"With America's sons in the fields far away," Lyndon said, "With America's future under challenge right here at home, with our hopes and the world's hopes for peace in the balance of every day, I do not believe that I should devote an hour or a day of my time to any personal partisan causes or to any duties other than the awesome duties of this office-the presidency of our country.

"Accordingly, I shall not seek, and I will not accept, the nomination of my party for another term as your President of the United States of America."

I was relieved to know that he wouldn't have to put up with a long abusive campaign where he would surely be cursed by thou sands, called a warmonger and murderer-not to mention the possibility of being an assassination target. He was out of it, free to pursue a lasting peace and bring our boys home before he left office.

Lyndon's popularity ratings soared. The bombing halt in Vietnam promised hopes of early peace. Instead of being cursed, Lyndon found cheering crowds. But the euphoria didn't last long. He struggled with an inflated economy and directed his efforts toward substantive negotiations in Paris. He wanted so badly to salvage his Great Society and Vietnam goals. But new frustrations appeared during the last ten months in office.

The nation endured again the shock of assassination-Or. Mar tin Luther King, Jr. and then Bobby Kennedy! The tensions came to a violent climax at the Democratic convention in Chicago where Lyndon had to suffer at a distance. Although he tried to hide his feelings, I knew how bitter he felt. He had hoped to make a graceful and triumphant exit from public life, but that would not be possible while the convention was under threats of violence by student radicals and other demonstrators against the war.

As I was recovering from my accident, I watched the convention on television and saw scenes of angry mobs around the major hotels. Mayor Daley had surrounded the convention hall with barbed wire reminiscent of Hitler's concentration camps and the police were prohibiting other anti-war demonstrators from entering the surrounding area.

As Hubert Humphrey accepted the nomination, there was also a certain hostility inside the convention hall itself that matched the anger of the demonstrators battling the police. I was glad that Lyndon had chosen to stay in Texas.

Richard Nixon won the election in early November. I won't bother to comment on his victory-too much has been written about that-but I will say that Lyndon was not exactly overjoyed.

When John Connally came out with "Democrats for Nixon" and staged an extravagant fund-raiser at his Floresville, Texas ranch, all the important wealthy king makers, were they Democrat or Re publican, joined forces to support the Republican candidate. Lyndon, a dyed-in-the-wool Democrat, told me that he should have kept a closer eye on John Connally. However, he was cordial to the incoming Nixon administration, participated in Nixon's inauguration, and presided over the tearful goodbyes at the White House.

Immediately following Nixon's inauguration, Lyndon and Lady Bird and daughters drove to Clark Clifford's home for a farewell luncheon. It was an assembling of old friends who had faithfully served Lyndon in his 31 years on Capitol Hill.

During this carefree occasion he bestowed five Medal of Freedom citations on Dean Rusk, Clark Clifford, Averell Harriman (the former Governor of New York and Ambassador to Russia was the subject of much gossip while courting Winston Churchill's ex-daughter-in-law, Pamela. Publisher's note: Pamela had always gotten around a great deal among men, married many of them including Harriman, and became our Ambassador to France where she died in 1997. It was a huge funeral, and the President of France was not alone in appearing to have suffered a personal loss), Walt Rostow, and William S. White.

With Lyndon's tongue-in-cheek attitude and smiling his little country boy smile, he told the group, "This was the most gratifying moment of Nixon's 'Big Day.'"

Now Lyndon was home in Texas, at his ranch in the hill country-with no job-no political role-defeated and disgraced.

33

"Who Am I?"

Since Lyndon brought NASA to South Texas, Nixon invited Lyndon to represent him at the blast-off of Apollo II.

Jesse called right after Apollo II's history-making return from the moon and said Lyndon would be attending a parade in Houston honoring the astronauts Neil Armstrong, Edwin "Buzz" Aldrin and Michael Collins.

"His heart is giving him hell again, Madeleine, and he wants to mend some fences. He really wants to see you."

By then surgery had largely repaired my features. Sensing this was to be our last goodbye. I was reminded, as the song says, that "the days dwindle down to a precious few."

It was August 1969, I flew immediately to Houston and caught a taxi to the Shamrock Hotel, where I checked into a room prearranged by Jesse. And waited.

A few hours later there was a knock at the door and I felt all the old rush of excitement and was breathless-my hands dripping with moisture. Yes, I loved him with all my heart. I simply couldn't help it.

I opened the door to find a crumpled, overweight, haggard looking Lyndon. His bout with heart trouble showed clearly in the lines of his face. But his craggy face was kind and mellow. His graying hair was long, sweeping back and curling on the ends. While his Secret Service escort waited discreetly in the hallway, a somewhat subdued Sandow entered the room.

He held me close with one of his bear hugs. We sat together,

Then I want you to hear something," I said angrily as Ire moved four handwritten notebook pages from my purse. "Your son wrote this at school while I was in the hospital."

Who Am I?
by Steven Mark Brown

I have a basic emotional pattern. Love, hate, anger, and pity. I say "basic" because I think these are the basic emotions of human beings. But although I say I have basic emotions like everybody else, I am an individual. To explain this is simple-my thoughts are my own.

> I do not hold with the statement that all humans have good and truth in them. The human mind that controls these traits can be controlled itself by another emotion or trait. For example, hate. Hate can destroy every thing good in a person, an individual. This goes for anyone.
>
> As I stated before, I am an individual. My thoughts on truth are extremely difficult to put into words. To be gin with, without truth, the truth of what a person speaks on every day of his life, there can be no happiness. To explain this, how can two humans, in close contact with each other, be happy when one or the other lies and deceives to the point where no respect is left? Go to connect these together, where there is no truth, there is no happiness. Where there is no truth, there is no respect.
>
> Next there is the truth of faith. Our whole existence is based upon the truth of some kind of religion. Catholic, Methodist, Buddhism, Episcopal or all the rest of the religions of the world. Without this, there would be no man.
>
> Then there is objective truth. When I say objective, I mean the facts that are supposed to be proven as true today, but may be disproved tomorrow.
>
> Several months ago I read somewhere a little bit of philosophy that I remembered distinctly. "There is a destiny that makes us brothers, none walks his way alone. All that we send into the lives of others, comes back into our own." I can relate this philosophy directly to my own life. But the first part, there is a destiny that makes us brothers, none walks his way alone, I don't believe to be true, it may be applied to the majority of people of the world, but there are a few individuals who are nobody's brothers and never will be and they walk their way alone.
>
> In conclusion, it might be said that this world of ours is in "orderly chaos." Chaos in the riot of emotions and events, and orderly in that we are under one God, I am an Episcopalian and from our morning prayer, as it was in the beginning, is now, and ever shall be, world without end-who am I?

Lyndon buried his face in his hands and began to cry. "Goddamn it, Madeleine, life is so unfair. Why can't things be different? Why did you wait so long to show me this?"

"Lyndon, Steven is so confused. His birth certificate says James Glynn Brown is his father, and he knows he can't be. Mr. Ragsdale goes with him to school functions and stands in as his dad. He's seen us together and knows you are someone special in my life. Please, please, Lyndon," I cried, "acknowledge Steven as your son. You owe it to him ... and to me."

Lyndon tore his eyes away from mine and looked toward the door. "It's been too many years. Madeleine. You and I are both older and Steven is a man now. Goddamn it, some things are better off left alone." Then he reached down and pulled me to him.

"I suppose you know what's best," I said. "It probably would only cause more hurt and pain to everyone if we told the truth now." "Don't worry, Madeleine. I've made arrangements with Ragsdale to make sure that you and Steven are well taken care of when the good Lord decides to cash in my poker chips."

"Quit talking like that," I scolded him as I put my arms around his neck. "I love you, my Sandow!"

"Goddamn it, you are something special, Madeleine Brown," he said as his arms went around my waist and he pulled me into him, "You are Annie Oakley with a shotgun, John Kinser with a golf club, and Jesus Christ, you can fuck the fuzz off a Georgia peach! You tum sex on and off like a light switch. It's like my Jewish friends say, 'you have chutzpa."'

"I love you, Lyndon, always have, and always will. You have been my great love, and there aren't too many women who can look back and say that they loved and slept with the President of the United States."

Lyndon's voice was low as his face moved closer to mine. "I love you, too, Madeleine, always have, always will."

As our lips met, he added, "I wish things could have been different, though, because you and I were made for each other. Ambitious and wild! But today is today-"

"And tomorrow is tomorrow," I answered, knowing full well that for the two of us, there would be no tomorrow.

34

Today is Today and the Tomorrow That Never Came

Although Mr. Ragsdale continued to provide us Lyndon's financial support, I still struggled from the burdens of my enormous hospital bills. I was unable to work. This was only the beginning of the lean years.

At one point, our only sources for funds were our friends, Pinto, his wife, Judy; and Don (Butch) Reynolds, the Jefferson Street pawn broker from whom I borrowed money-using as collateral the lovely jewelry that Lyndon had purchased for me.

Lyndon, however, had become the wealthiest ex-president in American history. He and Lady Bird owned interests in several businesses in Austin and real estate in Alabama and Mexico. They also sold KTBC for $9 million, which went mostly to Lady Bird and into trust funds for his two daughters.

Naive at the time, I cannot understand now why Lyndon didn't establish a discreet trust fund for Steven. Perhaps Lyndon secretly did, but a crucial safe deposit box entrusted to Mr. Ragsdale was drilled out and disappeared. I will never know for certain unless some one comes forward with its contents.

Although Lyndon and I would never see each other again, Jesse always kept me informed of his health and well-being. I learned that Lyndon had recent affairs with other women, some of them well known by now.

In March of 1970, Lyndon had suffered angina and was hospitalized in San Antonio.

On May 22, 1971, on a partly cloudy and very windy day. Steven attended the dedication of the Lyndon Baines Johnson Library and Lyndon Baines Johnson School of Public Affairs, 2313 Red River, located on the campus of the University of Texas at Austin. Also in attendance were Hubert Humphrey, Barry Goldwater, President Nixon and two thousand demonstrators who marred the opening by chanting "No more war," and

"Johnson's war." And again, "Hey, hey, LBJ, how many kids have you killed today?!"

In the spring of 1972, he suffered another heart attack while visiting his daughter Lynda and her family. Convinced Lyndon was dying, his doctors allowed him to be flown home to Texas to the Brooke Army Medical Center in San Antonio, the same hospital the Navy eventually would use for Steven's bone marrow test, a short distance from the LBJ ranch.

Lyndon refused to publicly comment on Nixon's dismantling of his Great Society programs, but he supported Nixon on Vietnam and was enthusiastic about his movements toward cease-fire. Because of his illness in 1972, Lyndon turned down repeated invitations to the White House. Yet, he was suspicious of Nixon's handling of the death of his close friend, J. Edgar Hoover, in May of 1972. Although Hoover reportedly suffered a fatal heart attack, Jesse said that Lyndon thought he may have been assassinated over the Watergate scandal.

Curiously, even though J. Edger Hoover maintained a position of importance in government, no post-mortem examination was permitted by Nixon to determine the exact cause of death. But Lyndon congratulated Nixon after his re-election. As a courtesy, Nixon in formed him that a cease-fire in Vietnam was near.

Lyndon made an unscheduled appearance at the Dallas Press Club in December 1972. Time did not permit me to see or talk to him. Jesse said, "Tomorrow, Madeleine, you'll be able to see him tomorrow." T hat tomorrow never came.

Steven saw his father for the last time during the inaugural for Texas Governor Dolph Briscoe. Lyndon called Steven "son" and re minded him that he was on his way to the White House, casually asking about me and my recuperation.

On January 22, 1973, I received a call from Jesse informing me that while resting in bed at the ranch, at 3:50p.m., Lyndon had suffered his fatal heart attack. He had called the switchboard and Secret Service agents responded with a portable oxygen unit. They found him on the floor next to his bed and were unable to revive him. Thus, Lyndon, my Sandow, died alone. Lady Bird had been at her Austin business office. I wish I had been there. I would have never left the house even though he probably would have cussed and screamed that it wasn't necessary.

The next several days have remained a blur in my mind for all these many years. Lyndon's body lay in state for a day at the LBJ Library. Lyndon wanted to be remembered as "Big." He wanted lots of people at his funeral service. Once he remarked, "I want everyone to know who's in the box."

Then, on January 24, reminiscent of Kennedy's funeral almost a decade before, Lyndon's casket was transported from the White House to the Capitol on a horse drawn caisson followed by a riderless horse. After lying in state for seventeen hours, services took place at the National City Christian Church. Lyndon's remains were released to the LBJ ranch. The Reverend Billy Graham, a favorite of the powerful Texas SF group, officiated at the grave site while Anita Bryant sang "The Battle Hymn of the Republic."

As I watched Lyndon's funeral on television, I saw brief but unforgettable images of twisted, grieving faces. Men and women, including Ethel Kennedy, were all crying openly without shame. At first, the crowd comforted me as we shared in a collective loss, then the surrealism of the scene became too much. I was no different from one of the weeping faces in the crowd. I had been crying off and on for three days. When I saw Lady Bird and his daughters, I realized I was on the outside, shut off from the real family structure of Lyndon's world. As I had loved him alone, I would have to grieve alone.

I was still mourning in May when Jesse called, requesting that I meet with Mr. Ragsdale and him at the Rice Hotel in Houston. Ten days after our meeting, I received a letter from Mr. Ragsdale reassuring me that the "financial arrangements" would continue as initiated by Lyndon for Steven and me as it had for the past twenty-three years. T he biggest question of all, of course, was-what, or when, would I tell Steven? Should I tell him anything? His father was gone. I had waited too long. Why did I wait? Why? I should have ignored what Lyndon had said about not telling him. I should have let Steven decide what to do about it. I should have given him at least that. Now it was too late. Steven would never be able to "know" his father, Lyndon.

35

Revealing the Truth

The years slipped away as I tried to reconstruct my life. But I only went through the motions of living. Sometimes, if I was busy, I would enjoy a few minutes or so without thinking of him. Lyndon's memory would not fade. Every time I looked at our strapping 6' 4"son with dark hair and that familiar hairline, I saw the mirror image of his father.

In 1975, the payments stopped when Jesse "put everything on hold," according to Mr. Ragsdale. I felt so utterly disappointed and betrayed when my old dear friend, Jesse, quit calling and would not return my calls.

My thoughts were of my son, Steven. Even though he was a womanizer like his father, one particular girl, Beverly Bucek, of Schulenburg, Texas, captured his imagination. In 1976, Steven began making plans to marry Beverly. She was the wealthy daughter of the owner of B and B Vending. Her father interfered with their marriage plans.

The company was the target of a Texas attorney general's investigation into the distribution of pornography. Ironically, Beverly's father felt that Steven was not of the financial caliber to be his daughter's husband. Steven was hurt, of course, and withdrew into himself for a long period of time.

I thought how unfortunate that Steven hadn't fallen in love with Jean MarDock now, rather than in the first grade, at St. George's Parochial School. She had always been my favorite. Jean's father, Dr. Julian MarDock, had been a World War II flying ace and pilot for General George Patton. He served as the Dallas County medical examiner and had become a legend in his own time, administering medicine to the needy, much like his father, Mr. Sam MarDock, of Tyler, Texas, had fed needy people during the Great Depression of the 1930s. T hey lived in my father's beloved community of Trinity Heights.

With welcome relief from more troubled days, I had retired to my lovely patio – surrounded by every color, shape and size of flower, vine, shrub and tree that only years of careful planting, nurturing and love can accomplish. Enjoying the pastoral beauty with me was my "pet" red cardinal bird that had nested in the honeysuckle for the last several years, faithfully guarding his dull-colored mate from the bachelor males of the neighborhood. After such a long time and buckets of bird seed and conversation, we were like an old married couple quietly comfortable with each other's presence. Yet at times when my soul is troubled, he will perch over my shoulder in a hanging basket of fuchsia or stray limbs of hedge and sing a song straight from God's heart. The beautiful red cardinal never failed to lift my spirits and make me smile.

My musings were interrupted by the ringing telephone. What a pleasant surprise! It was my good buddy, multimillionaire bachelor, Sam Park, of Harris County, calling me from his baronial South Texas ranch.

"Hey, Madeleine, have you been keeping up with the new South Texas banking scandal involving the Salinas family? It's even better than the Sharpstown Houston collapse! We've got a real star-studded cast of people with their fingers caught in the cookie jar-Enrique Salinas, Sammy Davis, Jr. , Lt. Governor Ben Barnes, and University of Texas Regent Dr. James E. Bauerle. Ben Barnes and former Governor Connally have filed for bankruptcy.

"It sure looks like ol' Lyndon's carpetbagger, Morris Jaffe, has done in Steve's pretty little girlfriend, Beth Horstmann, and her sister, Alex Short." Sam continued, "It was Jaffe who introduced Alex Short to the Salinas family, wasn't it? T he girls burned to death in a plane crash with $500,000 that the papers say is missing from the bank."

"Sam, no, no, no! It just can't be Beth and Alex. They were beautiful, sweet, darling girls ..."

San Antonio people called Jaffe a mystery, a tycoon, the Great Gatsby, a poor boy who had clawed his way to the top. He was resented by the country club crowd. Lyndon often remarked that Morris was no angel and loved money, although he was always very generous with it. Morris made his fortune in an array of ventures – oil and gas, home building, uranium, shopping malls, insurance, cattle, grain and land development. His name became popular in Texas when he stepped forward in 1962 and bought Billie Sol Estes' assets. When Speaker of the House Jim W right of Fort Worth stepped down in disgrace, Morris Jaffe's name became nationally known again-but all was quietly quashed.

Sam began to read the Eagle Pass newspaper and in sick sorrow confirmed the story of the two sisters. Alex had worked for Morris ten years. Morris Jaffe had been one of Lyndon's closest friends, and was an interesting and unusual character. A San Antonio native of Mexican-Jewish parentage, he grew up in the Alamo City and be came an aircraft engineering officer during the war. Upon his return from the army, he and his friend, David P. Martin, organized Jaffe and Martin Builders and went into construction work.

The girls had died in the fiery crash in remote northern Mexico near Atilano De La Garza, the same ranch that H.L. Hunt used as his retreat after President Kennedy's assassination. After he finished reading the article, Sam invited us down to his cowboy palace complete with golf course, swimming pool, tennis court, skeet range, trap range and a private airport befitting the Texas rich.

"Bring yourself, the boys, shotguns, and those magnificent Weimaraners of yours. I'll spot you and Jimmy five birds, but not that little 'shit' Steven: he's too damn good."

I answered him, "Sam, I'm afraid to come to South Texas because the La Raza Unida Party in Crystal City has things so stirred up. People are disappearing, getting murdered or brutally beaten, and I certainly don't want that to happen to us. I just saw where that good-looking County Judge, Jose Gutierrez, opened his office door and was greeted with a roomful of diamondback rattlers and copper head snakes. No thanks, Sam, but thanks for the invite."

Sam replied in his southern drawl, "Hell, girl, you may have tits, but you don't have any guts. Don't you know there's nothing like a good-juicy Texas scandal to stir the blood? No one knows who the screwee or the screwor is, but you can probably bet it's one of those University of Texas Kappa Sigmas. Don't tum your back or you're dead meat!"

I laughed at Sam's succinct words, then replied, "I better pass this time, Sam, because I'm helping my friend plan our country's 200th birthday."

With compassion in his voice, Sam told me, "Madeleine, if you will arrange a memorial for Beth and Alex, I'll reimburse you."

"How loving of you, Sam," I replied. "You are a true gentle man!" I sent him a kiss over the line and hung up.

It was hard to tum down an invitation to Sam's ranch, as one could get a real taste of Texas there with its contrast of manicured lawns, servants, and the wild open range crawling with diamondback rattlesnakes (Sam's flashy peacocks killed and ate them as much as possible). Oil derricks served as back scratchers for the sleek, pure bred cattle, as long-legged-jack rabbits raced for the horizon. A short distance away was Mexico, where "25 cent Margaritas reign supreme" and the "good times roll."

In October of 1977 Jesse Kellam died. I'm not going to say that I was overwhelmed with grief because that would not be true, but I was saddened by his death, just as I am saddened by anyone's death-friend or foe.

On March 12, 1978, the Dallas Morning News reported that city and county attorneys had filed a civil action against the Continental Theater, a pornographic movie house situated in a building owned by Mr. Ragsdale. Jerome had said if he had only one wish in life, he would have removed cigarettes from every shelf. His Continental Theater continued to operate long after Mr. Ragsdale's demise. I asked him once how he got away with operating an illegal porno house. He said by means of "payola" and the support of the organized crime syndicate that ran Dallas. Lyndon ordered Mr. Ragsdale to acquire the much publicized "Deep Throat" and "Behind the Green Door" long before the porno film controversy reached the Supreme Court. The two of us laughed heartily about "Things Go Better With Coke" and "Blue Cross/Blue Shield Card" inside jokes from Deep Throat. The civil action asked that a court classify the business as a public nuisance and issue an injunction closing it down.

John Dragna, head of Dragna Real Estate and director of Mer chants State Bank, Lawrence R. Burk, president of a real estate firm and son-in-law of the chairman of Zales Jewelers, and W.O. Bankston, a Lincoln automobile dealer, were among other professional businessmen named in the civil action. However, the pornographic business continued to operate for many years without interference from law enforcement.

Mr. Ragsdale requested that I meet with him in his office in the Mercantile Bank Building that March. He was suffering from lung cancer and doctors had told him to get his affairs in order. He confided in me that he was drawing up a will which would designate Steven and me as the inheritors of the bulk of his estate, which included automobiles, real estate holdings, oil and gas property and office buildings. Evidently, per Lyndon's request, Mr. Ragsdale had invested large sums of money on our behalf, only using what he personally needed. Lyndon often would laugh and say I was good for the economy. "Honey, you keep money in circulation." In addition, Ragsdale said that all confidential papers connecting us to Lyndon were in his personal safe deposit box, and he handed me a key. The key was marked Diebold, Inc., Canton, Ohio, and number 2042. It was manufactured by Independence Lock Co., with ILCO on one side, and stamped N on the other side.

The next month Mr. Ragsdale died, and I met with my attorney, Mr. Joe Hill Jones, a prominent Dallas lawyer. (At Mr. Ragsdale's urging, he had represented me in litigation involving my automobile accident.) I explained to him that Mr. Ragsdale had informed me of his intentions to write a will only weeks before his death, and then I provided him with the key to the safe deposit box.

The private investigator, Martin Cleary, hired by Jones, found Conrad Hilton's long-time business associate and companion, Margaret Elyn MacDonald, who also did stenographic work for Jerome Ragsdale.(In March 1987, Margaret, 95 years young, married a 50- year-old man on probation with a criminal sex record."Margaret," we asked," ...your sex life?" "Tain't bad," she said.)

She was the one who had typed Ragsdale's will, bequeathing the bulk of his estate to Steven and me. She had also typed the letter from Ragsdale to me confirming continued support. Martin Cleary also reported to Joe Hill Jones that the safe deposit box, with all its contents, had been drilled from the bank's wall. The bank would not offer any explanation for this mysterious incident.

When we finally appeared before the probate judge, everyone assumed that Mr. Ragsdale and I had had an affair and Steven was his son. Why else would he leave us the bulk of his estate? Even though Mrs. MacDonald testified, as well as two other witnesses, the icing on the cake came when the registrar of Steven's parochial school, Kearnie Adams, signed an affidavit stating that she saw the headmaster-a priest, Father John Worrell-destroy Steven's baptismal and school records. The judge ruled against us. Some time later, the present priest, St. George's David Mossbarger located the church pages that were rewritten.

Eventually, the attorney's for the Ragsdale estate sold off most of the property bequeathed to us, and liquidated the assets for attorney's fees.

In 1980, our appeal to the Texas Supreme Court was denied, and we settled out of court for the ridiculously insulting amount of ten thousand dollars. All the money in the estate was consumed by vicious lawyers dragging the contest for the will into long court proceedings.

Though ill-health and poor management drained my finances, over the next few years I took on the care of my blind, invalid mother and older sister, Neta Bell Duke. While Neta was in the hospital, her accounts were robbed, leaving her penniless. I have taken care of her ever since in my home. I guess we all fall victim to the cruelty, avarice, and desperation of others at one time or another in our lives.

In February of 1987, I was hospitalized after a heart attack and called Steven to my bedside. I wanted to get everything ready so I could go to the other side peacefully.

"Steven, I know there are things you have worried about," I said, "and I feel I have done you a great injustice. I want to ask your forgiveness for allowing something like this to happen."

He looked at me intently and asked, "Mother, who really is my father?"

"Lyndon Baines Johnson was your father." While in one sense blissful tranquility overcame me, I winced in agony, awaiting his reaction.

Steven flew into a rage. He felt cheated and deceived by his own mother, the same woman who, as his "best pal," had taught him to throw a baseball, shoot rifles, pistols and shotguns, and bought him a subscription to Playboy magazine when he had turned twenty-one.

He asked me why I had waited until now to tell him and I said it was because it was better for him not to have known.

After he calmed down, he confessed, "I suppose after all those years, the shock of what you said boggled my mind," He added, "I guess I inherited my father's temper."

But he didn't blame Lyndon for failing to acknowledge him. "I realize he had to think about his political position, the girls, and his legal wife. I think there was no other course open to Lyndon under the conditions. Although if he had acknowledged me during the period when I wondered why I didn't have a normal life, it probably would have kept me from the fears and anxieties I had to deal with as a child. "

Understanding as he appeared, I still found it impossible to talk to Steven about Lyndon and me. I could not tell him any of the details of the story. I simply wasn't ready. That made it worse. His bitterness returned and lasted for four months.

Then on June 18, 1987, Steven flied a $10.5 million suit against Lady Bird, claiming that Lady Bird, Jesse Kellam and Jerome Ragsdale had conspired to deny him his birthright and his fair share of Lyndon's inheritance.

"In a public forum, sooner or later, the truth comes out," Steven said, "That's what is important to me. I want my last name changed to Johnson, the way it should be."

Steven prepared to take the state bar exam in order to legally represent himself in his own lawsuit. It would be his first case, in fact, and he felt his success would be overwhelming. Steven was totally unlike his famous father where ambition and morals were involved. He had aspired to be an attorney from an early age. He hoped to write legislation one day that would revoke the double racial standard and improve Texas laws on a variety of progressive issues. He would have achieved this, I believe, had he lived.

I tried to discourage Steven from filing his lawsuit in Dallas County. The political arena there was influenced by the affluent echelons of the social register-who highly admire and respect Lady Bird Johnson.

"Remember, son, we are little people. Think of the insulting and degrading lies we suffered in Probate Court over the Jerome T. Ragsdale Estate. You know your identity now. Let bygones be bygones. Accept the things we cannot change, and continue your missionary life."

Much like his father, Steven ignored my pleas. His lawsuit was quickly perceived as the lawsuit of the decade in the Dallas County Court House, and many predicted it would become the most notorious case ever filed there. It was, however, the beginning of the end for my uncrowned prince.

Steven welcomed and appreciated the letter from Judge Harlin Martin outlining all the court procedures. He felt the judge's input came from personal interest, since we had supported him for election to the bench.

Our popularity soared as the Associated Press and United Press wire services spread the word around the world about us. We were invited to appear on the Phil Donahue, Sally Jesse Raphael and Geraldo Rivera shows to explain the details of our private lives. We traveled from coast to coast where we found audiences on local talk shows invariably treated us with warmth and understanding. Our mail box was filled with good luck notes and other tributes of affection from people around the world.

We both enjoyed the celebrity status. The elevation of our new lives filled us with delight. People now greeted Steven with comments like, "You look just like your famous father!" and Steven would always graciously thank them.

Then on a bitterly cold October morning, the harassment began. Telephone calls came day and night, the mail was tampered with, and strangers followed us. A pipe bomb was placed in my automobile and it blew away the entire exhaust system. Fortunately, I was not injured, but an examination of the car revealed that the brake lines had been severed.

We reported all this to the Dallas police. Sheriff Bowles' spokesman, Jim Ewell, could only offer us advice, urging us to be cautious and screen all calls by using an answering machine.

Then, on a Saturday afternoon, I received a devastating letter from the Grand Prairie Naval Air Station. This base was approximately ten minutes from our home, and was the same base Steven had received his military discharge from ten years earlier.

They claimed that Steven was a deserter!

There had to be a mistake. I was sure I could straighten the matter out with a telephone call. As it was Saturday, the Grand Prairie offices were closed, so I sent them a mailgram outlining their error, and forwarded copies to Senator Phil Gram (a Republican) and Congressman Martin

Frost (a Democrat). I pleaded with both for information about this sudden persecution. To this day, the U.S. Navy has never responded to my inquiry.

Congressman Frost agreed it was a puzzling case, but said that representatives are powerless over the military. They operate on their own, Steven and I were told, often without the knowledge of their Commander-in-Chief, the President.

I had worked as a volunteer in the offices of Senator Gramm. But they claimed to be helpless in finding answers to this dilemma.

My son, Steven, had always been an enthusiastic "doer," always engaged in one civic project or another. He had, it is true, been stopped by the Dallas police for speeding, and like everyone else, for auto insurance checks. Had there been any outstanding warrant, he would have been taken into custody and arrested on the spot. Why, after ten years, was the Navy pressing a case for desertion?

The harassment continued, and one bitterly cold October morning at 4:30 A.M. I was awakened by extremely loud banging on the antique oval door to my home.

When I went to investigate, two men-one black; one white immaculately dressed in dark blue suits, brutally pushed their way past me, shouting obscene remarks, "Where is that lowlife Steven Mark Brown? We're here to arrest him. We hate sorry bastards who commit treason against America! We're Vietnam vets!"

Overwhelmed and shocked, somehow I managed to reply, "I don't know where he is. Why don't you check his home or call him on the telephone?" Then I added, "He was discharged from the Navy ten years ago!"

I showed them the mailgram; and also a copy of Steven's medical report indicating a diagnosis of lymphatic cancer. I defended my son, pointing out that he had never been a deserter. The Navy had graciously issued Steven a discharge on humanitarian grounds ten years before. This was because of family emergencies involving his invalid and blind grandmother, and crippled aunt suffering from a series of strokes.

Their replies were caustic. They ignored the cries of my two frightened grandsons, Christopher and Jeffrey, who lived with me and whom I took care of. I had taken legal guardianship to keep them from being placed in foster homes. Lights were flashed in the faces of the children and my invalid sister by the screaming intruders. Then the strangers began ransacking our large two-story home like violent madmen on a mission to destroy. We were terrified.

Stunned and shocked, I demanded to see a search warrant, insisting, "I want to see one now, or you'll have to leave our home!" They responded defiantly, "We'll stay as long as we want!"

I was furious and getting more angry by the minute. I could easily have chewed the bark off the live oak tree in our yard. My red hair stood straight up like an attacking dog in full fury. I reached into my gun cabinet, pulled out my faithful Charles Daly shotgun, and turned the barrel on them, "Guess again, guys! You're on your way out of our home. We don't have to take this kind of treatment!"

As I began to march them to the front door at gun point, they belligerently yelled, "We'll be back for that traitor! We'll get him one way or the other!"

I felt so utterly helpless and hurt. All I could do was calm my innocent loved ones and hold them close to me. We loved Steven with all our hearts. He was a saint to us.

I tried to comfort the children, but their little hearts were bro ken. They sobbed for the rest of the day.

I pleaded with Steven to drop his lawsuit. It seemed to me that if he took that step, the harassment would end.

He replied, "Mother, that's what they want me to do!" While the two bullies never returned, a higher power was successful in having Steven's quest for justice ended. While I was attending my invalid sister. Steven was arrested in the presence of his two nephews. Although he showed the police his identification plus his medical record, he was taken to the Dallas County Court House and then to a hospital. It did not stop there. The Navy then sent personnel to the hospital, cuffed Steven's hands behind him, and threw him into a military van, where he was forced to endure the nine-hour drive to the Corpus Christi Texas Naval Air Station.

I still shed tears over the military's barbaric treatment of my son. It is difficult to believe that anyone deserved this kind of inhuman brutality, especially a man who was the son of the late President, Lyndon Johnson.

After forty-eight hours of unsuccessful attempts to reach Admiral Taylor of the Corpus Christi Naval Air Station, I finally made contact with one of the staff's top medical officers, a man who appeared to be somewhat sympathetic, who told me he would order a full investigation. He also agreed to release Steven so that my son could return home a few days before Christmas.

Instead, they transferred him to the Army's Brooks General Hospital in San Antonio, where his father's records were stored. There, the army gave him a bone marrow test.

I flew to San Antonio and had a conference with the medical staff, who indicated they would release Steven at 2 p.m. When I re turned to Brooks, I found my son's bed empty. Steven was gone! I almost collapsed on the spot. No one would talk to me. They acted like zombies.

Upon returning home I hired a Capitol Hill private detective. Finally, after two months, we located Steven in Bethesda Naval Hospital and brought him back to Texas where he was confined to a hospital until he died.

During this ordeal, Steven's lawsuit was dismissed on grounds that he had failed to appear for his court date.

Some weeks before Steven passed away, he looked up at me to say, "You know, you are right! Those people wield insurmountable power and clout. They realized I would have won my case the minute I walked into that courtroom."

"Steven," I said, in a voice as filled with as much love as I could muster, "you've won. You'll always be a winner. You wanted people to know your father was Lyndon Baines Johnson .. .and that news has gone around the world!"

Then I quickly changed the subject, because I realized how much pain and discomfort Steven was in.

"Hey, Big Guy, you know you have always been the apple of my eye. You know how much I love you!"

Steven's handsome face glowed. His accented dimpled cheeks wrinkled."Mother," he replied, "there just aren't enough measuring cups in the world!"

"Right," I agreed, blowing him kisses from my hand, and gently closed the door to his room so that he could finally get some rest.

Epilogue

Courage and Tears

When I began writing this book, I somehow summoned the courage to visit Lyndon's beloved plot on the LBJ Ranch, under the live oak tree in the Hill Country where he is buried near the Pedernales River. The former President is buried among the mockingbirds, jack rabbits, and beautiful Texas wild flowers where Lyndon had worked and played as a boy, building dreams of becoming a great leader.

Seeing his tombstone solidified the realization that he was gone. Oh sure, we had been separated many times before. Weeks, months, dark stretches of years, but he always came back. Not this time. He was dead and now Steven was dying of lymphatic cancer-just like Lyndon's mother, Rebekah Johnson, my son's grandmother.

Since the filing of Steven's lawsuit and the subsequent public reaction to the disclosure of my relationship with Lyndon, the differences between Steven and me had melted.

"One day, after holding the bitterness inside for so long, I realized that you never meant to hurt me," Steven said. "All those years you were really hurting and really suffering and no one to turn to!" Lasting tranquility came over me. Our son had truly forgiven me.

There remained the question of how to tell Steven the whole story. We couldn't just sit down on the sofa. It would take too long and I would cry too much. But Steven and others deserved to know it all, the good, the bad and the ugly.

Writing this book was the solution. My mind drifts back to a wild time when I was a young naive girl caught up in a world of passion, politics, and closely guarded secrets. I have sat long hours at the typewriter, forcing dark, painful memories to the surface. Some times they ease out naturally, sometimes I have been unable to go on, and sometimes I have allowed myself to cry.

I knelt close to Lyndon's grave. I knew there would never be another "Texas in the morning." I know he died tormented and I know in my heart that the torment came from his double life and the son he had never publicly acknowledged. A lot of other things must have tormented him, as well. My thoughts then turned to a more pleasant memory, the first-time we made love in 1948 in his suite at the Driskill Hotel.

"I promise you that from this night, nothing will keep us apart. I will always be there when you need me. I always keep my promises."

I smiled, "We shall see about that." "What do you want me to say?"

"Lyndon, we've been close tonight. We've been as intimate as two people could, but you're a married man and tomorrow you may…"

There was no mistaking the urgent passion in his kiss. "Today is today and tomorrow is tomorrow."

I know now that I could never have lived the life that Lyndon lived, but our love was like a calm sea after a storm. As long as we kept it a secret, no one could take it away from us. They couldn't rob us of memories.

I cling to mine! We had each other. I had our son … for a little while.

But the "little while" was all too short. It came before I had completely penned Texas In The Morning. My uncrowned prince went to sleep permanently on Friday, September 28, 1990 at 1:13 p.m., a haunting irony for me. Steven's departure was as beautiful as the caring life he lived.

His favorite nurse, Terry Phillips, entered the hospital room and said. "Steven, I need to take your vital signs."

Steven, looking up with the same eyes and smile of his father, said, "No, I am going to relieve you of your duties today." Then he looked at me, "Mother, I am going to relieve you of your duties also."

Although Steven was a giant of a man, he had again become a little boy to me. I said, "Doctor Cox has ordered more blood for you and it will be here shortly. I know you will feel better."

Steven, with a faint smile, said, "No, Mother, it is time for me to go."

Father David Mossbarger, St. George's Episcopal priest, read passages from his prayer book and anointed Steven and me with holy oil. A few minutes later, my son quietly stopped breathing.

Dr. Jack Barnett placed his arm around me and said softly, "Madeleine, you need to leave now. Michelle Hanks is here to take you home."

As tears flowed down my cheeks, I turned to take one final look at my son, no longer suffering. As I gently threw him a kiss, I could hear his words of wisdom-"Mother, lighten up! Don't sweat the small stuff."

I smiled and said, "Son, Mother has never told you 'Goodbye,' even when you went away to Texas A & M. I always said, 'I love you. Hey, I'll see you later."'

My heart still aches for Steven and Lyndon-their absence creates a great void in my life. I pray that Lyndon's torment has been replaced with peace. Hopefully, some day, I will join Steven and Lyndon, the eternal loves of my life. Then tomorrow will become today!

Afterword

Legacy

Madeleine gave me her memories for safekeeping in the 1990s and said I would know what to do with it when the time came.

I met Madeleine in 1975 at the Chateaubriand Restaurant on McKinney Avenue in downtown Dallas. We both had dinner dates and happened to be in the ladies' lounge at the mirror at the same time. I commented on how beautiful she looked. She had flaming red hair and was wearing a turquoise evening dress with beaded bag and shoes to match. She gave me card and said we should have lunch. Madeleine invited me to the Top of the Cliff private club at the Bank of America building in Oak Cliff. This was just the beginning of what turned out to be a lifetime friendship. Madeleine always treated me like a daughter. I was her confident for many years.

Madeleine and I had mutual friends and acquaintances in the Dallas area. She was friends with the older generation and me, with the younger generation, people I had gone to school with. Madeleine had two sons, both single.

I met her younger son Steven in 1976 and attended political fundraisers and other Bicentennial events that year with him and his mom.

I met her older son Jimmy in 1980 when he was honorable discharged from the US Navy after serving his country for eight years during the Vietnam War on a submarine I was not until years later that we dated and eventually married.

Most people don't know that Madeleine had an invalid sister that was bedridden after a stroke. Madeleine moved her sister into her home and cared for her and her needs. I would pick up the catholic priest and bring him to her house to pray for her and her sister.

During the filming of the *JFK* movie Madeleine and I socialized with the research community more often. She would entertain people at the Top of the Cliff. We also would attend parties at the other locations in addition to the dinners & conferences.

So many of our friends and family have passed, but her spirt lives on!

PHOTOGRAPHS

Madeleine Duncan Brown

Lyndon Baines Johnson in his prime--a classically handsome Texan.

Madeleine Brown's son, Steven Mark Brown, the only son of Lyndon Johnson.

Jimmy and Steven.

Madeleine and Steven

Madeleine Brown with son Jimmy (left) and Steven..

Mildred Teel, Duncan family companion.

Madeleine and her scout troop on the trip to Austin, ordered up by LBJ.

Young LBJ (right) with Bill Deason (left) and Jesse Kellam.

LBJ and John Connally in the Navy during World War II. They were always close friends. Connally was gravely wounded during the assassination of President John F. Kennedy. Johnson was two cars behind the President and Connally.

Young Congressman Lyndon Johnson with President Franklin Delano Roosevelt.

LBJ and Sam Rayburn, Speaker of the House.

The "Box 13" gang. This was the fraudulent 1948 election that put Johnson into the United States Senate, causing a massive scandal in Texas. Left to right, Deputy Sheriff Stokes Micenheimer, Hubert Sain, Givens Parr, Ed Lloyd and Barney Goldthorn.

The Johnson Ranch.

The very rich Sid Richardson with President Roosevelt. Richardson was already a power-broker in the 1930's as he rode with Roosevelt (in the right front seat). Later, the wealthy Texas oilmen backed and installed General Dwight David Eisenhower as President. Eight years after that, they financed his retirement farm near Gettysburg, Pennsylvania.

Sid Richardson (right) and his life-long buddy, oilman Clint Murchison, Sr. (left), on a hunting trip. They always slept in the same room and talked all night. Both men were fabulously wealthy, but stayed close to the soil and hunted varmints and real game. Murchison's sons became powerful men in their own right until Clint Jr's empire collapsed. The man in the middle is Clint's gun bearer.

H.L. Hunt, the wealthiest man in the world at the time John Kennedy was killed in his town, on the grounds of his Mt. Vernon estate in Dallas.

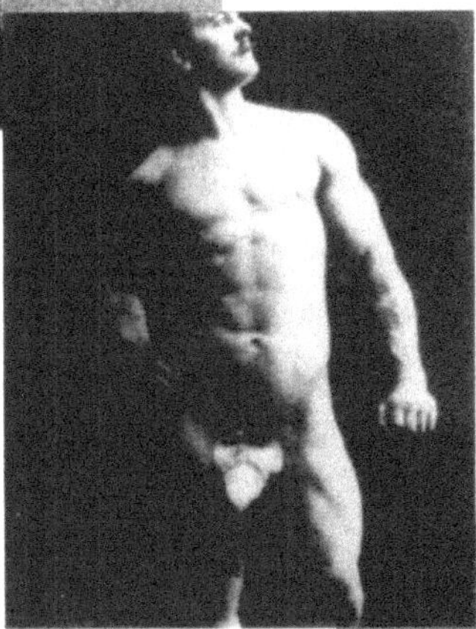

Sandow, greatly admired by Madeleine Brown, would have been *Playgirl*'s male pin-up of the decade. Madeleine always thought of Lyndon Johnson, who was equally strong, as her "Sandow." Women all over the country considered Sandow, who was discovered by Florenz Ziegfeld, the ideal strong man, and large numbers swooned over him and carried a torch.

Jerome Ragsdale, Lyndon's loyal attorney and intermediary, funneled money from Senator and later President Johnson to Madeleine for the upkeep of their son Steven.

The Driskill Hotel in Austin, a frequent trysting place for the lovers.

Jesse Jones (left) and Fred Florence (right) at the Lamar Hotel in Houston.

George and Mary Priscilla Lee Duncan, the author's parents.

Miss Laura and Joe G. Lee, the author's maternal grandparents. Brown suspects there may have been more than friendship between Miss Laura and Speaker of the House Sam Rayburn (insert).

Steven Mark Brown, age three.

Father and son on their favorite steeds.

The President at home on the LBJ Ranch.

JEROME T. RAGSDALE
ATTORNEY AND COUNSELOR AT LAW
1807 MERCANTILE BANK BUILDING
DALLAS, TEXAS 75201
May 18, 1973

Mrs. Madeleine Brown
218 South Windomere Avenue
Dallas, Texas

Dear Madeleine:

Thanks so much for breaking your plans and meeting with Jess and me in Houston last week. I sincerely hope we did not inconvenience you in any way.

Those of us that were close to Lyndon are saddened by his recent death. It is fortunate that he died at the ranch; he would have wanted it that way. It is unfortunate, however, that he died so bitter and tormented.

As we discussed in Houston, you have my personal assurance that I will continue with the financial arrangements that Lyndon provided for you and Steve throughout the past. I know you were very concerned about this and I simply wanted to relieve your mind.

As always, if you need additional funds for you and Steve's living expenses, please do not hesitate to call me. Of course, I will continue to make weekly home visits to verify you and Steve's welfare.

Sincerely yours,

Jerome T. Ragsdale

JTR:mm

Enc.

Madeleine's two sons, Jimmy Glynn (left) and Steven Mark Brown (right) playing "Cowboys". Lyndon's son Steven had much more of a hot temper, like his father, than his older brother. Good thing the gun wasn't loaded.

An older Steven with his nephews Chris and Jeffrey on a camping trip.

Vice President Lyndon Johnson and President John F. Kennedy. LBJ looks warily at Kennedy. Perhaps arrogantly and disdainfully. Neither could stand the other.

President Kennedy attempts to restrain Johnson as he explodes and curses the crowd, "I'll put the evil eye on you!" he screamed. This was not the only such incident.

President Kennedy in Texas hours before he was killed.

Johnson is sworn in as President on Air Force One soon after the assassination. Kennedy's body lies in a coffin in the rear of the plane. Note the smiles of those in the swearing in, and the stricken Jacqueline Kennedy on the right, forced to be on hand.

Serious trouble between the murdered president's brother, Robert Kennedy (on the left) and the new President. The White House photographer said Bobby hit the post and accused LBJ of killing his brother. "It was the first time I ever saw LBJ ever lose control like that," Madeleine said.

Madeleine Brown, son Steven, and his father, Senator Johnson (back to the camera) at a party.

Johnson with his long time friend and enemy, J. Edgar Hoover (left), who black-mailed everyone, including presidents. Hoover may have been assassinated. Robert Ludlum's best seller, *The Chancellor Manuscript*, focuses on this very question of Hoover's death. Hoover had too much on LBJ to be retired, including LBJ's relationship with Madeleine Brown. And everybody wanted Hoover to retire. It didn't happen. He got them before they got him. Were they co-conspirators?

President Lyndon Baines Johnson, looking presidential and not the earthy man he was to spite this pose. He was the 36th President. Among the lessons in hardball he taught is this from the master of the power game: "I never trust a man unless I've got his pecker in my pocket."

Madeleine Brown in recent years at her favorite club, The Top Of The Cliff.

LBJ's famous dog ear pulling incident, for which he was pilloried in the press.

President Johnson signs the Medicare Act, with Vice President Hubert Humphrey looking on, and former President Harry S. Truman and his wife Bess receiving the first Medicare cards.

The Reverend Martin Luther King and President Lyndon Johnson. Notice how serious some of the people look.

Lyndon Johnson's grave at his ranch in his beloved Hill Country, among the wild flowers and breezes where he played as a child and grew up.

Madeleine Duncan Brown and her daughter-in-law, Margaret.

L-R: Billy Sol Estes, Madeleine Brown, Estes' nurse, Margaret Brown, Jean Hill, Dr. Miller.

Jim Marrs & Madeleine Brown.

Madeleine Brown, Larry Ray Harris & Gary Shaw.

Madeleine Brown, Billy Sol Estes & Larry Howard.

Index

Symbols

A

B